BEYOND A FRINGE

BEYOND A FRINGE

TALES FROM A REFORMED ESTABLISHMENT LACKEY

ANDREW MITCHELL

Biteback Publishing

First published in Great Britain in 2021 by
Biteback Publishing Ltd, London
Copyright © Andrew Mitchell 2021

ISBN 978-1-78590-698-5

10 9 8 7 6 5 4 3 2 1

A CIP catalogue record for this book is available from the British Library.

Set in Adobe Caslon Pro

Printed and bound in Great Britain by
CPI Group (UK) Ltd, Croydon CR0 4YY

MIX
Paper from
responsible sources
FSC
www.fsc.org   FSC® C020471

To Sharon, Hannah and Rosie

CONTENTS

PREFACE

This is not a political work designed to justify or proselytise. I rather hope it may at least in part amuse. Mine is without question a privileged life. Born into a secure family, I learned about public service and politics around the kitchen table. Through my father, a respected member of the House of Commons, I had the considerable benefit of witnessing the pluses and minuses of a political career at one remove and before embarking on that journey.

Over the years, I seem to have passed through most British Establishment institutions: from prep and public school, the Army and Cambridge to the City of London, the House of Commons and the Cabinet. Many of these British institutions have changed beyond recognition, but the Establishment itself continues – an Establishment from which I resigned in 2013, becoming rather more sceptical, cynical and wary of views I had previously accepted without question.

CHAPTER 1

OF CANES, FLEET STREET AND PEACEKEEPERS

The first indication that her son was an arsonist came in a call to my mother from the headmistress, Mrs Wallbank.

The Gatehouse in Islington, where I was a pupil aged six, was one of Britain's first Montessori schools – a form of education designed by an Italian physician which at its heart gave children freedom to decide how to learn. It may have suited some children, but it clearly did not suit me, and faced with a choice of diligently studying or running around with my friend Alaric making plasticine models and causing chaos, I opted firmly for the latter.

One afternoon, Alaric and I discovered a box of matches and decided to mount a sophisticated scientific experiment, dropping lighted matches through the gaps between the floorboards to see the effects. Before long, smoke started wafting up from beneath the planks. Mass panic ensued as the school was evacuated and the fire brigade called. I seem to remember trying to blend into the background as hysteria gradually subsided outside the school when four large shiny red fire engines showed up.

My anxious parents were summoned by the headmistress – a formidable figure whose husband was the organist at St Bartholomew the Great, the school's church, where Sharon and I were later married. I can only imagine what was said, but my mother later told me that the punchline was: 'Your son is a thoroughly bad hat. We think his future probably lies in the Army.'

These unfortunate events coincided with the discovery by my parents that, having opted for the plasticine type of education, my ability to read, aged nearly seven, was non-existent. They set about finding a school where I could catch up and their eyes alighted on St David's in Elvaston Place. The headmaster, a genial old fellow called Dudley Durnford, was the public-facing image of the school. He had a sinister wife who taught the Winifred Durnford handwriting style with Stalinist menace, and a sadistic son, John, who regularly thrashed young children and was later convicted of actual bodily harm for caning a seven-year-old. I was absolutely terrified and apart from the fear I remember little except walking two-by-two past the Albert Memorial and learning to box in the school basement.

The cane was used vigorously as an instrument of discipline and encouragement, but within a year I could read, write and count to a sufficient standard to be accepted by Ashdown House, a well-respected school, now closed, located in beautiful countryside near Ashdown Forest in Sussex. Some years later, my brother Graham, who was also sent to St David's, was removed from the school. Our parents noticed that every morning he had to have his fingers prised off the railings outside our house by the *au pair* before he could be carted off and delivered to the school. I can vaguely remember his daily screams of protest.

Ashdown House was a new world. In spite of the daily shock therapy administered by St David's and the Durnfords, leaving the love and home comfort of my family was rather frightening. For the first month I was homesick: my teddy bear was dismembered by the head of my dormitory and I was deeply distressed to learn that Father Christmas was not preparing goodies to be delivered at the end of my first term. Like most other young English boys sent away to school at the age of eight, I soon had the open, sensitive disposition knocked out of me, replaced by closed, self-protective instincts.

The art mistress had custody of the new arrivals, and although I had (and have) zero talent for anything remotely artistic, I remember her as a warm and affectionate person. Amongst the other staff there were certainly misfits and perverts as well as talented teachers. I struggled with carpentry, run by a former RAF officer who gently warned me that my ambition to be an RAF pilot would flounder on account of my weak eyesight.

Colonel Fowler, a decorated officer who had fought against the Japanese in the Pacific and been twice wounded, taught geography. But we were far more interested in his war stories: 'Come on, sir, tell us about the time you were nearly killed.' The colonel would willingly oblige. He had been part of an ambush and had been charged by a Japanese soldier who had carried on racing down the track towards the colonel as the latter emptied his revolver into his attacker. The soldier dropped dead at his feet. I vividly remember too his telling us that a group of Queen Alexandra nurses had been murdered under the orders of a Japanese officer, whose trial and subsequent execution after the war the colonel had made a point of attending. One of his colleagues had been incarcerated by the

3

Japanese in particularly hideous conditions. On being liberated, he had joined his fellow PoWs in chasing after a cruel and sadistic Japanese camp guard. Once they caught him, they castrated him with his own samurai sword. The sword had been taken back to the UK and now hung over the colonel's friend's fireplace, still covered in the blood of its former owner. We boys listened agog, our eyes wide. No wonder I only scored 4 per cent in geography in my Common Entrance exam (hardly the best qualification for an International Development Secretary).

It was also suggested that the French master, Monsieur Gabain, had had a terrible war. A member of the French Resistance, he was said to have been caught by the Gestapo and hideously tortured. Boys would circle round him as he sat on his shooting stick, smoking his pipe and invigilating sports, surreptitiously eyeing up his shins, which were said to be scarred by appalling knife wounds inflicted on him by the Bosch. In hushed tones it was also confidently declared that he too had been castrated by the Germans – although with hindsight this seems unlikely since his wife was the school's head matron and he had a six-year-old son.

In those days, we read 'trash mags' late at night, stories in cartoon form from the Second World War. They were much enjoyed and did little harm while teaching us a somewhat select smattering of German. The need for this was heightened by the headmaster's insistence that each weekday morning the whole school 'paraded' on the square in front of the building before undertaking marching, which took place around the grounds. The headmaster recalled in solemn tones that before the First World War this prep school activity was the only 'training' that some boys from the school had had before being sent off to the Western Front. Many of their names appeared on a board in the school chapel under the slogan 'dulce et decorum est pro patria mori'. The headmaster was determined to continue the tradition in case the Germans decided to have another go.

Together with my friend Nicholas Coleridge, who later ran Condé Nast's UK interests, I set up the Ashdown House Stamp Club. We had a lot of fun. My modest selection of stamps from around the colonies was totally eclipsed by Nicholas's splendid and expansive worldwide collection. He even had a coveted Penny Black.

The legendary headmaster, Billy Williamson, was a twinkly eyed tyrant. The *omertà* about what went on there has recently been broken by Alex Renton, who has written about his schooldays with a sense of hurt and injustice which I do not personally share. But what he says is, I'm afraid, true. Billy Williamson was a terrifying, brutal but charismatic headmaster. He had his 'favourites' and they would be incarcerated with him in his exquisitely decorated and furnished study for suspicious lengths of time. He was a brilliant Classics teacher and would dictate the Bible story in Scripture lessons. I can still remember, more than fifty years later, vast chunks of it as he vividly brought the Old Testament to life. And yet quite apart from what can only be described as his paedophile disposition, his use of the cane was a study in casual sadism and violence.

On one occasion he beat the whole school. Every boy was lined up, bent over and received two strokes of the cane… except for me. Just before the headmaster descended into the main hall in a fit of rage because of noise levels, I had been despatched by a prefect to the kitchen to pick up a crate of half-bottles of milk. As I returned to the hall, I heard the headmaster, who had sent a boy to collect a selection of canes from his study, administer the early thrashings. I quietly put down the crate and tiptoed off to hide in the lavatories. Fortunately, no one noticed. Subsequently, the headmaster bragged that the exercise had done no end of good for his golf handicap.

Behind the school there was a play area known as 'the jungle', and in one bug- and insect-infested corner the school swimming pool was situated. The swimming lessons on Tuesday afternoons were obligatory. The school had a novel way of teaching swimming which involved throwing the hapless eight-year-old in while Mr Tidmarsh, a portly and unathletic teacher, stood at the side holding a pole with a piece of rope hanging off the end to which the drowning novice could in desperation cling. Mr Tidmarsh would only lower the aforementioned rope if he decided the weedy specimen thrashing about in the water really required it. This somewhat unusual teaching method worked with me and, as far as I can recall, no one ever drowned.

School food – which I remember being served in small portions – invariably consisted of spaghetti and paste. It left its mark. When they were young, my children asked, 'Daddy, why do you eat so fast?' I explained that when I was at Ashdown House if you did not eat quickly, you would not get a second helping. 'And if you did not get a second helping, you would die of malnutrition!' My children's eyes widened in genuine horror at their father's dreadful experience. Many years later, my daughter Hannah claimed I also followed this up with '… and look what happened to poor Rodgers, who was carried out in a body bag!' I don't recall saying that, but she has remembered his name so it must be true!

The most sophisticated and revered fellow pupil was a precocious American boy who for some unknown reason was allowed to sport a ponytail. He became the school hero at the age of twelve on account of being caught in bed with one of the two seventeen-year-old matrons who looked after us. She was summarily sacked and left the school while he became a prefect, his hero status reinforced.

At about the same time, one of my friends brought back to school a novel by Dennis Wheatley he had appropriated from his father's bookshelf called *The Sultan's Daughter*. Late at night in the dormitory, his voice trembling with excitement, he would read out page 64 with its erotic allusion to carnal lust and satiation. Sitting on our beds, we listened transfixed, begging for the chance to read for ourselves these exciting and suggestive words in black and white.

The headmaster would produce at the end of each term 'The School Bulletin', a small booklet reporting to parents on the school's activities and successes and the quite remarkable number of scholarships it regularly achieved to Eton and Winchester. The high point, on its front page, was an apocryphal conversation between the headmaster and an old and beautiful beech tree named Fagus, situated on the lawns in front of the fine Benjamin Latrobe façade. Fagus would dutifully listen attentively to Billy's right-wing prejudices and angry ramblings, normally directed towards Harold Wilson's Labour government, and retort with sympathetic agreement.

Looking back, I am amazed at the lack of transparency and passive acceptance of the unacceptable which accompanied our time in this extraordinary environment. While I do not believe it did me much emotional damage, my wife, a doctor, would beg to differ. But despite the apparent lack of trauma it appears to have caused most of us, for others it has led to lifelong misery and anguish over the way they were abused. As L. P. Hartley said, 'The past is a foreign country. They do things differently there.' But, in due course, I vowed never to send my own children away to boarding school.

My parents had decided I lacked the social class and pretension to go to Eton or the cleverness required for Winchester and so I was despatched to Rugby, an unpretentious but excellent school which educated the sons (and only the sons, of course) of the British middle classes, successful country solicitors, small-business people and the occasional foreigner. It is very different today. Rugby has changed more in the fifty years since I was a student there than in the previous 200.

The term before I arrived, if you left the boarding house without your cap in place on your head between the inner and outer doors, you attracted the mandatory punishment of a beating from the head of house. The rows of lavatories had only had doors installed to allow a modicum of privacy the previous year. The school's monosyllabic doctor was John Sparks, whose prescription in respect of almost all ailments was nose drops. (It could have been worse.) Masters wore gowns (some wore mortar boards) and the headmaster, Jim Woodhouse, called the 'Bodger', was a terrifying but respected figure of authority. Learning the school song – a three-verse Latin number – was a vital part of the new boys' initiation. At the end of their first term, all new members of the school house were required to sing it, in tune and word-perfect, in front of the prefects. Failure to accomplish this task meant that a glass of 'hall brew' had to be drunk. This was a hideous concoction to which each of the prefects would contribute an ingredient. I once saw a senior prefect and head of house cutting his toenails and contributing the clippings. As a result of this unconscionable threat, I can still perform all three verses perfectly today. I made friends easily, enjoyed the male camaraderie, acted in school plays and briefly joined the school Army corps, presided over by Regimental Sergeant Major Potter, a caricature of an Army sergeant major who believed it was the right of every free-born Englishman to eat roast beef on a Sunday. One English teacher, T. D. Tosswill, tall and austere, while always wearing a dark suit and gown, was much revered for his asides. Once questioned closely in class about the merits of a particularly moving piece of gay poetry, he responded, 'Good God, boy! When I was at school, we were all queer and proud of it!' It was not a good idea to appear too clever. Showing any sign of intellectual curiosity or academic brilliance was generally frowned upon, though exceptions were made for Anthony Horowitz and Denys Blakeway, respectively later a famous author and renowned documentary maker.

During my school holidays, I regularly worked in the family wine business, El Vino, which in those days had extensive cellars under its two branches – one in Fleet Street and the other in Martin Lane off Cannon Street.

Wines selected and imported by my father and my uncle would be stored in cellars under each branch and in a warehouse off Farringdon Street. It was there, as a cellarman, that I would work during my school holidays, and occasionally, when I was older, I was allowed to serve behind the bar. I loved it. I was paid up to £3 per day and learned how to bottle, cork and label a hogshead of wine (300 bottles) in a matter of hours. The trick was to keep the wine flowing continuously, fill all the bottles to precisely the same level and master the temperamental corking machine while

9

ensuring the consistency of gum for the labels was as thin as possible. We would 'bin' wine using laths between each row of bottles, sometimes ten feet high, for the wine then to mature until it was sold. All these processes well suited my obsessive-compulsive tendencies.

Working behind the El Vino bar in Fleet Street was wonderful. In those days, Fleet Street was the centre of the universe for news and journalism. We always knew everything first before it appeared on the billboards, let alone the newspapers and television. The bar at El Vino Fleet Street was run by a flamboyant prima donna, Geoffrey Van-Hay. Women were not allowed to stand at the bar and be served – sexism dressed up as old-world courtesy – and on one occasion a feminist riot took place. Fleet Street was brought to a halt and Geoffrey Van-Hay, half-strangled by the wing collar he always wore, passed out in front of the main doors and had to be revived with a large glass of El Vino VSOP brandy. Later, the Equal Opportunities Commission took El Vino to court – led by a young and effective solicitor called Harriet Harman – but it was difficult to find a judge to try the case who was not a customer. Eventually, one was found who promptly decided in El Vino's favour. When the EOC announced they would appeal, the company gave up, announcing that what had been a rule would now become a tradition. All the legal costs were debited to the advertising account.

I had always assumed that I would take over the business in due course, or certainly work there. When the time came, it was clear that my palate was simply not good enough. My family suggested I should go into the City and learn about finance. 'None of us know much about money, but we know a lot about wine,' they said. 'Why don't you go off and bring some financial skills back for the family team?'

I did finally, many years later, develop a palate – at least for white Burgundies and wines from the Bordeaux region, if nowhere else – something which certainly gave my father more pleasure than anything I ever did in politics; by then it was too late for me to go into the trade.

Back at Rugby, however, there was the school dance to be navigated. This was an annual event of supreme importance to many of us, involving the almost unimaginable excitement of meeting girls. I had zero experience (my mother and sister obviously did not count, and nor did aunts and grannies, who usually exuded a faint aroma of mothballs and lavender). Girls were a thrilling and exotic breed about which I knew nothing. The annual dance involved several busloads of girls from neighbouring boarding schools descending on Rugby and being offloaded and each arbitrarily allocated by the organisers to an appropriate boy. Dinner in the boarding houses would be followed by the dance itself in Old Big School, a large hall suitable for the occasion. There was, at least in theory, a 'six inches apart' rule.

During the school holidays that preceded the dance, I had struck up a tentative acquaintance with the sister of an old friend. With her long, fair hair and tall willowy figure, I found it hard to articulate complete sentences in her presence. She was intelligent and fun, and I managed to take her to the pub for a drink. I recently found a photograph of this vision sitting outside the Duke of Wellington on Eaton Terrace with a glass of wine, an unkempt, long-haired youth sitting desirously alongside her.

As the date of the dance approached, I summoned up the courage to ask her to come as my guest. I explained, as nonchalantly as possible, its innocent charms, and to my surprise and delight she agreed.

On the night of the dance, my suspicious but world-weary housemaster cross-questioned me closely and arranged for her to sleep in one of his bedrooms away from the boys' side of the house, located through an adjoining door. When she arrived at the house, my stock amongst my sixth form colleagues briefly rose to stratospheric heights never before or subsequently attained.

The dinner went well, and we all set off to the main dance. After an hour or so, I suggested we returned to the house as it was getting late (otherwise known as 9 p.m.) and to my incredulous excitement, she agreed. Avoiding the main road, which might have exposed us to officious schoolmasters, well trained by the Stasi, patrolling the area, we left the heaving mass of bodies on the dance floor, watched over by flustered and panicky staff.

By now I held her hand as we climbed over the back wall and in through a side door which acted as a fire escape, where earlier that day I had dismantled the lock. My heart thumping, we silently crept up the stairs to the corridor where my school study was located. I had carefully prepared my room, removing the obligatory pictures of Julie Christie which normally adorned the boys' walls. My comfortable couch was covered in elegant drapes and cushions. By now, I was in a state of almost uncontrollable excitement. Unable to believe my luck, I put my arm around her and clumsily reached for a first kiss. My head pounded and stars appeared before my eyes as our lips met.

At this point, there was a knock on the door. My house tutor, Mr

Ian Barlow, popped his head around the door and turned on the light. 'Ah, Andrew, sorry to intrude. Good evening, Miss. Andrew, the housemaster is very keen to show your dance partner where she is sleeping tonight. I think I'd better take her off there now.'

Time passed and others returned to the house as the dance came to an end. Couples were parted, sometimes with difficulty, sometimes vowing undying love, and the girls transported back to their school. I lay in my bed unable to sleep, waiting for the quiet of night to descend and for Plan B to begin.

At about 2 a.m. I crept along the passageway, stealthily descending the stairs, tiptoeing ninja-like past Matron's lair, where, encouragingly, the sound of steady snoring emanating from under the door suggested the coast was clear. Trembling with nervousness, I reached the interconnecting door which led to the housemaster's side. I knew that my friend was in the second room down on the left. As quietly as I could, I reached for the door handle and slowly turned it. It was locked; impossible! It was never locked! The doorway to paradise had been sealed by my canny housemaster. Deflated and miserable, I returned, thwarted, to my dormitory and my cold and lonely bed.

My last year at Rugby featured less frivolity. I played rugger badly but ended up captaining the Third XV – a bunch of thugs who were not allowed to play the top two school teams. This was because of the damage inflicted on the one occasion we had played against the First XV on the hallowed turf where William Webb Ellis first, 'with a fine disregard for the rules, picked up the ball and ran with it'. During our game, no fewer than five members of the opposing team had to be carried off the pitch injured. It somehow seemed appropriate that we were playing this brutal match adjacent to The Mound – the location of the last time the Riot Act was read by magistrates in Britain, when the Army was called in to disperse a serious disturbance taking place at the school. This resulted in desks being burned and the headmaster barricading himself into his house in 1797.

It is said that we all remember at least one teacher who made a huge difference to our lives. For me it was Warwick Hele, who taught me history and went on to be High Master of St Paul's. I attended his lectures and at the start of term occupied my place amongst the Awkward Squad at the back of the class. His subject was 'the governance of England throughout the Tudor and Stuart period'. From the beginning I was hooked as he explained the growth of Parliament's role and the skills used by different monarchs to control the burgeoning power of the middle classes. Soon I turned up early and took my place in the front row. It was undoubtedly due to Warwick Hele that I got into Cambridge.

Originally, I was still planning to go into the family wine business. The school suggested, however, that we sixth formers should go and visit Cambridge to see what it was like and to meet some undergraduates. I hadn't intended to go but changed my mind at the last minute when there was a spare place on the bus. Walking around Cambridge, I was transfixed by the beauty of the place, its architecture and the hundreds of undergraduates clearly enjoying themselves. I returned and told my teachers I was determined to go there; what did I need to do to secure a place? I worked flat-out for my A-levels. In those days, you stayed on for an extra term to do a specific exam. The school's opinion was clear: try to get in to read history.

'Mitchell, you are likely, I fear, to go towards a political career, so don't go either to a right-wing college, which will merely reinforce your prejudices, or to a left-wing one, which you will react against. Go to Jesus College, where Fascists drink happily with Communists at the college bar.'

It was excellent advice. That December, after the exam and interview, I secured my place at Jesus College for the following year. Meanwhile, there were nearly twelve months to fill.

Over the preceding year, I had wondered about joining the Army. I had seen friends spend their gap year in a variety of ways and I wanted to make the best use of mine. I had considered going abroad (I barely ever had) to Australia to work on a sheep ranch, but the Army's Short Service Limited Commission (SSLC) appeared as an interesting and useful way to spend the time. I decided I would apply to a 'Teeth Arm', which meant either infantry or armour. But walking everywhere in the infantry did not really appeal. I reckoned I lacked the money and social elevation to join a cavalry regiment. That left the Royal Tank Regiment – there were then four of them – and I duly went for interview at the regimental depot in London. There was also the Regular Commissions Board held at Westbury in Wiltshire to be negotiated and a daunting lunch in the officers' mess at Tidworth to attend and meet the regiment's top brass. And so it was, one Sunday night in January 1975, that I arrived at Victory College at Sandhurst, Salamanca Company, for officer training along with forty-two other young and green cadets.

The Army was ambivalent about Short Service Limited Commission officers – with good reason. By the time they had trained us up to be of any value, we would all be off to university. Our contribution was much less than that of others who took the Queen's shilling. We were expensive to train and the Army got precious few immediate dividends. But the SSLC contracted people who would not normally enter military service. Some stayed, like General David Richards, who went on to become Chief of the Defence Staff, but more, like me, went off afterwards to pursue other careers. We took with us a little knowledge of the military but a lifelong respect for the Armed Forces, their discipline, their bravery and their professionalism.

The experience was invaluable to me many years later as Secretary of State for International Development. Indeed, while in a previous era Cabinets had been full of those who had served in the Armed Forces, nowadays it is comparatively rare. Throughout most of the period of David Cameron's shadow Cabinet I was the only member with any military experience at all, and once we were in government in 2010 there was only me and Iain Duncan Smith, whose service, admittedly, was much longer and more distinguished than mine. But the point remains true that the Army's SSLC officers were often of greater value to the Armed Forces after they left than during their military service.

In 2009, Labour abolished the scheme, a decision I thought was short-sighted. Quite apart from the huge benefit – in every way – for me personally, I thought it was a foolish and unwarranted economy, depriving others of a valuable and worthwhile experience.

On our first day at Sandhurst, we met the Regimental Sergeant Major (RSM), who was to be our mentor and constant companion throughout our time. It became clear that a suspiciously large number of our intake were bound for Oxford or Cambridge. We were lined up by the RSM and each questioned in turn about how many A-levels and O-levels we possessed. A corporal followed the

RSM down the line with a pencil and clipboard, tabulating the numbers as we all proudly proclaimed our exam results. Once the necessary calculations had been made, the RSM looked us over.

'Right, you lot. I can now announce that you are the thickest, least-educated SSLC group we have ever had. Your tally of exam results is vastly inferior to those that preceded you.'

With that, we were marched down to the Sandhurst barber for the obligatory Army haircut and then to the hospital and dispensary, where we were weighed, inspected and vaccinated against every disease that could assail us in any part of the world where the British Army was deployed.

Training started in earnest and over the next four weeks I got fitter and more tired than I had ever been before. We were licked into shape by the RSM. One of our number provided much amusement as a dead ringer for John Le Mesurier's Sergeant Wilson in *Dad's Army*. He soon became the butt of the RSM's humour.

'You, sir. Why are you looking down at the man in front's backside while you are marching? We've all been warned about you public school boys, sir!'

The physical training instructors were the toughest, but their craft was laced with good-hearted humour (or at least I think it was).

'Mr Mitchell, you imbecile, that's not how you do it. You'd better take a break and lie down on the floor – but while you are down there, give me thirty press-ups. Go on, faster!'

At our first live shooting exercise, under the strict eye of a parachute sergeant we were exhaustively taught the need for absolute safety and rigour in our weapons training, as well as our responsibility for the safety of those around us. As we cleared our weapons, one of the cadets inadvertently let off an unintended discharge, which mercifully went down the range without harming any of the rest of us. I have seldom seen anyone more angry than the supervising staff, and the cadet left the premises that night.

As our time at Sandhurst drew to a close, we embarked on a 36-hour exercise – an advance to contact – designed to test what we had learned about basic infantry tactics. My platoon was led by a louche, amusing fellow and we were instructed to go to ground and evade being discovered by 'the enemy', who would attempt to launch a surprise attack on us during the night. As we dug in, our leader decided he was too tired to stay awake and needed to rest. Positioning himself in the middle of the hide, he arranged that pieces of string would be attached to various parts of his body from all of us around the perimeter of the area in which we were holed up, which could then be tugged if anything happened and his leadership skills were required. He then settled down for a good night's sleep as the rest of us manned our positions and prepared to ward off 'the enemy'.

At about 3 a.m. we were attacked. The noise was terrifying. Thunder flashes went off all around us, but the loudest noises heard were the screams of agony from our leader as the various parts of his anatomy were vigorously and simultaneously yanked by all of us in the shock of being so suddenly and comprehensively ambushed.

On our final day, after just four weeks, we proudly took part in the passing-out parade and received our 'pips' as Second Lieutenants in the British Army. Our short Sandhurst career concluded, we were sent off to join our units.

For me, this meant heading off to Lulworth Cove and Bovington Camp in Dorset. This was different from the rigours of Sandhurst. The training was more cerebral (TEWTs – Tactical Exercises

Without Troops) and gave us the chance to fire the weaponry on tracked vehicles, armoured cars and Chieftains, the main British Army battle tank, designed to take on the forces of the Warsaw Pact if they should ever storm across the plains of Central Europe. Firing the main armament on a Chieftain ranks as one of my all-time most exhilarating experiences.

To my surprise and good fortune, I was posted to A Squadron of the First Royal Tank Regiment as the most junior officer on a deployment to Cyprus, where we formed a key part of the United Nations forces there. The previous year, the Turks had invaded the island following a coup secretly instigated by the Greek government which overthrew Archbishop Makarios and declared Cyprus to be part of Greece.

Britain, along with Greece and Turkey, was a co-guarantor of Cypriot independence and after a faltering start the British Prime Minister had agreed that every serviceable armoured car in the two British sovereign bases at Dhekelia and Episkopi should be white-washed and deployed with soldiers issued with blue UN berets to try to stem the Turkish advance at the airport at Nicosia. In a stunning act of brinkmanship, in the early hours of the morning a British parachute sergeant had marched towards the Turkish lines demanding to see their commanding officer. Stamping to a halt and saluting, the para informed a bleary-eyed Turkish officer emerging from his tent that if he advanced one pace further, he would be up against the British Army. He saluted again, about-turned and marched back to his vehicle across the airport. Since that day in 1974, the Green Line, which partitions the island between the Turkish north and the Greek south, has remained firm and unchanged. From then on, the UN kept the peace.

The job of A Squadron, billeted in the main camp in Paphos, in Polis and in the defended villages high in the mountains, and commanded from the UN headquarters in Limassol, was to protect the minority Turkish population in the Greek south and in the Troodos Mountains. We worked alongside soldiers from Australia, Canada, Finland and Denmark. I flew out from RAF Brize Norton with the regimental adjutant on an RAF VC10. I remember that he carried with him six copies of *Playboy* magazine, which he studied assiduously throughout the flight. The plane made its way down to RAF Gibraltar, across to RAF Luqa in Malta, and finally into RAF Akrotiri in Cyprus.

I served with Lieutenant Nigel Lewis, who drew the short straw in having me in his troop as his No. 2. He was a tolerant and decent officer and we spent many hours, particularly in the Troodos Mountains, on patrol and playing backgammon. Technically, this was an 'active service' assignment, not usually available for SSLC officers, but I had slipped through the net. We patrolled in Ferret armoured cars, solid workhorses, which carried the accurate Browning .303 machine gun. Off duty, soldiers did not go out except in pairs and were always armed – usually with submachine guns. We spent a month at a time defending the Turkish minority in the mountains at a place called Vrecha, rotating thereafter to other remote outposts. There were long periods of boredom punctuated by occasional moments of tension, which spilled over into violence normally caused by disputes over land or goats. I acquired the nickname Cornflakes – my staple diet. I was given command of my own troop in the last few months of this six-month tour and left Cyprus with the UN Military Medal which I wear proudly on Remembrance Day in Sutton Coldfield.

While in Cyprus, I was put in charge of the Squadron sailing and helped run the water-skiing. I also learned to parachute, jumping out of planes at the British base at Dhekelia. On one occasion, racing to get over there from Paphos, I handed in my weapon to the armoury but failed to hand over two magazines of live ammunition. In the rush, I took a risk and stuffed them both in the bottom of a drawer in my room, hiding them under some clothes. Unluckily for me, a visiting general stayed in my room while I was away and while unpacking discovered my guilty secret. When I returned, I was made orderly officer on duty for the next three weeks.

On one occasion, the NAAFI tent – the dining area for the squaddies – erupted in violence as a group of paratroopers fell out with the tankies over some pretext, and a pitched battle ensued. The duty sergeant with a sense of humour rang the officers' mess and asked if the young orderly officer could 'go and sort it out'. I made my way nervously to the tent, stood on a chair and at the top of my voice demanded that they all desist. There was no reaction whatsoever as the two sides enthusiastically continued their punch-up. After a couple of minutes of further shouting, I shrugged my shoulders and returned to the officers' mess for a brandy sour and a game of backgammon.

Towards the end of my time in Cyprus, we were ordered to move the Turkish minority population who remained in the south out of the Greek area into the Turkish north, effectively partitioning the island. Long convoys of buses made their way along the coast through Limassol and up to Nicosia Airport, where the handover took place. It was our job to provide protection for these convoys as they passed through built-up Greek areas. I regarded this as a wholly immoral act and said so – to a general shrugging of shoulders by more senior officers, who suggested that we continue to do our duty. The Turks were loaded on the buses along with their possessions. I frequently witnessed the tears and hugs of the departing Turks with their Greek neighbours. In most cases they had all been living perfectly happily together and did not want to leave, yet they had little option but to obey the order from Ankara.

The UN forces in Cyprus were well equipped, with access to weaponry superior to anything that might confront us. This is a core requirement for the UN when deploying around the world, and when it isn't met, UN forces tend to have great difficulty performing their protection role. Our colonel, Tony Walker, commanded the operation from his helicopter, flying backwards and forwards over the convoys, and in case anything went wrong, we were watched over by the RAF at Akrotiri. It was exciting, certainly, but deeply depressing because I knew at the time that we should not have been involved in forcibly removing these long-standing Turkish villagers from their homes against their will. Our actions basically established the de facto partition of the island. This has made a political solution to the conflict (a dispute largely, at this point, between Ankara and Athens) virtually impossible for more than forty years.

Before finally leaving Cyprus and the Army, I was summoned for my exit interview and to say goodbye to Colonel Walker at Polymedia Camp in Limassol. He asked me if I would come back after university. I said I would not be returning but had learned a huge amount – some of it about soldiering – and had developed a great respect for the regiment and the British Army. I said that I thought as a career there was 'too much hanging around waiting to fill dead men's shoes'. The colonel laughed and said, 'Andrew, when I was your age I believed I could take over as colonel of the regiment without so much as a ripple across the water; now I am the colonel I know for certain I could not!'

The next time I saw Anthony Walker was thirty-seven years later at a Vintners' Company dinner at our livery hall on Lower Thames Street. The colonel (by now a general) was there as an honoured guest because the Vintners' Company is twinned with the Royal Tank Regiment, a relationship of which both parties are extremely proud. At the after-dinner drinks, I (now Secretary of State for International Development) was reintroduced to him.

'General, do you remember Andrew Mitchell? He once served under your command as a young SSLC.'

'I do indeed,' the general said. 'I remember him very well. When he left, he told me he could take over my job without so much as a ripple across the water.'

Some years later still, when I was in a terrible state over my conflict with the police, a letter arrived from my former commanding officer. He wrote: 'I have tarried too long before writing at this terrible time for you to offer my full support and best wishes. No one who served with you all those years ago in Cyprus will have any doubt whatsoever about your integrity.'

Even after so many years, the regiment rallied around. Long-forgotten brother officers came to see me at the House of Commons to offer their support. I learned anew that in the British Army, your regiment is truly your family.

CHAPTER 2

'MITCHELL, PAY
THE FUCKING FINE'

Forty-eight hours after leaving the Army, I stood proudly at
the end of 'the chimney' – the main entrance to Jesus College,
Cambridge – the first member of my family to go to university.

In those days, Cambridge was in transition. Previously, the
undergraduates were generally seen as a somewhat inconvenient
necessity, interrupting the research and high table activities of
the university's senior members. Now, student representation and
assertiveness was a live issue as undergraduates sought to play a
much bigger role in university life.

The Garden House riot had taken place a few years earlier, in
1970, unleashing considerable change. The Garden House Hotel
had decided to put on a 'Greek Week' at a time when the right-
wing junta controlling Greece was clamping down on the human
rights of its citizens and brutalising the student community
there. Left-wing student activists had rioted and run amok in the
hotel, causing damage to property and some injuries to innocent

bystanders. It was an echo of the student riots of 1968 which had occurred across Europe, particularly in France.

The old-fashioned system of policing undergraduates, where 'bulldogs' were answerable to university 'proctors', had broken down. In the old days, proctors would frequently give chase to students out late from their colleges without permission. On catching them, they would doff their hats and ask the undergraduate's name and college. This system was destroyed for ever when one of the proctors, Dr Charles Burford Goodhart, was hit by a brick and hospitalised during the riot. Order was restored by eighty policemen and their dogs. Six students were arrested, and the proctors gave the policemen the names of a further sixty students who had been present around the hotel.

The subsequent trial of fifteen students led to harsh punishment handed down by Justice Melford Stevenson, with six imprisoned, two sent to Borstal and two deported. The judge said he would have been more severe but for the 'evil influence' of some senior members of the university – a remark condemned by the vice-chancellor, Owen Chadwick.

By the time I arrived at Jesus, the memory of the riot was beginning to fade, although Senior Common Rooms remained significantly split on their judgement of these events and the fairness of the legal decisions.

In 1975, Cambridge was still male and very traditional, with three all-women colleges and the rest men-only. Paradoxically, my all-male college had originally been a nunnery, purged when visited in the fifteenth century by royal officials who discovered there were more men in residence than there were nuns (somewhat like Girton in the 1970s). The make-up of the university was caricatured by the left-wing student newspaper *Stop Press*. In a banner headline referring to one of the university's most traditional male right-wing colleges, they declared, 'Magdalene College to go coed – grammar school boys to be admitted'.

University politics were dominated by the left, with vigorous debates between different groups about whether the socialist revolution was coming next year or the year after. On the right, students tended to take a more laid-back view of life. In a poll in 1974, the university's undergraduate Conservatives had voted strongly for Ted Heath to remain and not for Margaret Thatcher to become leader of the party. Right-wing politics favoured black-tie dinner discussions. Political proselytising was largely regarded as a waste of time. On one occasion, in my first term, the left decided to mount a demonstration outside Barclays Bank, perfectly properly complaining about the failure of the bank to disinvest from South Africa and its apartheid regime. Unfortunately, they chose to stage their demonstration on a Saturday morning, when the branch was shut. Non-lefties turned up to laugh at them. It was a good analogy. In those days, the left was over-earnest and the right was over-frivolous. The tide was clearly receding from student activism, but at the same time student representation within university governance was advancing. It was still an era, unlike today, when those graduating with a degree had little to fear from unemployment, even though it was a time of high unemployment more generally.

I arrived straight from military service with short hair, in a suit and tie, fit, standing up straight and sober – unlike virtually everyone else queuing up at the porter's lodge on Jesus Lane. I was greeted by the head porter, Regimental Sergeant Major Reg West, whose healthy contempt for students was matched by a deep love of his college. Standing smartly to attention to greet me, he said, 'I give a special welcome to you, sir. You are a gentleman, an officer; very different from these left-wing layabouts and skivers.'

Alas, his judgement did not survive my first term. Some weeks later, attending formal hall, I arrived with my guest, an old school friend who was a monk, clad in his habit, with a large bottle of cheap red wine which during the formal Latin grace I inadvertently knocked over. As the emptying bottle spread across the table and the hallowed ancient words of the grace echoed around the hall, RSM West's head spun round to identify the miscreant. He alighted on me, by now transformed into a long-haired, jeans-wearing, slouching student, as the culprit of this heinous act. It was clear my privileged status was well and truly dead.

The monk came often to dinner. Because he was, by definition, chaste, he was extremely popular with a number of Cambridge's most beautiful women who were bored with unsophisticated male undergraduates slobbering all over them and preferred to spend time with a man whose sole interest lay in their brainpower and intellect. One particularly lovely girl would frequently accompany him around Cambridge. Towards the end of our university career, the pressure became too much for him and he resigned from the monastery, declining to take his further vows. That night, in a frenzy of release, he bicycled all the way to Madingley and at 2 a.m. banged on the door of the house where the girl lived. Roused from her slumbers, she threw open the upstairs window, demanding to know what he wanted. Standing there, beneath her window, habit gone, eyes ablaze, he told her that he had resigned from the monastery and had arrived to make love to her. 'Take me! Take me!' he said.

The lady in question looked down from her window. 'Certainly not! You're a monk. You must go straight back to Cambridge.' And with that, she shut the window and went back to bed while the monk, poor fellow, bicycled back to college. He later became editor of the *Daily Express*.

In those days, students were expected at least to go through the motions of attending to their studies. To the less industrious like me, it was necessary to ensure that tutorials were attended in the company of 'a swot' – someone more intelligent (not difficult) who had diligently mastered the subject of the day. On arrival at my first history tutorial, I discovered to my horror that I had been paired with George Plumptre – later a great expert on gardens – who was similarly ill-prepared for our tutor Norman Stone's interrogation. We were both sent away much chastened with his warning that we would not survive our first year unless we pulled up our socks. George and I promptly vowed to find tutorial partners of a more brainy and conscientious variety.

But I was fascinated by Norman Stone's mastery of Russia and the Eastern Front at the end of the First World War. Norman had unique access to original documentation because he had learned three of the local languages while imprisoned by the Soviet bloc for attempting to smuggle the girlfriend of one of his mates over the Iron Curtain in the boot of his car. Our subsequent meetings became a real pleasure as he teased me about my political views ('wishy-washy'), supervised me in history and taught me how to survive extraordinarily long drinking sessions without falling down the stairs on my way back to my rooms. Norman subsequently became my moral tutor – a position for which he was exceedingly ill-equipped (not least as on one occasion he tried to seduce my girlfriend) but which at least showed the college authorities had a sense of humour. He finally left Jesus, bound for Oxford, not because of his subversive views or his intellectual confrontations with lesser academics but because the college authorities tired of his girlfriend bicycling through the college quads. That, for them, was the final straw.

Later in my time at university I asked Norman if he would be my referee for my first job in the City of London, working for the investment bank Lazard Brothers. He generously consented. When I was interviewed there, I was asked if I knew what he had said (I didn't). The lengthy and witty piece, mainly dissecting my faults, with a nod to my questionable qualities, was gleefully read out by my interlocutor, ending with the wonderfully backhanded line: 'I like him – very much against my better judgement.'

I adored life in college. Being surrounded by hundreds of fellow students, all facing more or less the same problems – essay crises, running out of money, girlfriend/boyfriend issues – was reassuring. I was elected to the 'Jesus Genials', who met twice a term for breakfast in the Prioress's room. Over the course of a leisurely three hours, fruit juice, cereal, coffee, bacon, scrambled eggs, beans, mushrooms, egg-fried bread, black pudding, croissants, toast and marmalade were all consumed and washed down by copious amounts of beer. No words were permitted to be uttered for the first sixty minutes while the morning papers were also devoured in silence. I still have the club tie but have lost the appetite.

My college chums and I discovered early on that there was a considerable difference in the quality of wine consumed at high table and that available to undergraduates to purchase. Diligent research revealed that 'college societies' had access to the college cellars on the same terms as the fellows. And so it was that the 'Jesus Young Contemptibles' was formed to promote the noble game of backgammon. I was deputed to go to see the college's senior tutor, a taciturn geographer called Bruce Sparks, to explain with a straight face the importance of this club for college undergraduates and our intellectual development and to seek his agreement to it being set up.

'Mitchell, who is going to run this club?'

'It will be run by the Gammon, Ed Broadbent, and his deputy, Andy Barnes, will be the Backgammon,' I said.

'Indeed, and what role are you going to play?' he enquired.

'I am the honorary secretary and Keeper of the Board!'

With a look of total disbelief, he gave the necessary consent. For the rest of our university careers, fourteen of us would meet for dinner once a term in one of Jesus's magnificent private dining rooms, where the college's finest wines would be consumed – often at original cost price. On the first occasion, a backgammon board did indeed appear and made its way down the table before being jettisoned at the far end. Honour thus satisfied, it was never seen again. I remember that in the middle of our fifth term dinner, a reflective silence descended on those gathered around the table when one of our number pointed out that we were precisely halfway through our university careers. We understood all too well our good fortune and luck at being able to spend three years in such a wonderful place.

As Christmas approached at the end of my first term, it was suggested I seek election to the committee of the Cambridge University Conservative Association (CUCA). I did not take much persuading. As the snow fell across the beautiful main court of King's

College, I made my way from the Advent carol service in King's Chapel to the Chetwynd Room. I ended up tying for bottom place on the committee with my friend and later Appeal Court judge Jon Baker. The issue was decided on the toss of a coin, and I was the fortunate winner.

During the next summer term, I was sitting one Sunday in my room in North Court when there was a knock on the door. The visitor announced herself as an undergraduate of King's College and the Communist candidate seeking election to the Cambridge City Council. She was passionate, engaging and beautiful, and I asked her if she would like a cup of tea to take a break from canvassing and put her case to me. She agreed and we chatted for half an hour or so before she popped the question – would I consider voting for her? I suggested that I couldn't really as I was on the Conservative committee. Outraged, her eyes flashing, she demanded to know why I had wasted her time in futile conversation. I explained that – it got worse – my father was a Conservative Member of Parliament and I had been told that if a canvasser came calling for another party it was standard practice to keep them talking for as long as possible to delay them contacting floating voters whom they might then persuade to support them. Tossing her long fair hair, she stalked off.

A few days later, Pippa and I met on King's Parade as I was going to a student meeting and, in the hope of making amends, I persuaded her to come along as well and meet some of my friends. She could then discuss with them the forthcoming revolution she hoped to bring about in Cambridge city politics. She went down extremely well in Conservative circles, most of whom had never met a Communist before, and especially not such a good-looking one. High Tories christened her 'Pipska'. In the subsequent city council elections, she produced an unusually high vote – bolstered by a considerable number of Conservative students who voted for her.

I found new and yet more ingenious ways of getting in touch. My interest in Marxist dialectical materialism acted as a suitable bridgehead and we started a liaison, necessarily secret since she was paranoid about being seen with me. She had been spotted by a comrade talking to a Tory outside St John's College already and had been lucky not to face a motion of censure.

In great excitement, I found a loose railing at the perimeter of King's College on the Backs and managed to creep in late at night to see her. In turn, she would come over the wall at the back of Jesus College grounds, where I would meet her. Hugging the shadows, we would avoid the porters on their evening rounds as we made our way back to North Court for further discussions about Marx, Engels and the impending revolution.

In those days there was a rule that no member of college could have any guest to stay over for more than three nights on the trot. On a number of occasions, my Marxism tutorials went on for longer than the rules permitted, and I was confronted by the head porter, RSM West. Ever mindful of the Army officer in whom he had placed such high hopes and my subsequent fall from grace, he gleefully announced that I had been caught, that I was in breach of college rules and was to report to the senior tutor. Not for the first or last time, I duly reported to his rooms.

'Ah, Mitchell,' he started. 'You've had your lady friend staying with you for more than three nights in a row. You know perfectly well this is a breach of the college rules and I'm fining you £5.'

'But Senior Tutor, the college rules encourage promiscuity and should be amended.' By now my thumbs were behind my lapels as I warmed to my role as a barrack-room lawyer. 'If I'd stayed with three different guests, each for two nights, I'd have had guests for six nights without incurring any fine.'

A look of tired disdain appeared on the senior tutor's face.

'Mitchell, pay the fucking fine!'

Outside of my college life at university and my somewhat limited study of history – and Marxism – I got elected to the lower reaches of the Cambridge Union as well as CUCA. The Tories were ruled over by David Prior – later a colleague at Lazard Brothers and a distinguished minister who to great excitement invited Mrs Thatcher to speak at the start of her time as party leader. We were lucky enough to hear most of the leading lights in the Tory Party in those days and the centre right started to build amongst undergraduates – though not in the Senior Common Rooms, which broadly regarded Mrs Thatcher's views with distaste. Only in Peterhouse, which Michael Portillo had recently left, was there an extrovert right-wing fellowship. Edward Norman, the right-wing cleric, held court there as Dean. In the opposing corner was the left-winger Stanley Booth-Clibborn, rector of Great St Mary's in Cambridge and future Bishop of Manchester. Identified Tories were summoned to Peterhouse to be looked over by Maurice Cowling, whose contribution to Conservative thinking and philosophy was well known. I was invited in my turn to have tea with him, but I was judged to be somewhat wet and centrist in my politics.

In due course I became chairman of CUCA and mounted a recruiting campaign for new members. Our president was Rab Butler, Master of Trinity College, who lived in the magnificent lodge in

Trinity Great Court with his wife, Mollie, a Courtauld, whose art decorated the lodge walls and whose photographic memory meant she could greet almost all the college undergraduates by name. Rab was a celebrated figure around the university. As CUCA's president he would preside once a year at a black-tie dinner held in his college for Conservative undergraduates. Playing us like a fiddle, he would announce to thunderous applause that his college had not only taught more crowned heads of Europe than anywhere else but received more Nobel Prizes than all of France – a comment that resulted in prolonged cheering and foot-stamping as bread rolls were hurled in all directions while Rab sat beaming in his seat amidst the growing mayhem around him.

At the start of my term as chairman, I asked Rab somewhat cheekily if I could bring my committee to meet him in his lodge. He agreed. 'You had better bring them in the back so no one sees.'

We all arrived and were taken up to the magnificent first-floor sitting room, where we literally sat at his feet, hanging on his every word as he reminisced about his long political career, making amusing and off-colour remarks about our leader, Mrs Thatcher. At one point he told us that Mrs Thatcher thought that Sinai was a nasal complaint. I persuaded Rab to have a photograph taken with all the CUCA committee in front of the fountain in Trinity Great Court into which, after the aforementioned dinner, various undergraduates tended to end up. The picture still hangs above my desk.

Thanks to Rab's encouragement and the prevailing political wind, the recruitment campaign for which I was responsible in autumn 1978 increased CUCA's membership to over 1,000 for the first time, making us the largest political organisation in Cambridge. Fuelled by our excellent results, I was invited to the Conservative

Party conference in Blackpool. On the day in question, there was a controversial speech by a Young Conservative, forcefully denouncing party policy and its support for Rhodesia. Needless to say, this had not gone down well amongst the assembled representatives. The party high command thought it would be helpful to restore the reputation of the party's youth and for a tamer, less high-profile Young Conservative to address the conference to reassure the old guard. I was asked to speak.

It started well enough, with thunderous applause as I announced that 'I have come hot-foot from Cambridge, where for the first time we have recruited more than 1,000 members'. I then turned to the issue being debated, namely the House of Lords, which I suggested should be reformed, with a regional element and the removal of most of the hereditary peers. The applause grew thinner and thinner as I developed what seemed to me a perfectly reasonable argument. When the next speaker rose, playing to the audience, he sneakily pointed out that I had delivered my speech 'in the presence on this platform of the flower of their Lordships' House, the finest example of hereditary service and duty, the Lord Carrington'. The subsequent applause nearly lifted the roof off the conference hall as I and my arguments for reform slunk away. (It is authoritatively said that on the day of his death Lord Carrington departed with a smile on his face, because it was the day after Boris Johnson resigned as Foreign Secretary.) It was on the following day that William Hague made his memorable conference contribution as a sixteen-year-old youth from Yorkshire.

Back in Cambridge, the Labour Club had had to be wound up as a result of mischievous entryism by frivolous Conservative elements. The left had splintered, but the more centrist of their number regrouped into the Fabians. Over the summer long vacation – the period between June and October when the university was without its undergraduates – I had stayed up in college organising the CUCA programme for the following term. I bumped into Robert Harris, who was similarly organising a Labour programme for the Fabians and more importantly writing a guide to Cambridge for the next year's freshers. Robert had discovered a highly effective wheeze whereby he'd write to restaurants throughout the Cambridge area impressing on them the importance of providing a free meal for two so that he could write up the full glories of their culinary offering and congenial ambience in his new guide.

Alas, he was without transport, whereas I had a battered Morris 1100 which I ran on my savings from the Army. During the summer of 1977, we toured the outlying villages around Cambridge in what was essentially a sophisticated form of protection racket, as it was made clear to the owners that unless they gave us free meals their existence would not be mentioned. A firm friendship was formed over Château Cissac at the Chestnuts Restaurant in Madingley.

On one occasion the next term, when he was running the Cambridge left and I, the Cambridge right, we'd agreed to meet for dinner, and I rushed through the doors of his Selwyn College rooms. Robert was chairing a meeting of the Cambridge Organisation of Labour Students, a dour group of comrades, one of whom actually had the initials 'NKDV'. There were dropped jaws and looks of surprise from the Labour student leadership at the evidence before them that Robert was on speaking terms with a known Tory. I quickly reversed out of the room, leaving Robert with some explaining to do.

It is striking how few of my generation at Cambridge went into national politics – in contrast to Oxford, which has provided no fewer than three Prime Ministers from my generation in the past ten years alone. And Oxford sent at least three others into the House of Commons who might also (at least in their own estimation) have reached No. 10. From Cambridge, apart from David Lidington and Bernard Jenkin, who joined in the intake after mine, and Oliver Letwin and Owen Paterson a little later, none opted to do so. There were far more lawyers and journalists. In Trinity there was a distinguished and elite group bound for national journalism. My old friend Nick Coleridge was there, along with Charles Moore, who occupied rooms above Justin Welby. Oliver Letwin, who disdained CUCA but was seen as a fearsome intellectual, was amongst them, alongside the future BBC broadcaster Ed Stourton, who was widely regarded by the female undergraduates as the most beautiful man in the university.

During my first term at Cambridge, the president of the Cambridge Union was Peter Bazalgette, a larger-than-life extrovert and showman. He conducted the campaign to recruit new arrivals along with David Johnson, later a Church of England vicar and the most gifted and amusing speaker of his generation. Together they made a remarkable team. I remember in one debate a speaker had asked all the men to raise their hands and then all the women. David Johnson leapt to his feet: 'On a point of order, Mr President, Mr Bazalgette has voted twice.' Peter Bazalgette as president immediately responded, 'On a further point of order, Mr Johnson hasn't voted at all!' As soon as I met them both I was hooked and decided that given half a chance I would very much like to be president of the Union myself.

During Peter's term in office, he embarked enthusiastically

on the traditional mischief of sending up the Oxford Union. He unveiled a character called 'Colonel Rowland Wetherby-Johnston' and included him in his programme for the following term, giving a lecture entitled 'Idi Amin – apostle or oppressor?' This was proudly emblazoned on his term card. Having established Wetherby-Johnston's credentials, he suggested to the Oxford president that he might also persuade Wetherby-Johnston to come to speak so that Oxford undergraduates too could enjoy his lecture.

In due course, the colonel cancelled his appearance at Cambridge. A bad case of dengue fever was blamed. The Oxford president, suspicious, asked if he could speak to the colonel, so Peter persuaded his father to appear on the end of a phone from his City office, barking down the line at being disturbed. The Oxford president was duly reassured.

Peter now set about his prank with vigour. Because I owned a car, I was drafted in as Wetherby-Johnston's driver, and a Cambridge schoolmaster who fancied his grasp of amateur dramatics was roped in and kitted out with a suitable regimental tie. As we arrived in Oxford for his lecture, the library at the Union was packed with undergraduates. The colonel was introduced by the president and began his address. Fuelled by copious quantities of gin, which he proceeded to consume as he spoke, his meaningless ramblings became more and more incoherent and obscene, while the Oxford Union president started to fidget and look uncomfortable as he glared at Peter and me.

I cringe with embarrassment at what happened next. In our defence, I should say that Idi Amin at this stage was the butt of media humour in Britain and not yet revealed as the tyrant and human rights abuser that he was. Suddenly, a genuine Ugandan student – a refugee from Amin's brutal regime – stood up and denounced the colonel as an impostor and the audience started to rustle uneasily as mounting anger developed. Several students started to heckle, and it looked as if – with some justification – the Cambridge team might be assaulted.

And then – I have no idea how such a providential event took place – a fire alarm went off and the Union building was evacuated. In the confusion, the colonel, Peter and I sprinted down the High to my car and escaped back to Cambridge under cover of darkness. The *Daily Mail* duly reported the story in Nigel Dempster's column, under the headline 'Who was dat Man at de Union?'

Oxford's revenge was swift. David Johnson, the Cambridge Union secretary, was kidnapped and subsequently paraded, all trussed up, in a supermarket trolley at a debate in the Oxford Union. They also displayed him, thus restrained, in a shop window in the middle of Oxford.

In order to become president, you first had to be elected as honorary secretary. Once this hurdle was cleared, usually – though not always – the presidency was yours. As Jesus College was near the Union, I needed to ensure that the college turned out to support me if I was to win. But there was a problem. I was known as a Tory and the college (as foreshadowed by my teacher at Rugby) was politically very divided. I needed to secure the support of the college left.

One afternoon I spotted Geoff Hoon, then a graduate at Jesus studying for his LLB, walking through the college quad. Geoff Hoon was known to be on the left of politics in Cambridge and was subsequently a Labour MP and distinguished Secretary of State for Defence. I knew that Geoff was hoping to become president of the Junior Common Room, a post reserved for the leading student representative within college. We arranged to meet. That night, over several pints of Abbot Ale, then the Cambridge student's drink of choice, we did a deal in the college bar. He would tell his left-wing supporters, 'I know Andrew is a Tory, but he is a college man and we should all rally round and support him in spite of his ghastly political views.' I, in my turn, would tell my friends and supporters of the centre right and in the boat club circles, 'Look, I know Geoff is a socialist, but if he's elected he will run the college bar efficiently and ensure the price of beer is kept down.' Shortly after, we both attained the respective positions we sought.

Once elected to serve as president of the Cambridge Union for the Lent term in 1978, I set about organising my programme of events. I held a debate on the death penalty, which was supported by Group Captain Douglas Bader, the flying ace of the Second World War, and Teddy Taylor, a Scottish MP. It was opposed by Dick Taverne, the independent MP, and by Albert Pierrepoint, Britain's most famous hangman. At this point in his life Mr Pierrepoint had decided he was against the profession of which he, his father and his uncle had been a part (though he later appeared ambivalent).

The Cambridge Union rejected the death penalty by a substantial margin on that occasion, but my main memory of the debate was when Albert Pierrepoint stunned the attending students by announcing that he had become a hangman 'because I wanted to travel the world and meet interesting people'.

When the debate was over, I took him back to the hotel where he was staying – in his retirement he was running a pub in Oldham called, ironically, 'Help the Poor Struggler', with a sign above the door saying, 'No hanging around the bar'. I stayed with him for several hours. He drank lager in half-pint measures and told me tales of all the different people he had hanged – 433 men and seventeen women, by his reckoning. His record was seventeen in one day. His proud boast was that he could get a prisoner out of his cell with a noose round his neck and hanging dead between the first and last chimes of the prison clock at eight in the morning. I listened spellbound, but just before I left, I noticed that unlike most people, whose eyes are alive and tend to be a window into their souls, Albert Pierrepoint's eyes were cold and dead. It was a chilling revelation I have never forgotten.

The most memorable debate of my term turned out to be more exciting than I had planned. I wanted to do something for the charity Save the Children and decided to hold a celebrity debate with four famous national figures. By tradition, there was always a funny debate every term on a frivolous motion. Recent examples included 'A cigarette before and a brandy after are three of the best things in life'.

With an insensitivity that today makes me recoil, I decided my celebrity funny debate would be on the motion 'A woman's place is in the harem'. Robert Morley and Stirling Moss proposed the motion. Derek Nimmo and Felicity Kendall opposed it. On this occasion we charged undergraduates a pound a ticket and they were all sold out within an hour – the queue ran all the way around the Union and out on to Sidney Street. Ed Stourton commissioned Kit Hunter Gordon – subsequently a City magnate who both won and lost a billion-dollar fortune – to produce a suitable poster advertising the debate which included a scantily clad female at its centre. To top off my inadvertent bid to be the most politically in-correct undergraduate in the UK, I arranged for the whole thing to be sponsored by the pro-apartheid regime Barclays Bank.

I invited Her Royal Highness Princess Anne to preside over the evening in her role as president of Save the Children. The evening started well enough – all the speakers arrived and were presented to HRH at the Master's lodge at Jesus College. I even witnessed the moment when Robert Harris joined the Establishment and delivered the lowest bow to the royal personage.

As we made our way towards the Union after dinner, I could not help noticing a rather large police presence and the growing noise of chanting. As we rounded the corner, I saw that the whole front of the Union building had been besieged by placard-waving women, outraged at my choice of subject for the debate. I quickly met the leader of the demonstration and pointed out that it was a humorous debate to raise money for a good cause, but she was having none of it.

The attempt to bar our entry was thwarted by a chain of stout dinner-jacketed fellows protecting our royal guest from the yelling mob of Cambridge feminists, roused from their political slumbers both by my political provocation and by the even more provoca-tive poster. I heard Derek Nimmo say to Robert Morley, 'Do you think it's all right for us to go in? Aren't we crossing a picket line?' and Morley's response, 'Don't worry, old boy, it's only a bunch of students.'

The debate started with undergraduate contributions, brilliantly funny from Adrian Sells and Rory McGrath. With Princess Anne alongside me as I sat in the president's chair, with Wesley Kerr, subsequently the BBC's royal correspondent, appropriately sitting along the bench from HRH, Rory ended with a song about being a rock in the Rocky Mountains. The punchline, ending his speech, was 'Oh fuck! I've forgotten the words!' (which he certainly hadn't). As I nervously turned to see Princess Anne's reaction, the audience roared its approval for his wonderful performance. Fortunately, she too was amused.

As Robert Morley got to his feet, I saw to my horror that the demonstrating mob had moved round to the back of the Union Society, where they were trying to gain entry to the chamber through the fire doors. They pushed against the hinges and the doors bulged. Some of the audience moved to lean against the doors to stop them from being forced open. My admittedly brief life passed before my eyes as I realised the carnage that would follow if the doors were breached. Mercifully, they weren't.

By the time the debate was over, a brilliant evening had raised substantial sums for Save the Children, and fifty police officers were encircling the building. The headlines the next morning were lurid. In the national press, the *Mirror*'s front page ran with 'ANNE – MOB FURY' in block capitals, leaving little room for any text after. The *Evening Standard* read 'MOB THAT JEERED ANNE WAS A DISGRACE' and 'PIN-UPS STARTED ANNE DEMO'. Another red-top had 'STUDENTS IN FOUR-LETTER FURY'. Budding student journalists wrote it all up in sundry magazines including the *New Statesman*, but as the week went by I recognised that my attempts at a bit of worthwhile fun were unlikely to lead to a career in public relations.

At the end of my term, Robert Harris took over as president and I headed off to try to secure a degree and work out what to do next.

As I was walking past the college chapel shortly thereafter, out of the shadows jumped one of the fellows – a professor in the law faculty. He was widely thought amongst undergraduates to be a 'spotter' for the Secret Intelligence Service, MI6.

'Andrew – have you got a moment? I was wondering what you were thinking of doing when you leave. Have you decided?'

I said I hadn't really made up my mind but thought a spell at a merchant bank might be interesting.

Conspiratorially moving towards me, he whispered in a low voice in my ear, 'I wonder if you have ever considered working for Her Majesty's Government in an informal capacity?'

My eyes lit up. 'Are you suggesting I should join MI6? I'm not sure that's a very good idea. I'm far too indiscreet.'

And with that, he turned around and shot back into the Senior Common Room.

I left Cambridge in June 1978, having secured a job with Lazard Brothers. Going to and fro on the milk round between different merchant banks, I'd found myself in the lift at Rothschild's with another applicant from Oxford, Duncan Budge. As the lift ascended and we eyed each other up as competition, I muttered to him that I hoped our prospective employer did not know that I had originally failed my maths O-level.

'Goodness!' he said. 'I failed mine too.'

Before starting in the City, I managed to prolong my student days by undertaking a three-week debating tour to Australia and, more seriously, a ten-week debating tour of the United States.

Along with two debating companions from the Union – Daphne Romney and Daniel Janner, both now successful lawyers – we made our way down to the Antipodes via Bangkok, where, for reasons I cannot immediately recall, the No. 2 in the Australian Embassy arranged for us to visit a huge local massage parlour. The girls were lined up behind a glass screen, fluttering their eyelids at potential customers, each with a number. I remember it as a relatively chaste and innocent experience.

I also remember an amusing exchange with an Australian diplomat who said that the trouble with British diplomats was that they were all so uptight, and when confronted with a photograph of them in a compromising position would feel obliged to spy for the Russians. 'It wouldn't happen to me,' he said. 'I'm gay and proud of it. If a Russian spy sidled up to me with that picture, I'd say, "Oh, thank you! Can I have an enlargement of this one, and that one nicely framed?"'

In Australia, we debated in Sydney, Melbourne and Adelaide, including against Malcolm Turnbull, the future Australian Prime Minister, who subsequently ran rings around the British government in the *Spycatcher* saga.

Once back home, I set off with Adair Turner, also a former president of the Union, for the US debating tour. Each year the US sent two debaters to speak in British universities, and Adair and I were the lucky two selected for the return match. For ten weeks we crisscrossed the USA, speaking at thirty universities and boarding seventy flights. We seemed to spend an extraordinary amount of time in Kansas City Airport, where, on hearing my voice, a lady serving coffee said, 'Say, where is your accent from?' I owned up to coming from England.

'Say,' she said, 'is that an American state?'

With all the arrogance of youth, Adair and I had submitted ten motions for debate. We blithely said we'd speak on either side, whichever our hosts preferred. Our motions were clearly designed to provoke middle America: 'Big government is economically superior and morally essential' or 'Abortion on demand is every woman's right'.

In Iowa we stayed with a staunch Republican family who, not content with mere guns, kept a tracked armoured vehicle in their garage. With another family in Oklahoma, ahead of our debate at Oral Roberts University, we joined hands around the family dining table to pray for the return of our luggage, which Ozark Airlines had mislaid. Literally five minutes later our luggage turned up. Our God-fearing hosts announced that the Lord's loving care had been visited on Andrew and Adair.

When asked on Kansas public radio whether our hosts at the local community college had entertained us well, it probably would have been better not to announce in a completely dry county that we had enjoyed being introduced to the joys of drinking tequila. Later, in Texas, we felt our hosts were taking our support for liberal values and fun a little too literally when we arrived at our hotel to find we had been given a very pleasant room with one double bed. In the subsequent debate I said that while we were both strongly in favour of gay rights, we didn't think they should be made compulsory. The audience might not have agreed with the sentiment nor understood that the second part was a joke.

Where we really got our comeuppance was at Colorado State University. The topic of the day was 'Christianity is an elaborate superstition'. We opted to propose. When we arrived at the huge auditorium, there were nearly 1,000 students beaming at us. It was clear that the audience was largely drawn from the student Christian Union, and the selection of British university jokes which laced our speeches did not attract the usual merriment and laughter. When we sat down, the leader of the opposing team took to the podium and spoke: 'Before I demolish the arguments of our English guests, I'd like to invite everyone to join me in praying for the immortal souls of Andrew and Adair.' There and then, some with their arms in the air, 1,000 American students prayed for us to be saved. At the end of the evening, we secured fewer than fifty votes.

All good things must come to an end and Adair and I returned to the UK having finished off our extraordinarily fortunate university careers with a truly life-enhancing experience. We ended up shortly afterwards living together in the shadow of the Arsenal stadium in London. I had got to know a bit about America and started a lifelong love affair with that great country.

CHAPTER 3

TOP HATS AND DILDOS

With what would undoubtedly have been regarded then as comprehensive diversity, two graduate trainees, one from Oxford and one from Cambridge – naturally both pale, male and public school-educated, and both having failed maths O-level first time round – were admitted to Lazard Brothers and Co., Ltd in 1978. One of them was me. I was immediately despatched to start my training in the cash department – working for the chief cashier, Squadron Leader Sparrow. He had been wounded in the war and had a wooden leg. As the day went on, he became increasingly grumpy as the pain from his stump grew worse. My task was to count £10 notes – large quantities of them – and precious little else. My enquiries about what more I could do to help were met with a grunt.

In the evening, the other graduate trainee, Duncan Budge, who had arrived in October, came down to meet me. I asked him if the training was as bad as it seemed. 'I'm afraid it's rather worse,' he said, and we went off to the pub to swap notes. Visiting a pub in Highgate approximately twice a month on a Tuesday is something Duncan and I have done assiduously for the past forty-one years, until Covid intervened.

In the late 1970s, the City of London was, as in the sunset state of England before the First World War, enjoying what turned out to be the last phase before revolutionary change overwhelmed it. The 'Big Bang' which would change everything was coming, but when I arrived in the City many of its existing practices could be traced back a century or more. The accepting houses (merchant banks) had to be located within a mile of the Bank of England. The Bank lending rate was physically announced on the steps of the Bank of England and Lazard's head messenger, George Crown, would sprint back to the Bank and literally run around the different floors breathlessly shouting, 'No change.' There were no mobile phones and long-distance communication was transacted mainly by telex. A physical stock exchange offered market prices on blackboards in an entirely male environment where public school boys played pranks on each other. When I was sent down there for a week of training, one fellow quietly reading *The Times* in a corner had it set on fire. Another bald chap ended up having stamps surreptitiously stuck on his head.

The City of London was basically a huge closed shop run by the English (not British) Establishment, where officers mixed with 'other ranks' – often bright working-class chaps most frequently from Essex. It was designed to limit competition through a careful system of demarcation. Stockbrokers dealt with investors but could not make markets in shares. A system of fixed commissions meant that there was no price competition between them. Jobbers could make markets but not deal with investors. Merchant banks could underwrite share issues but not distribute the shares to investors (that was only for the brokers, who could not underwrite the issues they distributed). And the merchant banks, by convention, agreed not to poach each other's clients and, if they did, it was only after an embarrassed personal apology to the other bank. One firm of stockbrokers, Mullens and Co., had the monopoly of acting for the government in the gilt (government bond) market. Even when I arrived, its partners were required to wear top hats on the floor of the exchange. The discount market, where short-term bills of exchange were traded, was another closed shop operated by the discount houses with privileged access to the Bank of England. The whole system was designed to protect the established firms from competition and enabled the system to operate with surprisingly little capital. It permitted a comfortable, complacent, not very hard-working but self-satisfied life for those inside the protective barricades. But it also turned out, like Singapore in 1941, to be perfectly designed to be utterly overrun, practically overnight, as soon as all its restrictive practices were blown away in one fell swoop. But that was still in the future when I rocked up into one of the haughtiest pillars of all this seemingly rock-solid world.

Ironically, Lazard had almost come to grief in the early part of the twentieth century at the hands of a trader in the Low Countries. He had nearly bankrupted the bank but did the decent thing when presented with a revolver and a glass of whisky. The Bank of England had asked the French partners of Lazard in Paris to recapitalise the London firm, but they refused to do so and the Governor of the Bank of England persuaded the Pearson family to take over the ownership.

The merchant banks were a collection of fifteen accepting houses and all their graduate intake teamed up occasionally for dinners so we could get to know each other. This was the first year that Lazard Brothers had ever run a graduate trainee scheme – recruitment previously had been as a result of being known to a director, sometimes as a godson or a relation. The same families tended to run things down the generations. As George Soros said before leaving London for the US, it was almost impossible to transact business without having a personal relationship. The City of London institutions stayed English and small. Clients were taken to Glyndebourne and the Royal Opera House. You might take someone to Lords, but no one took anyone to Stamford Bridge to watch Chelsea. However, a senior director from Lazard did take an important prospective client whom he was wooing to a performance by Dame Edna Everage – the brilliantly funny one-man show by Barry Humphries, the well-known Australian comedian and sage. Having made the mistake of ordering front-row seats, he compounded his folly by arriving late. He was hauled up on stage with his client and they were ritually humiliated for the first twenty minutes of the show. The client never returned to Lazard nor hired our professional services. All this was gleefully witnessed by Duncan Budge from the safety of the back row of the stalls and joyously reported back to the Bank in full detail the next morning.

In spite of their social exclusivity, the London merchant banks were not really that profitable, one of the reasons they were so easily taken out later. Huge pay cheques were very much a thing of the future – not least because top rates of tax were over 80 per cent, rising to a staggering 98 per cent on unearned income. People were supposed to be dismissive about money; it was regarded as rather tasteless to talk about it. Indeed, at Lazard Brothers, revealing your salary to a fellow employee was a sackable offence. Getting married, however, secured a payment of £50, though only on the first occasion. There was a supportive paternalism about the place. One colleague whose wife, sadly, had had a miscarriage, was told that the board had decided to pay for him and his wife to go on a cruise to South Africa for a holiday.

This was my first experience of the 'old boy network' in action. We were well paid – £3,750 per year, with a small staff bonus at Christmas time – usually 3 per cent of salary – and normally given out on the afternoon of the annual carol service, which staff were expected to attend and where the chairman read the last lesson, starting with the words 'I am the alpha and the omega'. Archie Norman, seeking recruitment the previous year, had decided not to go to a merchant bank and signed up to Citibank because they paid £1,000 more per annum and their training programme was far more professional. This was, with hindsight, very much the way of the future for subsequent generations joining the City.

Sometime later I asked why Lazard had recruited Duncan and me through a transparent selection process rather than the more traditional hiring route (the personnel director, Brigadier Walker, had recruited from Oxford, Cambridge and Exeter – a university close to his weekend home). We were told that some of the directors thought they should recruit some young men 'with a bit more shittiness about them'.

Following the secondary banking crisis in 1973–75, Lord Poole, chairman of Lazard (and of the Conservative Party), was asked to set out his criteria for successful lending. 'It's quite simple,' he said. 'I only lend money to people who have been at Eton.' (He later suggested, however, that 'there are too many Etonians at Lazard; we should have more Scotchmen and more Jews'.)

This total closed shop was blown apart in 1985 when Big Bang opened up the City of London to competition. The Americans arrived, with a business model based on integrating merchant banks, brokers, jobbing and bill discounting, all supported by substantial balance sheets. They were ferociously driven by money, building organisations and making capital. It was as if a huge predator had been released into a pool of elegant, lazy, fat trout. Above the trading floor of one American bank was hung a mission statement: 'Let's make nothing but money'. Most of the accepting houses disappeared and were bought for very little. Warburg's, by then the leader, took some time to die before being gobbled up by UBS. Lazard Brothers and Rothschild's were the only ones to survive, essentially because they were advisory houses not competing with the new, capital-intensive, much larger-scale US business model.

As the 1980s advanced, Lazard Brothers got to know better its two sister houses, in New York and in Paris. Lazard Frères in New York was tiny, employing fewer than 400 people, but its influence was immense. It had been run until recently by André Meyer, described by Forbes as 'the most important investment banker in the Western world' and having 'an almost erotic attachment to money', and by one financial journalist as 'comparing unfavourably with Satan'. He lived in a suite in the Carlyle Hotel and even in the 1970s was worth hundreds of millions of pounds. He and the legendary Felix Rohatyn literally invented the mergers and acquisitions business. He despised the English firm, thinking that they were bone-headed antisemites. (Indeed, in those early days Lazard London had a clear streak of antisemitism about it. On one occasion an executive in London had agreed to receive the Mayor of Jerusalem for a business meeting and was told by the vice chairman that if he ever did anything like that again he'd be fired.)

Lazard Paris has probably changed the least. Populated by French énarques and mostly aristocratic haut banquiers – clever, secretive and serpentine – it was the only private bank to avoid nationalisation under President Mitterrand. The French would occasionally do business with Lazard London. Their technique was to offer their roast-beef visitors an exquisite lunch in a private dining room in their Boulevard Haussmann headquarters, washed down by bottles of Château Latour, which they knew no Englishman could resist – all prior to being ruthlessly legged over by the French in the negotiations in the afternoon.

Michel David-Weill presided over New York and Paris as the owner-manager, described as the last emperor of Wall Street and thought to be Concorde's most frequent flyer. He always booked two seats, 1A and 1B, on the supersonic airline. He said this was so he could go through confidential papers, but more likely it was to avoid an uncontrolled seating plan. His brilliant skill was to manage people. He could motivate egocentric geniuses and megalomaniacs with the promise that if they brought him 'a big bag of money' he'd allow them to keep some of it. Paris was his spiritual home, but he was clearly comfortable amongst the big characters in New York, where, after all, everyone was a foreigner. He used to encourage those who were downcast with the words, 'If you are not dead, you are alive!'

London was a different world. Michel's cultural hinterland clashed with City culture. He was – and indeed still is – a connoisseur who loved art and wine and was a trustee of the Met, the Guggenheim and the Morgan Library in New York, while in Paris he was intimately involved in the French Académie des Beaux-Arts and a director of ICOM, the International Council of

Museums. He was more at ease with women than men. A subtle urban operator with a jaundiced view of human nature, he'd been forced to flee from Paris as a Jewish child under Nazi occupation and been hidden in the Vichy south, where he lived under a false name. He used to tell his partners, 'Your first duty is to survive,' and believed everyone had their price. He once said that it isn't difficult to identify a man's strengths; the test is to learn their weaknesses. In London we were fascinated by him – his wealth, his power and his Frenchness. In 1987, according to an interview at the time, he earned more than $25 million and his family's net worth was close to £1 billion. But he never felt at ease with the English upper-class elite that then ran the City, with their attitude towards wealth and their longing to retreat at the weekends to their country houses to garden and shoot small animals.

This culture clash was equally notable on a weekend visit by an American colleague to stay with an English director of Lazard at his country home in Hampshire. After being shown to their comfortable suite by the butler, the Americans descended for pre-dinner drinks in the drawing room. Taking aside their English host, one of the Americans, looking awkward and embarrassed, said, 'Say, John, I didn't want to worry you or anything but beside our bed are what look like three large dog turds.' Doubtless deposited by one or more of their owner's magnificent black Labradors. 'Oh, don't worry at all about that,' said their host. 'We let them dry out and then flick 'em out the window with a golf club.'

Michel's undoing was his son-in-law, Édouard Stern. Michel must have known Stern's faults but was attracted by his evident ability to make huge amounts of money. Michel persisted in the teeth of the opposition of his New York, French and British partners in promoting him as his heir apparent. Ultimately, Stern tried to organise a coup against his father-in-law amongst the Paris partnership and Michel then sacked him. By that time, however, his support for Stern had cost him the confidence of his partners and he was now without an heir apparent. This led to him bringing in Bruce Wasserstein, to whom he ultimately lost control of the firm.

Some time later, to the incredulity and disbelief of the strait-laced Lazard London fraternity, Stern died in unusual circum-stances. He was found dead by the police in his Geneva apartment, dressed head to toe in latex. He had been shot by his mistress and the latex had closed over the bullet wound so the cause of death was not immediately discernible. Apparently, he had promised her money but failed to honour the deal, so she had returned and killed him. The police also noted that he was found with a dildo up his bottom, something that caused a good deal of confusion, wonderment and teeth-sucking amongst his less adventurous former London colleagues. Allegedly, when told of his death and before the mistress's role was uncovered, Michel was asked who he thought could have done it. After pausing and sucking on his cigar, he is said to have replied, 'Well, it could have been anyone.'

When I joined in 1979, Lazard Brothers was a sleepy blue-chip merchant bank with a superb list of clients. The Queen Mother and the Beatles came to lunch. The culture was underlined by seeing in my first week two young members of staff, Ned Dawnay, who later played a key role in the privatisation of British Airways, and Simon Miller, subsequently a leader amongst the Edinburgh financial Establishment, heading off for lunch at midday, returning just after three o'clock up the escalators towards the Bank's front door smoking enormous cigars. In those days, the City was awash with alcohol. Everyone drank. The traders would drink beer in enormous quantities at lunchtime. On my first business lunch at NatWest, sherry was consumed before lunch, white then red wine with the meal, followed by a sweet wine for pudding and brandy and port (and cigars) afterwards. Lazard, curiously, was one of the first to forswear lunchtime drinking and while a can of beer was offered before lunch, only different types of water accompanied the meal. Although the firm bought Château Latour for the Pearsons, wine could only be served to clients with the specific permission of the chairman.

But the cultural change after Big Bang was immense. Instead of making do with one jacket and two pairs of trousers, staff increasingly instructed their City tailors to make one pair of trousers and two jackets, so that a jacket could be left permanently on the back of their chair in the office, giving an impression of employee diligence and permanent attendance at meetings.

Not long after my first week, Ned Dawnay was given the job of recruiting staff for the bank. His first question to any applicant would be 'Do you like dogs?' If the answer was no, they didn't get a job offer. It was also clear, as I learned from my fellow graduate trainee, that the bank's idea of training was to send the two of us round the bank's constituent parts – banking, corporate finance and investment management – to learn on the job with some occasional outside tuition.

No doubt I was full of myself – just back from the US debating tour, fresh from Cambridge and my stint as president of the Union – but I found the internal culture increasingly burdensome and unwisely showed it. The clerks who came in each day from

Essex resented opportunities being given to these two new graduates which would in all likelihood be denied to them. To be fair, they had a point in my case; my lack of an eye for detail in filling in forms which then had to be checked by them underlined how right they were. One of them, an elderly man who had a particular grudge against graduate trainees, caused us some trouble. So Duncan and I arranged, as one could in those days, and with the knowledge of all those who worked in the open-plan office around him, for a phone call to be put through to him of a taped message from a highly imaginative prostitute offering him a menu of unusual – at least in our circles – services. As he picked up the phone, his concentration deepened and his eyes bulged. There were a few strangulated gasps of 'yes, yes' which escaped from his lips until finally he dropped the phone, slumped in his chair and had to be carted off to the first aid room. On another occasion I was asked by a director if I was free for the evening. He teasingly told me that there could be a spare seat at the opera house in the Lazard box at Covent Garden or perhaps something more mundane. I immediately volunteered my services and instead of the opera was sent down to Bexley to supervise the sending out of telexes – all night until ten the next morning – all around the world for a bond issue.

During my brief time in the investment management side, my alienation grew as I encountered a group of public school alumni who were clearly there because of their connections and the culture that pervaded the place. The director in charge used to stride through the back office banging a hunting whip against his thigh like a cross between a concentration camp guard and a master of fox hounds. He was variously known as 'Flashman' and 'Bungalow' on account of his lack of a top storey. Sporting a large pair of red braces with socks to match, he would put his head around the door of his office and shout, 'BOY!' and the hapless fellow who worked for him would sprint from his nearby desk to do his master's bidding in much the same way as if he were still fagging at Eton. I remember one of his colleagues looking me over and announcing, 'This chap's family comes from trade' – a reference to my family's business in wine. Another colleague engaged in the process of recruitment was confronted by an applicant with a first-class degree. 'You've got a First,' he said. 'It would never do for us. We don't like too much cleverness.'

As our so-called training continued, Duncan and I sought a meeting with the head of the banking department, Mr Butterwick, a Pickwickian character who was nominally responsible for the graduate training programme. When we protested at the way we were being treated, we were told we would have to make our way through the engine room. Butterwick said, 'I started as a clerk at Willie Glyn's. It was good enough for me, so this is good enough for you.' I thought Duncan might be about to hit him. A week or so later I was summoned by Mr Butterwick, who said he was considering sacking me and was most concerned about my attitude. He said he would let me know at the end of the week. Fortunately, he relented.

At the end of the eighteen-month induction period, I was sent to the credits department to analyse company accounts. My first assignment was to check out BP's balance sheet to see if Lazard's line of credit for £2 million was safe. It was clear even to my unmathematical eye that the inquiry was ridiculous. BP could buy Lazard Brothers out of its petty cash. By then I had set my heart on working in corporate finance – the SAS of the merchant banking army – and sought an interview with one of their directors to ask if I could come to work for him. He told me the answer was no and while he couldn't say it was no for ever, he thought it most unlikely I had the skills required.

It was clearly time to move on. I'd realised my face did not fit, and I realised, too, that I had not handled myself well, nor had I respectfully listened and accepted without complaint whatever tedious task was thought appropriate to my grub-like status.

Duncan had been offered a place in corporate finance and subsequently became a key aide to the chairman, Ian Fraser. This was a dangerous role since one of his predecessors had, presumably as a result of irritating the chairman, been despatched to South Korea – in those days very much a hardship posting – for two years, managing a remarkably courageous investment that Lazard had made in setting up the first merchant bank there. At that time Lazard thought twice before lending to the British government, so an investment in Korea – a country little known and under a right-wing dictatorship – was a very brave act indeed. Ian Fraser had, however, been brought in to change the nature of the bank, and he proceeded to do so. Having had a successful career in Warburg's, he was the right choice to wake up a sleepy aristocratic institution and bring it up to date.

The winds of change were now blowing, and a more diverse and meritocratic group took over the main part of Lazard Brothers, if not the investment management side. One of those was a former Rhodesian, David Gemmill, educated at Oxford, who was now responsible for the international activities of Lazard Brothers, which attracted a more entrepreneurial type with its emphasis on project and export finance in the developing world and international advisory work. David had made his name at Lazard while he was our man in Hong Kong, organising the finance for the Mass Rapid Transit (MRT) railway system. He brought to the international division, along with Peter Godwin his deputy, an ability to secure and keep clients by his energy, manner and financial engineering skills. Hearing that I was leaving, he asked me whether I'd be interested in joining his new team. I immediately agreed.

For the next six years I spent a great deal of time abroad, away from the stultifying conditions and constraints of the old English City. We worked long hours and won interesting assignments. In those days, if we travelled for more than six hours, we always flew first class (something I would not dream of doing now). We stayed in the best hotels and on returning from an overseas visit were entitled to buy the finest bottle from duty-free to compensate for being away from home and working over a weekend.

On one occasion after taking off in a small plane from East Midlands Airport bound for Heathrow, I was alarmed to see the stewardess running down the aisle and fiddling with the controls at the rear of the aircraft. A little later, with studied calm, the pilot announced that there was a problem with the landing gear. Feeling rather unnerved, I was greatly reassured by the calm of the man sitting beside me – obviously a seasoned traveller – who continued to study with close attention the value of stocks and shares in his *Financial Times*. As the aircraft approached Heathrow, there was further running up and down the aisle and the pilot announced, 'I'm afraid we still don't seem able to lower the front wheel, so we are going to perform a manoeuvre which goes back to the First World War. We will fly over the tower and they will look up and examine our wheel with binoculars.' My rising panic levels were calmed by

my neighbour, who, unperturbed, was now studying closely investment trust valuations without showing a flicker of fear. After twice
flying over the tower, the pilot – his voice a study in nonchalance
– announced that we would be landing shortly and while 'there is
no need for alarm' asked us to adopt the brace position. My anxiety
level shot through the roof as I saw through the window two fire
engines racing down the runway – but we came into land safe and
sound. As the aircraft drew to a halt, my companion, who had said
not a word while continuing to study his *FT*, was a paragon of
calm and British stiff upper lip in what had clearly been a minor
crisis. 'Goodness,' I said. 'What a turn up for the books; I don't
know how you stayed so calm!' The fellow saw me talking to him,
put down his paper and said, 'I am so sorry, I can't hear you. I'm
afraid I am completely deaf.'

In my new posting, I worked for Douglas Bolam, a remarkable
septuagenarian who'd arrived at Lazard from MI6, where in his
time he'd been our man in Vietnam when the French were beaten
at Dien Bien Phu. To get to know me, he'd invited me to dinner
at his home in Sussex and to walk the Seven Sisters – a half-day's
hike along the clifftops. I'd assumed I'd need to stop and wait for
him to catch up but in the event found myself huffing and puffing
along in his slipstream.

Soon after, we set off together to do business in Algeria, Moroc-
co and Tunisia. On our first night in Algiers, we ventured out from
the Aurassi Hotel, built by the Chinese, which was gradually sink-
ing beneath its foundations, to the pêcherie down by the docks. As
we drank the local wine, pelure d'oignon, and chose our fish fresh
from the water, Douglas confided in me that he had worked for the
Secret Intelligence Service, then of course much more hidden and

secretive than it is today, before the decision to place it on a statutory footing in the late 1990s. He'd have been mortified to know that all of us in the engine room at Lazard knew about his past. That night in Algiers, Douglas eyed me shovelling food into my mouth. 'You eat like a British public school boy, but you know a bit about wine so you may be redeemable. I'm not sure how much I am going to teach you about banking, but I'll try to remedy your lack of knowledge about food.' And so he did, as we went along the north African coast (where on decolonisation the French had often left their chefs behind), working, amongst others, with British shipbuilders, trying to sell the vessels that would keep the British shipyards in business.

Back in London, it was decided I should have a go in west Africa, with occasional wider African forays. I had worked up a deal involving Lonrho and Tiny Rowland and went to get clearance from Tom Manners, a director from the old school of banking. In those days if you weren't wearing a jacket and arrived on the directors' floor, you'd be sent back to get it by the bank messengers. The loos were segregated: men, women, and directors only. Approaching Tom Manners's desk, I started setting out the details of the Lonrho deal I was organising, the fee arrangement and so forth. Without looking up, Tom heard me out before commenting, 'I'm afraid, Andrew, Lazard simply doesn't do business with people like Tiny Rowland.' And that was that. On another occasion I told him I was off to a meeting in St James's. Today much of the cream of British finance is situated there, but back then it was nearly all in the City of London, the Square Mile. Tom Manners wrinkled his nose: 'I wouldn't spend too much time in St James's, Andrew; only spivs and ne'er-do-wells operate from there.'

That August I headed off to Salcombe, looking forward to a week's sailing along the Devon and Cornwall coast in *Curlew*, a gaff-rigged cutter. Eight crew members, including a skipper and a mate, met at the Ferry Inn that Saturday night, together with a doctor called Sharon with an air of authority. Although twenty-five, I was rather baby-faced in those days and the doctor, fearing I was underage, offered to buy me a shandy. For the next seven days we sailed between picturesque seaside ports, and the six men and two women got on well – with most of the men, including me, seeking to ingratiate ourselves with Sharon. Each night when at sea, there would be two of us on watch and I sidled up to the captain to ask if I could go on watch late at night with Sharon – preferably for the 2 till 4 a.m. slot. Unfortunately, most of the other men were also manoeuvring for the same watch, which became unusually popular.

Once the week was over, we said our fond farewells and Sharon headed back to work at the Princess Margaret Hospital in Swindon. A few days later I called the hospital to enquire whether she might be free for lunch, as I just happened to be passing through Swindon every day the following week. Apparently three of the other men had also been ringing with similarly spurious reasons for visiting the area.

It was clear that something more subtle was required. I had discovered that Sharon was a skilled windsurfer. So my next call suggested that we meet and go windsurfing. She agreed. There was, however, a problem – I had no idea how to windsurf. For the next three days, with an old university friend who had windsurfed before, I spent time training at Thorpe Water alongside the M3. It was clear I was not a natural, but having spent hours falling off the board and climbing back on again, I eventually managed to stay upright for short periods of time.

When the day of our date arrived, I turned up at the Cotswold Windsurfing Club at the agreed time to be met by Bruce, a fit and tough Australian with a roll-up cigarette permanently glued to his lower lip, who was in charge of the club. He looked me up and down in my ill-fitting wetsuit, clearly wondering what this pathetic specimen was doing there.

Our windsurfing outing went just about OK and I was awarded brownie points for enthusiasm rather than skill. I was aware that Sharon had another suitor, also a doctor, and Bruce, having watched my weedy efforts on the water, informed me that the doctor was part of the British Olympic Windsurfing Squad. Having seen off my rival, notwithstanding his windsurfing prowess, some years later I finally persuaded Sharon to marry me – on one knee in a Sussex field.

In the early hours of one morning, Sharon and I returned home simultaneously as dawn broke. I had been working as a minor cog on a deal at Lazard throughout most of the night. Sharon had been operating with a team at St Mary's Hospital when the Regent's and Hyde Park bombs had gone off, killing eleven soldiers and seven horses. An urgent announcement had gone out that all routine operation work be stopped and preparations made to receive the many casualties. The injuries were appalling, and Sharon was involved in the team fighting to save lives. One patient had four separate teams working on him simultaneously – orthopaedic, maxillofacial, vascular and neurosurgeons – battling to save his life throughout the night. I particularly remember Sharon saying when she got home ashen-faced and exhausted that she had spoken to relatives who said that they'd lived in permanent fear when their loved ones were serving in Northern Ireland but had breathed a sigh of relief once they were safely home on the mainland. It was a powerful reminder of the big discrepancies in terms of relevant value to society of what we were both doing.

As my involvement in west Africa grew, I was asked to accompany the vice-chairman of Lazard Brothers, Lord Kindersley, on a visit to west Africa led by the Duke of Kent, President of the Board of Trade. This government trade mission, organised by the Department of Trade and Industry, was to take place with eight captains of industry and the use of an RAF VC10 to travel across French west Africa – first to Gabon then to the Cameroons then on to the Ivory Coast. It was an extraordinary opportunity for me being in such interesting company, as well as a business opportunity on the back of it. I made myself useful too as a reasonably fluent French speaker – I'd spent eight weeks as a sixteen-year-old working in the Bordeaux vineyards where no one spoke a word of English.

On one occasion during the visit, Lord Kindersley travelled from the Cameroons to the Ivory Coast in his tennis clothes, exasperating our civil servants who were organising the trip, as his time on the Ambassador's tennis court had overrun and he was late for our plane. As we arrived in Abidjan, it was clear that a televised reception awaited the Duke of Kent and his entourage on the tarmac. Kindersley immediately ordered me to let him have my suit jacket, thrust his tennis racquet into my hands and grabbed my briefcase before he could be photographed by the waiting news crews. I imagine the local TV assumed his half-business half-tennis attire was how all English aristocrats dressed.

In Gabon, the delegation was received by the diminutive

President Omár Bongo. Sitting high on a throne with all of us congregated at his feet, he wore boots up to his knees and a long black cape. It all looked every bit like a scene from Evelyn Waugh's *Black Mischief*.

Once back in the UK, my boss, David, asked Lord Kindersley whether Mitchell had performed to his satisfaction. Kindersley said that during a ride in a lift he'd been horrified to spot me reading upside down the briefing notes of Lord Jellicoe, chairman of Warburg's and Tate & Lyle. He thought this quite appalling behaviour. David gleefully repeated this conversation to me but told me that he disagreed. 'If you hadn't read his notes, I'd have fired you,' he said. It was a good metaphor for the difference between the old Lazard (Kindersley was the third generation of his family to grace the Lazard boardroom, to which he was elevated at an abnormally young age) and the new dynamic meritocratic regime that had succeeded it.

In the early part of 1982, I had managed to persuade the British company GEC to hire Lazard to finance a deal in Upper Volta in central Africa. The deal involved selling about £3 million of telecoms equipment to the government there. The idea of doing anything in Upper Volta at Lazard was faintly absurd, but since I'd also negotiated a decent fee, the bank decided amidst some hilarity that I should go to Ouagadougou, the capital of Upper Volta, which was changing its name to Burkina Faso, meaning in the local dialect 'country of incorruptible people' – a name which was certainly a breach of the Trade Descriptions Act. Once there, my instructions from London ordered me not to return until I had a cheque from the Upper Volta central bank in my hands. 'The path of true love does not run straight. Stay until you've got it,' the telex read.

With a weekend to fill in Ouagadougou, I headed off on Friday night to have dinner with one of the Europeans I'd been introduced to. As we returned to the centre of the capital, across the causeway the lights had gone off and come back on again twice. My German companion and I rounded the corner by the President's palace and there in front of us was a tank with soldiers firing into the ground-floor windows. I do not speak any German, but even I could manage the exclamation from my companion, 'Scheiße! Ein coup d'état! Scheiße, scheiße!' as he spun the steering wheel and headed off at speed, dropping me off at my hotel before heading to his. I quickly walked into the lobby, where staff were in tears and already blockading the doors. Throughout the rest of the night, sporadic machine-gun fire echoed across the city. I sat in my room, trying to read Kenneth Harris's biography of Clement Attlee, listening each hour to the World Service on my small travelling radio. I remember being outraged that these dramatic events in a far-off place were not being given, as I saw it, correct prominence at the top of the international news bulletins. Finally, at 4 a.m., at the end of the news bulletin (and following tedious stories about the balance of payments), I heard: 'Reports are coming in of fighting in the west African capital of Upper Volta, Ouagadougou.'

At eight o'clock the next morning, a car carrying a Frenchwoman tried to run the blockade outside my hotel, The Independence. The car was fired on and the woman killed. A curfew was imposed. When, after forty-eight hours, the curfew was lifted, I set off in my jeans and T-shirt to the office of our local lawyer, Maître Vimal. I was acutely conscious that I had been doing a deal with a government that had now been forcibly removed. I knew that the former President had been deposed and it seemed sensible to get the paperwork to a safe hiding place. Maître Vimal was most disconcerting: 'I cannot take these documents. You must get rid of them immediately. You have been in cahoots with the old regime! They'll put you in the pot.'

Thoroughly alarmed by this conversation, I went straight to the Canadian Embassy, which looked after UK interests there, clutching my bulging briefcase. As I walked, I was conscious of being watched by the gun-toting soldiers who were checking on people and asking for their identity papers. Fortunately, they showed no interest in a foreigner. The Canadian Embassy agreed to take my documents and return them to the UK in the diplomatic bag. They suggested I go to the US Embassy and register my presence in case of any difficulty. At the US Embassy, the American Ambassador was wandering around in a Stetson hat. He helpfully offered to get a message to my parents telling them I was OK. The phone lines had all been cut, and only the Americans had the communications capacity to make calls out of the country. The US Ambassador was as good as his word and my mother was astonished to receive a call from the US Embassy in London to reassure her that her son was all right. 'Where is he?' she asked. 'He's in Upper Volta,' they said. 'Where's that?' she enquired.

Back in Ouagadougou, the clean water was running out in the Hotel Independence. The Canadian Ambassador had told me that he thought there was another Brit staying in a more modern hotel not far away. So, when the curfew lifted, I went straight over, only to be informed by the receptionist that there were no rooms free. I enquired if there was another Englishman around. 'Ah l'Anglais. He's upstairs on the first floor,' I was told. And there, I kid you not, on a sun lounger with a gin in one hand and a Graham Greene novel in the other, reddening in the sunshine, was Richard Marsden. I'd last seen him behind the bar at Jesus College dispensing the cheaper beer organised by Geoff Hoon.

After Richard had had a swift word with the manager, a free room was found. 'How did you do that?' I asked. 'I handed over some notes with pictures of Her Majesty the Queen on them.' I raced back to the Hotel Independence, settled my bill and rushed to my new digs just as the curfew was reimposed. And there I stayed, assisting Richard in drinking their cellar dry, playing backgammon and discussing in somewhat surreal circumstances our student days.

Meanwhile in London there was moderate concern at Lazard as they made unofficial enquiries about extracting me should the need arise. GEC rang up in some anxiety to find out what had happened to their documents. David Gemmill mentioned that the bank was slightly concerned about one of their staff being stuck in Ouagadougou. 'Never mind about him,' GEC responded. 'We need to get those documents back.'

After about a week, anxiety about it all had given way to boredom. I was woken at 3 a.m. by Richard Marsden to say that he had heard a flight was about to leave carrying a team of World Bank officials. 'Why don't you tag along and see if you can get on it?' He, however, had bravely decided to stay; he was there selling grain to the government. 'Whichever government is in power, they've still got to eat.'

I raced to the airport and saw a group of foreigners waiting to proceed through what passed for Passport Control, where a bored official was stamping their documents. So I just joined the back of the queue and was waved through in my turn. Heading off down the runway, I noticed on either side that artillery and field guns had been dug in – put there by the new regime in case the French government decided to intervene on behalf of the old. But the French had already decided that the days of that kind of neocolonial intervention were over.

Lazard decided we should put some effort into financing our clients who were bidding for the Singapore mass transit railway, given our credentials and the reputation David Gemmill had won for us in Hong Kong. In late 1982, I was asked to go and live in Singapore for six months and act as the eyes and ears of Lazard for what was then the biggest civil engineering project in the world. As well as this role in Singapore, I was to pursue business opportunities in Indonesia and Malaysia.

One of my more bizarre experiences took place at the British Embassy in a tropical location nearby. During a marketing visit, I asked to see one of the British Ambassador's deputies to gather information about major industrial projects then being considered by the government there which could be of interest to our clients in the UK. Although the Foreign Office was then erratic in its commercial intelligence on opportunities for British business, diplomats in that particular country had a good record for spotting potentially interesting opportunities for UK plc. On my arrival in the diplomat's office, it was clear that he was not having a good day. He went through the motions of answering my questions, but his eyes were wandering and opening and shutting in an alarming manner. After about twenty minutes I made my excuses and expressed the hope that on a subsequent visit I might take him out for a more relaxed lunch, whereupon he rose to his feet, seized a handful of buff-coloured folders that were lying on his desk and hurled them against the wall, loudly exclaiming, 'I hate this fucking country and its food!' He then jumped up and down three times on the spot. 'I hate it! I hate it! I hate it!' As I sat there, astounded, he mounted his chair and, assuming the position of an ape, said, 'Now you can write to your MP and say that you have met a mad diplomat.' At this point his secretary appeared in the doorway. I noticed she did not look surprised at what was going on. 'Well,' I said, 'I can see you are having a difficult day, and I must take my leave.' As the secretary and I descended the stairs, I suggested he might need some time off. 'He's just returned from the UK. Thank you, Mr Mitchell.' At which I shot out the door in a state of shock.

I was returning to Singapore that evening and was not sure what I should do. I was worried that if the diplomat harmed himself, or worse, it would be profoundly remiss of me not to have told anyone, but equally I did not want to damage his career. I determined to tell the titular head of the British business community there. He had been particularly kind to me and interested in what I was doing, so young and so far from home. So I rang him up and told him what had happened. Chortling, he told me he would deal with the matter. I subsequently heard that he had seen the diplomat privately and told him he simply could not behave in such a way in front of young and impressionable British bankers.

Nearly fifteen years later, I was part of a delegation to another tropical location on a parliamentary visit together with Gwyneth Dunwoody, the redoubtable Labour Member for Crewe and Nantwich. I failed to read the brief before leaving the UK, but on the plane, to my alarm, I saw that the Head of Mission in the country we were visiting was none other than the aforementioned diplomat, who was scheduled to meet us on arrival at the airport. Once we landed, I rushed off the plane ahead of the rest of the delegates, found him, warmly shook his hand and said I'd not seen him since we had met years earlier. 'Ah yes,' he said, looking uneasy. 'It was Lazard, wasn't it?' The visit went well and on the last night there was a reception for local worthies at his residence. I had made the mistake of recounting the story to Gwyneth, who hooted with laughter and went round telling everyone. As the gin circulated and the ceiling fans whirred to diminish the rising temperature, she repeatedly dug me in the ribs. 'He's coming for you – look, his eyes are swivelling.'

In Singapore, I had an office in Jardine Fleming, then a successful investment management joint venture between Jardines, the major Hong Kong trading house, and the family-owned Fleming bank. Jardine Fleming in Singapore was run by a larger-than-life Brit, Roddie Fleming, who even in the heat of midday Singapore insisted on wearing a three-piece suit. In the first week I went with Roddie to the MAS, the Monetary Authority of Singapore, where the financial regulators – overwhelmingly fierce and clever Singaporean women – were based. It was clear from their attention to Roddie that he was in their sights over some minor infraction of the rules. In Singapore, everything is either compulsory or forbidden.

It later emerged that Roddie had been 'round-tripping' – arbitraging the difference between the Singapore interest rate and others. In due course, Roddie was told the time had come for him to leave town. The Singapore authorities were even less amused to hear that at his final goodbye party, held at the magnificent old black and white house where he lived – several of which still survive from colonial times – he had driven a Mini into the swimming pool.

I lived in considerably less splendour in the Goodwood Park Hotel, which had been the headquarters of the Kempeitai (the Japanese secret police) during the Second World War. In the early 1980s, Singaporean citizens would cross the road to avoid walking past it too closely, in view of its bad feng shui. Returning to my quarters one afternoon, I heard screams of a different nature emanating from the next-door room and assumed two young Australian lovers were probably pleasuring each other. Some hours later I bumped into my two neighbours as they came out of their room. They were both Japanese; I don't think either of them was under the age of eighty. It shows how misleading stereotypical thinking can be!

While I was making inroads in Indonesia and Malaysia, it was soon clear that the central objective of my time in Singapore – to secure successful contracts for our clients on the MRT – was most unlikely to happen. I wrote a note back to London saying that I thought the Japanese were going to clean up on the civil engineering contracts and the Germans would do likewise on the electrical and mechanical work. Our mainly UK clients did not look well placed. And so, with a heavy heart, I returned to London.

Sad to be back in England, I decided every cloud had a silver lining and I would see if I could fight a Labour seat in the general election that would have to take place in the next few months. I'd left it pretty late. Previously I had decided that the opportunity to go to south-east Asia was more appealing than starting out on a political career. On enquiring, I discovered that there were only three seats with strong Labour majorities left to select their candidates: Islington South, Jarrow and Sunderland South. I immediately applied to all three and asked Conservative Central Office if

I could have 'one-seat clearance' as I was not on the party's candidates list.

Islington South turned me down flat. There were far too many competitors on the selection committee to give one of their own a leg up. But both Jarrow and Sunderland South invited me for interview. Unfortunately, they were both selecting on the same night so I went for Sunderland South on the grounds that Jarrow, with its iconic history, would be the more sought-after seat.

I managed to find a family connection in the north-east; most candidates manage to dredge up local connections, however tenuous, and I had a grandfather who had worked in a shipyard there seventy years earlier. I did my homework and saw that one of the largest private sector businesses was the Vaux Brewery. As I got out of my taxi at the place where the first round of the selection was being held, I asked the taxi driver about 'Vaux', pronouncing it 'Vo', beer. 'It's pronounced Vox, bonny lad, Vox', he said, thus saving me from what would have been utter humiliation at the meeting.

When I went into the hall where the assembled hopefuls were waiting to be called for interview, I was the complete outsider. All of the others had been on the candidate circuit hoping for safe seats. But with the election approaching they had been unsuccessful and were looking for a bolthole to keep themselves in play for the future. I delivered a workmanlike speech and scraped through to the final three who would be interviewed the next day.

As we were leaving, one of the others who had got through to the final came up to me and said, 'You do realise neither of us have a chance tomorrow? It's all been set up for the other guy, a management consultant and the son of the borough engineer.' I believed her and was outraged: I'd come all the way from London at my own expense, paid for the hotel overnight and was now hearing it was all a fix.

I spent much of the night working on a speech designed to answer the question on the doorstep: 'The pits have shut, the ship-yards are dying: what have you lot ever done for the unemployed?' When it was my turn to speak, I gave it my best shot and when the ballot was counted, I had beaten the borough engineer's son by one vote. As I stood at the door saying goodbye and thank you to my new party workers for choosing me, one elderly lady came and shook my hand. 'Floreat rugbeia,' she said – my old school motto. She had been a matron at Rugby. It was clear that I had secured the nomination on the basis of my old school tie. Two days later, Margaret Thatcher asked the Queen to dissolve Parliament and fired the starting gun for the 1983 election.

I went straight back to London and on Monday asked Lazard for leave of absence for the four weeks to polling day. I pointed out to David Gemmill that there was zero chance of my winning and I'd take all my time off as holiday. Lazard could not have been more supportive. David told me he had to clear it with Ian Fraser, the chairman, who agreed to my going, saying, 'These young men need to get the lust for political power out of their system.'

The campaign passed in a blizzard of energetic activity. It was not a difficult election to fight; Labour under Michael Foot was never going to win. The worst moment came when Conservative Central Office told me that mine was the last Labour seat they thought would fall to the Tories! I wore the Sunderland Football Club tie every day throughout the four weeks and spoke from a bridge above the marketplace with a loudhailer, challenging Gordon Bagier, the long-serving sitting MP, to come out and debate the issues of the day. He naturally ignored such effrontery and I in turn accused him of cowardice.

On the final Saturday of the campaign, things hotted up. There was an unusually large crowd who came to heckle me on my bridge. When I invited questions, the first demanded that I name at least three members of the Sunderland Football Club team and the positions where they played, since I was proudly wearing their tie. Not knowing any names at all, let alone the positions, I dismissed the question as entirely frivolous: 'I'm not demeaning the vital issues in this election for such trivia.' As the hostility grew and I was coming down from the bridge, I was punched by a lady festooned in Labour badges who was literally foaming at the mouth. Fortunately for me, the incident was witnessed by a journalist from the *Newcastle Journal* who had heard about my market forays and decided to come along and watch the fun. The incident made the evening news – 'Young Tory candidate assaulted' – and elicited the only communication from the sitting MP to me – a short note of apology.

On the Tuesday before polling day, Chris Lewis, the Conservative candidate for Sunderland North, and I went down in our loudspeaker car to meet the men ending their shift at Sunderland Shipbuilders and to hand out our leaflets. On this occasion we were accompanied by Chris's mother, Lady Lewis, a formidable woman whose manner and comportment were reminiscent of Lady Bracknell. Having announced our presence over our loudspeaker, Chris and I got out to shake hands and distribute leaflets. Unfortunately, we left the loudspeaker on in the car, which was covered with Conservative posters. Lady Lewis was sitting on the back seat in twinset and pearls sporting a very Tory hat, and the car was surrounded by irate shipyard workers who started rocking it back and forth on its springs. Suddenly across the yard, echoing off the tall buildings, boomed the voice of her ladyship as she blasted out, 'Why don't you lot bugger off – just bugger off!' Chris and I looked at each other in horror, and with that we legged it.

On the night of the count, the Labour agent said to me, 'If you get our majority below 10,000, bonny lad, I'll give you a fiver.' And sure enough, much later on, as we all mounted the platform for the returning officer to announce the result, I felt a rolled-up piece of paper being stuffed into my hand from behind. It was a five-pound note. We'd done well but were undoubtedly helped by the fact that it was the election in which Labour had delivered as their manifesto the 'longest suicide note in history'.

As I headed back to London, I knew that I had truly got the political bug. I had really enjoyed my concentrated time in Sunderland and made many new friends there amongst that tough breed of resilient Tories in the north-east. Over the next two years I returned every month for a weekend to campaign and help in council contests. The chairman of the Conservative association was Tom Cowie, who was also the chairman of Sunderland Football Club. The fortunes of the Tories in the town tended to mirror the fortunes of the team.

Returning to Lazard, the international division was expanding its work in a way which was genuinely exciting: we had discovered our counterparts in the other two Lazard houses. The international division in New York was led by the diminutive Wall Street figure Frank Zarb, who was as unknown to all of us as his counterpart in Lazard Paris, Hélie de Pourtalès – a polo-playing blond giant who could trace his ancestry directly back to Talleyrand; his wife traced hers back to Napoleon Bonaparte. His advice on recruiting staff was: 'Never employ an ugly person.' I had been sent by David Gemmill to spend a fortnight in Paris: 'You're a political type: go over there and work out the chain of command. Find out who does what to whom.' I had a wonderful time during those two weeks, being wined and dined with sumptuous cuisine and meeting a very engaging group of French haut banquiers, but I learned rather more about the French than about Lazard. They were all wonderful companions: clever, engaging, witty and good-looking. When I went through what I learned about their business – how much they had shared – there was precious little. All the information was one-way.

We started to have three-house meetings where the French énarques, the preppy New Yorkers and the Oxbridge London bankers would meet and bring to the table their very different skills, connections, backgrounds and businesses, and I began to work closely with Craig Macnab, a South African who had left because of the apartheid regime and settled in New York. We tried to assist businesses in Zambia – often with debts from the copper industry – and on the way there Craig suggested that I join him for a weekend in South Africa with his family. 'You look to me as if you're going into politics and you oppose the apartheid regime. Come and see for yourself.' We stayed with his parents, whose pride in their son and pain at his exile was all too evident. I met both his liberal friends ('It's an awful regime, but what can we do?') and his Afrikaner friends ('We built this country; it's ours and we're not going anywhere!'). I left with a rather greater respect for the latter group, because of their honesty. They weren't just parading their moral consciences while enjoying the fruits of an evil regime.

In Zambia, we met up with our French colleague Paul Ragetly. Many of our meetings were conducted in the colonial splendour of Government House in Lusaka, with its enormous lion skin on the floor in the main entrance. The meeting rooms were in the basement, where there was a warren of offices, many of them containing state artefacts. In one particular room where we met officials, there was an enormous bronze carving of Her Majesty the Queen with an African hairdo and bone structure. I insisted on sitting with my back to it. My French colleague gleefully demanded a photograph.

Preoccupied with getting married and pulling my weight at Lazard, I had assumed I would be fighting Sunderland South again and had deliberately kept involved with the local party and the North East Conservatives. But I put in for the safe Conservative seat of Wokingham mainly to test the waters rather than in any expectation of getting very far. To my considerable surprise, I ended up coming second to John Redwood (in fact, on the first ballot I was ahead), a senior Downing Street adviser, older and far better connected in the party than me. Realising my chances were better than I had thought, I applied for Gedling, where Philip Holland, the sitting MP, had announced his retirement. During the selection process, wives (trial by sherry) were presented with flowers, with very high marks allotted for how they responded. Sharon was the only partner who responded verbally – a departure which subsequently became increasingly common for male candidates' other halves.

A week later, Sharon and I were married and headed off on honeymoon to Kenya.

As the date of the 1987 election approached, I nursed my new constituency and made a point of continuing to try to pull my weight at Lazard. After all, one never knows what's around the corner in politics. The bank was undergoing another internal up-heaval which in time would see the merger of the three Lazard houses. This new phase was led by Sir John Nott as our chairman, recently released from government and the House of Commons. His mercurial temperament and can-do approach greatly widened Lazard's business and reach as we set up and took on new sorts of work. Indeed, it was under John Nott's leadership that the London arm started to make serious money.

My early years at Lazard taught me a great deal. I was never really an investment banker, which requires skills and a rigour I do not possess. But if you are well organised and energetic, you can make a contribution. Lazard certainly did more for me than I did for them. With its broad reach, quite extraordinary connections and geographic diversity, Lazard was a flag around which some fas-cinating and unusual people camped. There was a conceit, certainly, that the Lazard boardroom could do a better job than the Cabinet, but there was also an integrity and an innate decency. Amongst my closest friends are members of that Lazard group.

Those friendships, networks and experiences helped and sus-tained me as I set off in 1987 for the House of Commons.

CHAPTER 4

THE HOUSE AND THE HEADMISTRESS

In the spring of 1987, some months before the looming general election, the Konrad-Adenauer-Stiftung invited sixteen aspiring Conservative parliamentary candidates to visit a still-divided Germany. This well-funded German think tank is closely allied to the Christian Democratic Union, the sister party of the Conservatives in London. It was a useful, indeed extraordinary, visit. We went first to see a joint exercise between the British and German Armed Forces. There was something of a contrast between the two, with the German unit made up of long-haired and bored conscripts who were neither as fit nor anything like as professional as their British counterparts. Had the Russians stormed across the plains of central Europe, they'd not have had much difficulty seeing off that lot.

We moved across the Berlin Wall, heading down the empty autobahns of East Germany, little changed since Hitler built them. We arrived in Weimar, where we stayed at the Hotel Elephant

– one of the Führer's favourite haunts, from whose balcony he memorably addressed the crowds below.

When we arrived, we were told by the management that there were no single rooms available and we would all have to double up. There were also only rooms available on the second floor. It is not easy to remember what it was like in those days before the Berlin Wall came down and East Germany collapsed, but it was pretty clear that we were to be accommodated in this way so East German security could listen to our conversations and indiscretions. I pitied the poor Feldwebel in the basement with a pair of headphones clamped to his ears, transcribing what he heard.

As the sixteen of us in the Elephant reception area divided into pairs, I teamed up with James Arbuthnot, who had brought with him some vodka. Our colleague David Nicholson, who enjoyed his high camp reputation, was allocated the honeymoon suite and chose as his roommate the young and good-looking Simon Burns, whose loud expletives and adamant refusal caused great amusement.

The next day, we toured Weimar and visited Pushkin's house. Older than most of us was Quentin Davies, soon to be elected for Stamford and Spalding. Highly intelligent and well read, he was noted as something of a know-it-all. As we walked up the steps, he started talking very knowledgably about Pushkin's poetry in English to us and in German to our local guide. In an effort to tease him, I asked him if Pushkin's poetry was not in fact Russian, and Quentin immediately recited several verses fluently in Pushkin's native tongue.

Many years later, Quentin crossed the floor and became a Labour minister. He had been badly treated by the Conservative Party, who thought him 'too clever by half' – the ultimate sin for a

Tory MP – and refused to promote him or take him seriously. He was also very pro-European (the second most pernicious Tory sin) but, treated respectfully, he served perfectly happily in Iain Duncan Smith's shadow Cabinet.

We drove to the former concentration camp at Buchenwald, not far away. As we passed a major Russian Army camp, with row upon row of tanks, we were joined by a Russian guide as well as our West and East German ones. It was a dyspeptic visit. Our West German guide had insisted that there had been no concentration camps on German soil – clearly untrue. The Russian guide laid into the Nazis and the Germans over their brutality without acknowledging that as soon as the Russians liberated this camp, they merely changed the guards and incarcerated their own political prisoners there. The East German guide who told us the history of the place omitted to mention the dozens of RAF officers held at the camp, two of whom died there. As we listened to this tri-national dishonesty, I noticed that across the wooded area outside there were none of the normal sounds of bird life. Not even the humour and good company of Anthony Coombs – the future Member for Wyre Forest and Brummie businessman, and very much the well-dressed man about town – was able to lift our spirits.

On the day of our return across the Berlin Wall, we visited the German Parliament and stood on the balcony which overlooked the wall itself and was overshadowed by an East German guard tower. The body of an East German man shot while trying to escape the night before had been left lying where he fell to discourage others from any escape attempt. As we took pictures of the scene and the East German tower, their guards ostentatiously took photographs of us.

Our visit finished with a high-level meeting with some of German Chancellor Helmut Kohl's most senior advisers, organised by the Stiftung. Their agenda was to ensure that we, a possible new generation of future Conservative MPs, supported a reunited Germany. No such luck. The majority of us – but not Quentin Davies, I recall – camped on the words of the French novelist François Mauriac: 'I love Germany so much that I am glad there are two of them.' Our German hosts were appalled at our lukewarm attitude to the reunification of their country. They'd have been even more horrified if they had known what advice Norman Stone, my former moral tutor at Cambridge, later gave Margaret Thatcher at the famous Chequers seminar. To assuage Thatcher's concerns about the prospect of German reunification, Stone reassured her that in taking over East Germany, West Germany was only getting 'twelve enormous Liverpools'.

Not many weeks later, the electorate delivered fourteen of the sixteen of us to the House of Commons. I had had a 'safety first' campaign in Gedling, where Philip Holland had been a popular though old-fashioned MP. The leader of Gedling Council told me: 'We liked Philip. We never saw much of him, of course, because he held the highly prestigious job of chairman of the Committee of Selection, which kept him in Westminster.' Subsequently, the chairman of the 1922 Committee told me: 'We never saw much of Philip in Westminster because he was so busy in Gedling.' Clearly my predecessor had things running pretty smoothly.

Once I had been elected, John Nott asked me to remain as an adviser. Lazard generously agreed to match my parliamentary salary – about £18,000 per year. As now, if you are not a minister (another job in itself), MPs are allowed to have properly declared and regulated outside interests as long as their constituents' interests come first. I have personally always thought that having outside interests makes for better MPs, who, if solely left pounding the House of Commons corridors, may be less effective representatives of their constituents and are more likely to succumb to one of the House of Commons' twin curses, alcoholism or adultery – or both. (The House of Lords, of course, being too ancient to indulge in the latter.)

The House of Commons I so proudly entered in June 1987 was most unlike today. It was rather like turning up to your first term at a boys' boarding school. There were the staff, the prefects, the senior and junior boys, and of course the headmistress. The club-like atmosphere was epitomised by the Smoking Room (known to the Labour women as the Leather Room in those days), where groups of male Tory and Labour MPs would pass the evening drinking and smoking and voting as required.

In those days, the House was very much a community, sitting from 2.30 p.m. until late into the night. The bars and restaurants would be full. The Members' Dining Room, full at lunchtime, was packed for dinner. The Labour Party sat down one end and we at the other. The rules were that you made up tables as you arrived, so no one knew whether they would be sitting next to me – the most junior Conservative Member – or Mrs Thatcher. In the middle were two large tables, one for the Liberals and the other for the Ulster Unionists. The more senior House of Commons clerks might also be there. A table for four in the corner was reserved for the Conservative Chief Whip. There he would sit, with his back to the wall (probably an unnecessary precaution) surveying his charges. To be invited to dine at the Chief Whip's table was a rare and coveted privilege. One evening I sat, along with other newcomers, at a table with one of the older Members of the House. Spellbound, we listened to his wonderful stories for what was an extremely entertaining evening. A fortnight later, I spotted him going into dinner and rushed to sit next to him again so that I could savour more of his wit and repartee. Alas, he told all the same stories, in the same order, with precisely the same timing and inflection. Today, because of the changed sitting hours, the Members' Dining Room is invariably empty. The Churchill Room – previously the best restaurant in the House – is now closed.

The Tearoom is less changed. Labour occupy the front end while we Tories camp at the back. Conversations held there are supposed to be private, but usually someone can be relied upon to leak anything spicy to the media. A few years ago, Claire Perry came in protesting furiously, having failed to catch the Speaker's attention throughout Question Time. She mused out loud about whether she'd have to give the Speaker a blowjob to get a hearing. Her comments were all over the papers the next day, allegedly leaked by three different sources.

When I arrived, I was almost immediately written up in the 'New Boys' column in *Private Eye*. By comparison with others, it was a pretty benign piece, though it included the untrue story that 'his nickname was Thrasher at Rugby because, like Douglas "Hitler Hurd" at Eton, he was a stern disciplinarian'. The story seemed too good to correct at the time and it would have been churlish to denounce it.

At about the same time, the political editor of the *Daily Mirror*, Alastair Campbell, rang me and asked for an interview: 'I'm writing up six of the future movers and shakers – three Tory and three

Labour, and you are one of them.' He came and interviewed me at home in Islington, taking a lovely photo of me holding up my baby daughter Hannah like the scene in *The Lion King* when Simba is presented. His six were Tony Blair, Gordon Brown, Mo Mowlam, John Major, Michael Portillo and Andrew Mitchell. Many years later he laughingly told me, 'Five out of six ain't bad.'

The greatest danger for any Tory backbencher was to be cornered by Mrs Thatcher in the Tearoom on one of her not infrequent visits. On hearing she was coming, many would bolt down their tea and scarper, but there were always some enthusiastic toadies to make her welcome. The Prime Minister would sit down next door to you, plonking down her handbag carefully, fix you with a steely look and ask your views on the money supply figures published that morning. Everyone would freeze as whichever hapless colleague she lighted upon stammered out what was usually judged to be an inadequate reply. I was completely in awe of Mrs Thatcher. My father, with whom I sat in the Commons for ten years, was amongst her most fervent admirers. To me, she was like a goddess. Along with her entourage, she would swish past me in the corridors at high speed as she moved between meetings. I would stand smartly to attention facing straight ahead hoping to avoid her eye.

There was just one occasion when I met her almost alone for a meeting. The miners' strike had been and gone, but a deep legacy of bitterness remained. I represented a coalfield seat. The 100-year-old Gedling pit had remained open during the strike, manned by the UDM – the Union of Democratic Mineworkers – who helped break the strike. They were the reincarnation of the Spencerite union of the 1920s and 1930s.

I used to go down the pit at Gedling on a Friday twice a year, normally on the early shift around 5.30 a.m. I sometimes arrived direct from the House of Commons due to late-night votes. It was an extraordinary experience: the heat, the dust and the man-rider conveyor belt to the coal face. There I would usually meet Dennis Skinner's brother, Gordon, who'd been lurking, waiting to berate me as a representative of the Conservative government. The overseer laughingly told me he was known as 'Man Friday' as he'd only turn up on that day to collect his wages. What the lads really wanted to see was whether I would crawl along the High Hazels seam, the face from which the coal was cut, on my hands and with kneepads strapped on. I always did. That seam supplied big cobs of high-quality coal destined for home burning, including by the Queen at Sandringham.

Following the strike, the coal industry contracted sharply. We fought to keep the Gedling pit open and succeeded for a while, but its fortunes were always incredibly precarious. So much hung on the size and quality of the seam being mined. Huge investment – but never safety – risks were taken. Gedling village fought to support the pit even though few people living there worked down it and the dust and noise as lorries transported coal down the little roads was burdensome. Miners fought for the right for their sons to follow in their footsteps. It is a culture now completely gone. I advised my daughters to read D. H. Lawrence to understand the history and life of Nottinghamshire, where they were living, which was vanishing before their eyes – though Ken Clarke told me he remembers people bridling in Nottingham at the mention of D. H. Lawrence's name. He was the fellow from Eastwood who wrote those dirty books.

As the pits were closing, my parliamentary near neighbour

Patrick McLoughlin (who had been a miner before becoming an MP) and I became very concerned that the government was shutting UDM pits rather than the Scargillite NUM ones. At great and often personal risk, the UDM had kept the lights on during the strike and saved the Tory government's bacon. Were we really cynically going to let them down?

I asked Mrs Thatcher's parliamentary private secretary, Mark Lennox-Boyd, if Patrick and I could have a meeting with her. She not only agreed but suggested the three of us have dinner in the Members' Dining Room. We waited nervously together, and she joined us. I started by saying, 'Prime Minister, we both represent constituencies in which the UDM pits saved the government and are now facing closure, when it is the NUM pits that should bear the brunt.' They were the last words either of us got in edgeways for the next twenty-five minutes as Mrs Thatcher explained in detail the difficulties facing the coal industry and the consequences. I had just managed to intervene as she drew breath when Mark Lennox-Boyd hoved into view and came over to our table. 'Prime Minister, I'm afraid a bomb has gone off over Lockerbie and a PanAm jet loaded with passengers has been destroyed.' Clearly deeply shocked, the Prime Minister issued a series of instructions and took her leave from Patrick and me. I remember being particularly impressed that she said to Mark, 'Please ensure Hector is on my plane with me tomorrow.' Hector Monro was the Lockerbie MP. Not all her successors as Prime Minister would have taken the trouble to do that.

The closure of UDM pits came to a head when Michael Heseltine was at the Department of Trade and Industry as President of the Board of Trade. Sharon was at a party in London while I was at the party conference in Blackpool. A junior energy minister told her that her husband would be very upset next week when the closure of a large number of pits was to be announced. Later that night she phoned and relayed this conversation. I simply did not believe it and assumed the minister was having her on. Sure enough, a few days later such plans were announced. By then I was at Central Office as a party vice-chairman and reluctantly called Norman Fowler, the chairman of the party, to say that if the plans went ahead, I'd have to resign from his team. There was no way Gedling's Member of Parliament could possibly support such measures and look his constituents in the eye again. Norman, wise as ever, suggested I wait and do nothing as he did not see how the plans would get through the Commons. Many Conservative colleagues, including William Hague – knowing what it would mean for the few Conservative coalfield MPs left – rang to express support. I spoke to Michael Heseltine and – always the consummate politician – he queried the spelling of one of the UDM pits that was close to my constituency and which I said must be saved. Of course, he knew how to spell all of them. The government relented in the end, though it wasn't long before most of them were shut down anyway.

When my eldest daughter, Hannah, was born in December 1987, I decided I'd like her to come to tea every Tuesday in the Strangers' Cafeteria – the only suitable venue. I was told that there were no high chairs available at the House of Commons. So, along with Simon Burns, whose daughter was the same age as mine, I started a campaign to persuade the House of Commons authorities to provide more support for children. Eventually they agreed. At that time our children were an unusual sight in the Commons, sitting in their high chairs. When my daughters were slightly older, Gre-ville Janner, a Labour MP, used to perform conjuring tricks for them if they bumped into him and I remember Tony Benn once gave Hannah a fifty pence piece. But children weren't encouraged. On one occasion Paul Boateng, the Labour MP for Brent, and I worked up a proposal for a children's Christmas party. He was to be the black Father Christmas and I the white one. But the House authorities, fearful of jelly besmirching the priceless wallpaper, de-clined our proposal.

At the end of my first year or so, my whips' report would proba-bly have said that I was 'too anxious to please'. When a whip sidled up and mentioned speaking opportunities – often defending the government on some spot of bother it had got into – I was their man. I was put on the Community Charge (Poll Tax) Commit-tee, studying the Bill line by line. I sat next to Sir George Young, the Conservative token rebel allowed on to the committee by the whips. (In those days the whips wholly controlled the composition of all committees.) Sir George's measured warnings and forensic demolition of the government's case sent a chill down my spine. The committee was whipped by Peter Lloyd, one of Parliament's saints, whose wife had terrible arthritis and who would arrive home in the small hours of the morning to do all the housework while she slept. Whenever I went to see him meekly to voice reservations about the Poll Tax, he'd pull out of his folder an analysis of my constituency and point out how many of my constituents would gain from this local government reform. Reassured (until the next time I heard Sir George speak), I'd get back into line.

Other opportunities to be a whip's nark would present them-selves on Fridays, when an exotic group of MPs would assemble

– normally to talk at length on a Bill we wanted to succeed, thereby squeezing out of time an opposition-supported Private Member's Bill which we did not. Ian Gow, Mrs Thatcher's skilful parliamentary private secretary and an old family friend of ours, would often be there. He was particularly kind to me, frequently taking me off for a 'white lady' – his favourite drink. He was on close terms with both Mrs Thatcher and Geoffrey Howe, and his absence from the field when they finally fell out helped define the final chapter of that relationship, with its serious consequences. I adored him. Nicholas Soames would be there in extraordinarily loud socks ('It's Friday, for goodness' sake') leading to opposition taunts that he was going ratting. Michael Brown – utterly loyal, a fine whip and a skilful parliamentarian – was a regular. On one occasion I seem to remember speaking for forty-five minutes on the relative merits of low-volume alcohol being defined as 0.5 per cent as opposed to 1.2 per cent. Intervening on me to help me keep going, Ian Gow would muse about whether I was 'the son of my father' or 'my father's son'.

At the end of 1988, I was asked to be parliamentary private secretary to William Waldegrave. A PPS is the lowest form of parliamentary life and the first step on the ministerial ladder. PPSs are a good deal for the whips because if you hold this minor post, you are part of the payroll (though unpaid), and you cannot vote against the government without resigning. No fewer than three senior whips privately took me aside to confide that my 'elevation' was as a result of their personal recommendation. I was the first of my intake to get promoted – thus occasioning the genuine pleasure of two or three of my peers and the irritation and disgust of most of the others. I greatly enjoyed working for William, who was a senior Foreign Minister and one of the cleverest members of the government. He dealt with the complexities of the Middle East, and I was in awe of his intellect. But I noted that he tended to discount all his successes without really savouring them while being consumed with misery whenever anything went wrong. I defended him ferociously whenever he was under attack.

On one occasion a shadow fell over him following a visit to Palestine and a meeting with Yasser Arafat, the chairman of the Palestine Liberation Organization. A chilling note from No. 10 arrived on his desk which started: 'The PM is surprised to hear...' Under serious attack, he was summoned to the Despatch Box in the House of Commons. I organised support, including from Greville Janner, a leading member of the Board of Deputies of British Jews on the Labour side, to help shore up William's position. As I was not really on his wing of the party, William never quite trusted me until I had worked for him for a while, but he treated me very well indeed, including me in what he was doing whenever he could. After eighteen months with William, I went to work for John Wakeham – a promotion, as John was in the Cabinet.

For the next three years I carried John's bags while he was Secretary of State for Energy and later leader in the Lords. John was a class act. He was Mrs Thatcher's fixer, remedying the electricity privatisation which under Cecil Parkinson had gone off the rails. With his Chief Whip's network, his close relationship to Mrs Thatcher, and the deep affection of the party – not least following the terrible wounds he had sustained after the Brighton bombing when his wife was killed – he was much sought after. Unusually for a former government Chief Whip, he was remarkably charitable about human nature, tending to see the best in people even when they failed him, so long as he thought they were on his side, or at least one of the good guys.

As it happens, John Wakeham was a critical player in the ensuing drama as the Conservative tribe ruthlessly despatched Mrs Thatcher. It was a psychodrama from which the Conservative Party is still today recovering. I was in the House the night Mrs Thatcher decided she had to go. I had not supported her in the first ballot of the leadership election against Michael Heseltine. With a heavy heart I had concluded her time was up. If she had taken Denis's advice and told the annual party conference celebrating her decade in government that she was going, the conference floor would have been knee-deep in tears. She would have gone out on a high. I thought she'd done a brilliant job and should retire when the going was good. So I voted for Michael Heseltine, who I thought was magnificent. His One Nation Conservatism, his energy and his work in Liverpool and compassion for the less well-off were very attractive – besides which there was an almost chemical excitement and animal charisma about Michael. I had invited him to speak at the annual dinner in Gedling, knowing he would accept because he was running for the leadership by this time and wanted my vote. The senior Tories in Gedling were appalled at the idea as they thought him disloyal, but when he strode into the dinner, they all rose as one to their feet to give him a standing ovation. He played them brilliantly, but the vote he was after was mine. His speech was directed at me and indeed at Sharon, whom he completely won over. To this day she regrets that he never became Prime Minister. His premiership would certainly not have been dull.

Following the first ballot, in which Mrs Thatcher fell four votes short of an outright win, John Wakeham arranged for her to see each of her Cabinet ministers separately. This would prove to be the last afternoon before she resigned. Various conspiracy theories abounded afterwards, but I remember John saying that in these difficult circumstances, order needed to be restored. There were only two ways a Prime Minister could be removed. One was through a vote in the House of Commons – well, that was never going to happen – and the other through losing the support of her Cabinet. He acted as he did to end the chaos then engulfing the government. He was asked at the eleventh hour if he would take over and chair her leadership team, which he agreed to do. I declined his request to join it. By then it looked as though the die was cast and any attempt to fight on would prolong the agony for the party and demean her colossal reputation.

After the Cabinet had seen the Prime Minister, most of them trooped up to John's office on the Cabinet corridor behind the Speaker's chair. He said I could stay and hear what was said. Once they'd all left, he spoke by phone to Denis in No. 10. He turned to me and said, 'She's going tomorrow morning.' At that time, probably fewer than ten people knew this was about to happen. I remember arriving home just before the BBC midnight news, which announced that she was fighting on, and telling Sharon the truth.

Shocked by the damage and division in the party following Mrs Thatcher's departure, I concluded that Hezza was too divisive to lead and might even have split the party, so in spite of his attractions I voted – and worked hard – for John Major to take over instead. I thought he was an election winner who, after Mrs Thatcher, would be a more comfortable and less controversial figure ushering in a period of good and godly government.

When the general election came just over a year later, I was gloomy about our prospects. After nearly thirteen years in office, any government is vulnerable to the opposition cry of 'time for a change'. I thought we had a better chance under a John Major-led team, with the wounds of the Poll Tax now cauterised and a gentler, less ideological approach. Also, the party had at least superficially reunited, with Michael Portillo, Hezza, Ken Clarke, Peter Lilley and Chris Patten all serving happily in the same Cabinet. But I never thought we'd win, and it turned out not many others thought we'd win either, not least because the 1992 manifesto was extremely thin on new ideas. As it turned out, John Major led us to a surprise victory, with the largest number of votes received by any party in British history – perhaps helped by the fact that the country felt there had already been an election because the Prime Minister had changed.

I spent the campaign working in my constituency and looking after the Conservative students, who were now under the stern direction of an MP. Left to their own devices they had proved too much even for Norman Tebbit, who as chairman of the party had them disbanded for being too ideologically right-wing and causing damage to property at their annual conference in Loughborough, where some of them had sported badges reading: 'Hang Nelson Mandela'. Chris Patten as party chairman had asked first David Davis and then me to police them vigorously. After a couple of years of DD's discipline, they had been thoroughly brought to heel, and when I took them over they were a most impressive bunch. I remember Andrew Griffith, now a Conservative MP elected in 2019, being one of their leading lights.

When I returned to Westminster in 1992 for my second term

with an increased majority, the Labour Party was flat on its back. Robert Harris, then political editor of the *Sunday Times*, wrote an article suggesting that now politics was all about management; the age of ideology was dead. Geoff Hoon, having transferred from the European Parliament to Westminster, told me in his cups that he thought his party would struggle to be in government again. But, as ever, you never know what's around the corner in politics and not long after, Black Wednesday took place and the Conservative Party lost its reputation for economic competence. It was to be a generation before we recovered it.

Despite the record number of votes, we now had a rather smaller parliamentary majority, and I realised I needed a 'pair' – a Member from the other main political party with whom I could agree not to vote on specific issues if either of us needed to be away. Pairing gives you the ability to be absent from the House of Commons without affecting the government majority. My father's pair had been Roy Hattersley, the former Labour *bon viveur*, leadership contender and author. Every Christmas my father gave him a bottle of exceptional wine and Roy would send over his latest publication, appropriately signed. In a tight parliament, a reliable and congenial pair is absolutely essential. Indeed, I'd been told by an old sweat that after your wife or husband, your pair would be the most important person in your life. Peter Mandelson, whom I knew through Robert Harris, agreed that we should pair together. It was an excellent arrangement. Busily engaged in making the Labour Party electable, he was the ideal pair for a harassed junior minister because he frequently had to be away from Parliament and unable to vote while engineering Labour's revival. I would call him from my car as I headed to London from Gedling on a Sunday evening and we would agree our whipping arrangements for the week ahead. 'Oh no, Andrew,' he'd say, 'I can't possibly vote then. I've got a very good party to go to.'

I was also lucky enough to be elected to the One Nation group of Tory MPs, a group of about twenty-five who met for dinner each Wednesday evening under the chairmanship of David Howell, one of Margaret Thatcher's early Cabinet ministers, whose career as a minister stretched from 1970 to 2016. I was shortly afterwards made secretary of the One Nation group – a post I held on and off until 2020, when I became the chairman. The reason I was elected secretary at such a young age was because the other members hoped my El Vino connection would improve the quality of the wine at our dinners. I managed to negotiate an excellent deal with the parliamentary banqueting manager which subsequently had to be amended so that it would last 'only so long as you remain in the Commons'. Unfortunately for the palates of the One Nation members, my exit would take place rather earlier than I had hoped.

Having completed my three years in the government Whips' Office (about which more later), in June 1995 I was informed by Richard Ryder that it was time for me to head off towards a department. I told him I'd rather stay in the Whips' Office, but he was adamant that it was time for me to go. I had been the whip responsible for the Department of Social Security and got to know Peter Lilley well. But as a result of that experience I had also decided that I definitely didn't want to serve in the Ministry of Social Security as I didn't think I'd be any good at it. So in the subsequent reshuffle, when I got the call to go to see the Prime Minister in No. 10, I walked across Whitehall saying under my breath, 'Anything but Social Security, anything!' In the Cabinet Room John Major thanked me for my time in the Whips' Office and asked me to go to… Social Security. I must have looked rather crestfallen, as he leant forward and asked, 'Is that OK? Don't you want to go?'

I replied, 'I'm not sure, Prime Minister, that such limited talents as I possess lend themselves to Social Security.'

'But I started there,' said the Prime Minister.

I pulled myself together. 'If you want me to do it, I'll do it to the best of my ability.' And with that my nearly three years as a government whip drew to an abrupt close.

Richard Ryder, who was also moving on from his role as Chief Whip, asked if I would have his wonderful driver, Janet, and I was very pleased when she agreed to take me on. My children loved her. Over the next two years of growing crises, she would collect me in the morning from my home and drop me back at the end of the parliamentary day. My children's schools were on a direct route to Westminster, so I would usually give them a lift in, and they would order a story to entertain them on the way. I'd offer them a menu the day before from which they'd select the ingredients. Janet used to remind me, as she dropped me off exhausted last thing in the evening, 'Don't you forget, Minister, you promised them both a story and for tomorrow they have ordered a unicorn, a snow leopard and Rosie's cat!'

Once in the department, I asked Peter Lilley if I could have responsibility within his ministerial team for the Child Support Agency. I had worked out that all the most interesting stuff would be done by the Secretary of State, so as a junior minister it was important to secure responsibility for something that was either too detailed for a Secretary of State's daily input or which they were not interested in. Peter readily agreed to my request. My predecessor, Alistair Burt, now a Minister of State in the department, had previously had responsibility for the CSA and was very glad to be rid of it. He had had protesters sitting on his roof at home and on several occasions had required a police escort.

I was also given responsibility for the disability living allowance and some other benefits. There was a general view in the Conservative Party that benefits were 'out of control' and needed to be reined back. I quickly learned that the enemy, if you are a minister in a large-spending department, is not the opposition but the Treasury. I also learned that in spite of his reputation as a hatchet-faced right-winger, Peter Lilley was humane and decent when it came to cutting back spending. I had responsibility for in-work benefits and the Treasury was forever sending notes about the need to get mothers with very young children off benefits and back into work. I refused to do this, telling officials that I'd not come into politics to make poor people poorer, and under Peter Lilley we as the government refused to do so. As it turned out, it was the Blair Labour government which cut benefits for single-parent families.

The CSA had started on a tide of goodwill. Virtually no one voted against the legislation when it came before Parliament. Everyone believed it was a means for going after 'feckless fathers' who'd run off, often with a younger woman, and who refused to pay for the upkeep of their former families. This was unfair on taxpayers, who were left picking up the bill. But the reality was sadly different. Although in theory the actions of the CSA were all about money and not about the rights and wrongs within personal relationships, inevitably the state was dipping its fingers into the emotional tensions and misery of broken homes. As pressure mounted, concessions were made, with the result that the formula for what the 'absent parent' would pay became ever more intricate. It took me a long time to grip the complications of the formula – complexities which Parliament had decided were preferable to a broad-brush approach but which made the system incredibly difficult to operate and explain. Eventually, I got to the point where I could more or less tell those who came to see me what the result of their assessment would be, within a few minutes and within a few pence. Before I took on this responsibility, I used to write fierce letters to Alistair Burt, remonstrating with him about the way my constituents were being treated. Now I was in receipt of such letters. Thousands of them. On one Thursday morning, all the ministerial team trooped into my office to see what 1,000 'yellow jackets' – the folders storing each reply drafted by officials – looked like as they waited for my signature. At the weekend sometimes eight red boxes would be delivered to my constituency home, five or six of them full of letters to be signed. I had agreed specific paragraphs that should be used addressing similar points to shorten the time that I took in reading, approving and signing a response. The two or three other boxes would contain the tightly written policy documents which made Social Security – now the Department for Work and Pensions – one of the most complicated and detailed briefs in Whitehall.

My children used to hate those red boxes. When they arrived on a Saturday morning, my elder daughter Hannah used to count them. If there were four or fewer, she knew I'd be around for most of the weekend, as I could leave them to be dealt with after she and her sister Rosie had gone to bed. But if there were more, I'd be out of commission and there would be no fun and games in the car on Sunday night on the way back to London. I'd sometimes be woken on Saturday morning as she hit me over the head with a pillow, loudly complaining after she had conducted her count.

To reform the Child Support Agency, I had a piece of exceptional good fortune. On my watch a new chief executive of the agency had been appointed – Ann Chant. When Ann had left school, she had worked on the public counter and on visiting duties on the then National Assistance Board. She worked her way up to the top of the Social Security Department and had come to the CSA from running the Contributions Agency. She had forgotten more about human nature than most of us will ever know. She was the ablest of officials and the Permanent Secretary told me I was very lucky to have her. With Ann Chant's words of advice ringing in my ears ('I wouldn't do that if I were you, Minister'), we made over fifty reforms, some of them fundamental and all designed to civilise the system. We persuaded the Treasury to allocate more funding to us, telling their officials that otherwise the system would collapse and they would lose even more.

Dealing with the Treasury was at the heart of everything we did at Social Security. When the budgets were set each year, very clever Treasury officials would come over the road to the Social Security Department and negotiate with ours. It often felt like the SAS arriving to deal with the Poor Bloody Infantry. But like the tortoise and the hare, the savings the Treasury demanded often proved illusory, and common sense won eventually. If you press in on one side of a balloon, the bump invariably appears on the other side. So it is with Social Security spending. And the Social Security officials, many with a long and deep experience of the system, honed over countless public spending rounds, were usually right. Each year, in the end the Treasury would give up and the balancing figures would be achieved by 'efficiency savings' or the ingenious 'spend to save' measures, whereby money allocated would expect to secure many times that amount in subsequent savings over the ensuing year, most of which would never materialise.

Colleagues in the House of Commons continued to remonstrate as their CSA constituency caseload failed to diminish. To some amusement, my father, the MP for Hampshire North West, had a go at me on the subject in Social Security Oral Questions in the House, referring to me within the normal conventions as 'my Honourable and Filial Friend'. Back in my constituency, the numbers seeking to come to my surgeries included those from all across the Midlands, and I would often agree to see them. The format was invariably the same: an older man would arrive with his younger second partner. The man would start explaining, but within a short time the exasperated younger woman would take over, ramming home the point that his first wife was getting all the money and there was nothing left for the new family. I would try patiently to explain that we are responsible for the cost of all of our children – even if they are spread beyond one family unit. If we didn't meet those costs, our neighbour the taxpayer would have to pick them up. Occasionally I'd let a non-constituent have it with both barrels: 'Dr Mitchell and I would also quite like another child, but we can't afford it.' 'Your former partner also has your children to support, so you will be short of money.'

One of my constituents, Richard Robinson, was a regular visitor to my surgeries. He was determined not to pay a penny to his ex-partner and as time ticked by and his daughter approached eighteen, he found increasingly ingenious ways to avoid paying. I would jolly him along and he became a friend. By coincidence he had decorated Ann Chant's home in Fernleigh Avenue in my constituency some years earlier. He and his colleague, Nigel Woolley,

were superb decorators and years later decorated our home in Screveton. (Indeed, as I write this, Nigel is repainting our front door.)
Richard was also extremely helpful in crafting our reforms. He had
started a local organisation called APART (Absent Parents Asking
for Reasonable Treatment), which went national. When the election came in 1997, he and Nigel joined my campaign team and put
up more posters around the constituency than anyone had ever
seen before or since.

I believed that all our reforms, painfully crafted, were enough to
civilise the system and ensure it would endure after we left government. But Labour had a manifesto commitment to change the
CSA and so come the election its provisions were effectively neu-
tralised, and the Treasury had to fork out and buy the pain.

I also had responsibility for in-work benefits – trying to use the
benefit system to help those on low pay into work and give them a
leg up. I enjoyed this and was particularly interested in understanding what other countries were doing. Nick Ridley, a senior Cabinet
minister and one of Mrs Thatcher's closest supporters, had told me
that all junior ministers should have one overseas trip per year, and
they should make sure it was a good one! I decided to visit the
GAIN programme in California, which was having real success in
getting women back into work. The guy who ran it used to leap out
of his car on the way into work when he passed a restaurant and
ask how many vacancies they had, which he could help fill.

I then planned to fly over the Pacific and meet my CSA counterparts in New Zealand and Australia, which had similar benefit
systems to ours and were struggling with the same problems. As I
was part of the Prime Minister's group of ministers looking at juvenile crime, it seemed sensible to visit Singapore on the way back

to investigate why juvenile crime was almost non-existent there, thus completing a round-the-world visit. To undertake this mission, I would need a selection of civil service skills to accompany me and a quite extraordinary number of officials offered to come. I sent a note to the Secretary of State seeking his permission and justifying the public expenditure involved. But it has to be said it was an exotic trip by Social Security standards, where a day trip to the Wigan benefits office was more our staple diet.

We set off to California, where the GAIN programme was indeed impressive and, as we learned, successful. Thereafter we arrived in Auckland and I noted the large number of grannies at the airport, dispensing tea to disorientated families who were emigrating from the UK and who arrived jetlagged and bewildered after the long journey. I remember in Wellington visiting the enormously moving war memorial and staying with the British High Commissioner in his beautiful residence – rather more impressive than the Prime Minister's house further down the hill. We arrived on a Sunday and, knowing of my interest in the wine industry, he generously took me to visit some vineyards before organising dinner with the CSA officials and the government Chief Whip. As I went off to bed after having consumed the best of New Zealand's white wines, I felt the room shake beneath my feet. I nervously mentioned to the High Commissioner the next morning that I hoped I hadn't drunk too much of his excellent wine. He told me that as I went to bed quite a severe earthquake, rather than alcohol, had made the earth move.

From New Zealand we went on to Australia, calling in at Melbourne and Sydney, before our final stop in Singapore. We had a detailed discussion with the authorities there about juvenile crime and justice. We visited Singapore Boys Home A, where young men who had misbehaved were incarcerated. When a whistle blew, all the inmates would rush into line like soldiers on parade. There was plenty of physical education and exercise. There was also a facility for parents to admit their children if they were 'beyond parental control' (BPCs). For a period of time, they would be taken from their homes and disciplined. I talked to one of them, who was only ten years old. 'What are you doing here?' I bent down and asked this little chap. 'I'm a BPC and I'm never coming here again,' his little tear-stained lips opined.

In one of the corners of the facility stood a flogging block where rule-breakers would be thrashed by the superintendent. Back in his office I picked up one of his canes and swished it through the air while the accompanying British civil servants had an attack of the vapours and nearly passed out. Even for an old Tory like me, their disciplinary regime was excessive. Once home, over a family dinner, I told Sharon about this tough regime while my wide-eyed children listened. A few days later my younger daughter, Rosie, stormed into our bedroom, hands on hips, to announce that her elder sister was definitely a BPC and needed to be taken away.

After the sad death of John Smith in 1994, the Labour Party elected Tony Blair and we soon knew that the Tory goose had been cooked. We limped on in what I thought was a good government, introducing social reform and rebuilding the economy under Ken Clarke's practical middle-of-the-road policies. But the country was tired of the Conservatives after eighteen years and wanted something new. With Tony Blair they got Tory economic restraint with social justice, and it was clear that we were on the way out. The only question was how big Blair's majority would be.

I knew I was in trouble in Gedling. The seat, running round the eastern side of the city of Nottingham, was changing and large houses on the city border once lived in by Tory families had morphed into flats and new buildings which were heavily Labour. In addition, between 1987 and 1992 the Liberals had lost almost 1.5 million voters, who transferred almost in full to Labour.

Candidates in parliamentary elections can usually tell what is happening to their vote on the ground. Until the final week of the 1997 campaign, I felt I'd just about got my head above water. It was an extraordinarily vigorous campaign. Under Mel Shepherd and Alan Bexon, my two loyal and hard-working campaign managers, we flooded the constituency with workers, literature and canvassing.

In a key moment, pressing the flesh in Netherfield as we worked our way down the main street, I saw a family coming towards us. It was one of those I had really helped. I'd sorted out granny's benefit problems and found a nursery place for the child in the pushchair, which the mother was manoeuvring along the pavement.

'Ah,' I said to those helping me, 'this will be encouraging,' as I advanced with outstretched hands and an open, hopeful smile. 'Hello. How good to see you. I very much hope you will support me next Thursday.'

'Well, Andrew, we have talked about this as a family and we are going to support Mr Blair.'

'Well, he's going to win anyway,' I said pleadingly, 'so if you vote for me, you'll have Mr Blair in No. 10 and me as your MP here.'

The mother smiled. I remember her precise words.

'No, Andrew, you're an excellent MP, none better, and you've helped us as a family, but it is time for Mr Blair.'

That night I reported this conversation to John Wakeham, who was in Conservative Central Office in London as he was retiring as an MP and without a constituency to fight. He confirmed it wasn't looking good.

All candidates hope for a miracle, but the evidence from that last week suggested that our vote was slipping away. I spent twenty-seven hours without stopping signing letters to voters we had identified who had been Conservative in the past but had expressed doubts about supporting us this time. I was fed fish and chips and Hamlet cigars by those who generously stayed with me in relay to print off the letters, fold them and stuff them into envelopes in our headquarters on Carlton Hill.

On Wednesday, my driver Janet came to collect my last red box. Unable to meet my eye, she said she'd been instructed to collect my ministerial red box keys as well.

As polling day dawned, I was delivering our final leaflets at 5 a.m. and hoping I might just scrape through. It had been an exhausting campaign and afterwards when I came to thank everyone who had helped, the list of those who had supported me in one way or another was over 300 strong.

I ended my campaign at 9.45 p.m. in Woodthorpe, one of our best areas, and went to my friends and supporters Andrew and Jenny Collinsons' home to await the BBC exit poll. Sitting in Andrew's large black leather armchair as the bongs of Big Ben rang out, I learned my fate.

In the two previous elections I had written my speech thanking the returning officer and scribbled a few notes in case I lost. This time it was the other way around. At the count it looked for a time that we might buck the trend, but the truth soon became clear. The

Labour activists could not believe their good fortune, and as the results were announced, some of them were dancing at the front of the hall.

I shook hands with the victor, Vernon Coaker, who had fought a straight and principled fight against me at both previous elections and was now third time lucky. He was decent in his acceptance speech, saying, 'Whatever reasons have led to tonight, it is no reflection on Andrew Mitchell's work as our local MP' – something he repeated in the House of Commons when he came to make his maiden speech, to the disapproval of his Whips' Office.

When it was my turn to speak, I said what a privilege it had been to represent Gedling for ten years and how much I would miss my constituents. I also said that I thought that history would treat John Major's period as Prime Minister with rather greater respect and admiration than his contemporaries. I think history now, twenty-five years later, might well concur. Along the front by the returning officer's dais, many of my supporters and key party workers were in tears.

After a large number of hugs and handshakes, we left to go home to Tithby. TV cameras had dashed over from Nottingham once they'd heard that Gedling was almost certain to fall to Labour. One fellow with a camera was rushing down the centre of the road towards the sports hall where the count had been taking place. Sharon accelerated towards him. I urged caution, pointing out that he was not responsible for my defeat. As we came down the ramp and on to the main road just as dawn was breaking, there at the crossroads was a fox, languidly washing his whiskers and stretching. It was, in truth, a new Labour dawn – a Britain where it would shortly be safe for foxes to roam free.

Once back in Tithby, we called our London home, where Hannah, aged nine, had been allowed to stay up with her nanny, SizBiz, to watch the result. She'd fallen asleep, but Siz had woken her at the key moment.

'Well done, Dad.'

'Thank you, darling, but I'm afraid I did not win.'

'Never mind, Dad, you came second and that's pretty good too.'

CHAPTER 5

ON THE OUT

Losing your seat is a bruising experience. On polling day, I had been a Minister of the Crown and a Member of Parliament. On Friday morning, I was unemployed. It is a very strange feeling being rejected by the voters. Members of Parliament get a worse press than they generally deserve – on both sides of the House. Most want to do a good job for their constituents. We fight hard for the privilege of having those two letters after our name.

Without an income, I sat down to work out how long we could meet our current financial commitments without surgery. I was lucky that we had been a two-income family, but our mortgage and outgoings definitely required those incomes. I was also concerned as the country fell in love with New Labour that finding employment might be difficult. I might end up rather like a wounded Italian veteran after the Second World War, waiting outside the Vatican but ignored by the prelates because I'd been part of a bad lot – a relic of the failed Majorite junta; part of the past not of the future.

Without a ministerial car, I bought myself a bicycle which I used in all weathers and I normally rode in a suit – though until I returned I could not bring myself to cycle anywhere near to Parliament. I had a 25-minute rule for plausible journeys and a wicker basket for my foul weather gear. In 1997, a fraction of the number of people bicycled around London that do so today, and I enjoyed calculating how much I was saving in taxi fares and petrol costs – perhaps an inheritance of sorts from my Scottish grandmother.

If ever I left the house without wearing a cycling helmet, my two daughters would stand on the doorstep and shout to their mother, 'Daddy's going to die! He's not wearing a helmet!' So I quickly got into the habit of always wearing one.

I used to take the children to school by putting them on the No. 4 or No. 43 bus at the Angel Islington, cycling down behind them, then helping them across the main road outside the Barbican Underground station and in through the doors of Charterhouse Square School. On one occasion as they travelled on the bus, I was pedalling alongside them using my mobile phone. The children froze as they heard someone sitting near them say 'Look at that tosser using a phone on his bike?'

One call I greatly appreciated was from David Verey, the young chairman of Lazard who had recently taken over from John Nott. Over lunch, David very generously indicated that if I had any interest in resuming a City career, I would be welcome to rejoin the firm. He told me, 'Either come back as a full-time director and make your way and your career here or come back as a non-exec, but you won't get paid much for that.' In the end, rather to his irritation we agreed that I would return for two days a week, working with some of the old international division survivors. I would make Lazard my base, with my office and secretary there, and in return they would get more than the two days contractually due. It was, for me at least, a superb arrangement.

My new life had broadly fallen into place by the beginning of 1998, so with great relief I settled down to a plural business career with a portfolio of advisory and non-executive roles. The main part was Lazard, which was once again in transition. That autumn the firm was on a roll. On 10 October, there were five major international merger and acquisition deals announced around the world, and Lazard in London was on one side or another of four of them. Under David Verey and Marcus Agius's leadership, the firm benefited from an extraordinary collection of talent, many hired by John Nott. This included John Nelson, Nigel Turner and Nick Jones (with whom I shared an office), later joined by Peter Kiernan, bolstering the home-trained and highly skilled talent of Jeremy Sillem, Michael Baughan and Michael Bottenheim, who together propelled Lazard London to the top of the league tables. I made myself useful in a series of non-executive roles in the bank as well as working with the American Lazard in asset management in the Gulf, capital markets in Eastern Europe and some overseas advisory work.

Since my first Lazard innings, Adrian Evans had arrived and become the chief executive. His mother had starred with Noël Coward in the wartime film classic *In Which We Serve*. His own personality combined the dashing charm of Coward with a sensitivity and understanding of human nature that inspired affection and admiration in equal measure. He had run Grindlays in India. At a pivotal time, his human relations skills had resolved a serious national banking strike centred on Mumbai. He had an extraordinary rapport with members of the wider Lazard fraternity in New York and Paris and for a brief period he played a part in guiding Lazard's destiny towards being one firm. I joined Adrian on the

Lazard India board and visiting Mumbai saw the breadth of his friendships and contacts. Staying at the Taj Hotel, one of the most romantic and engaging hotels in the world, he secured the famous John Lennon and Yoko Ono Suite for Sharon and me when she accompanied me on one of my visits there.

In life you can often remember where you were when you heard shocking news – the death of Diana, the assassination of John F. Kennedy. I was at the Nottinghamshire Showground at Newark at midday one Sunday when my phone rang and David Verey suggested I go somewhere private to talk. He told me the dreadful news that Adrian had gone jogging that morning in central London and on his return told Ingela, his wife, that he did not feel well. She immediately said she would take him straight to hospital, but as he went through their front door, he looked at her, said, 'Too late' and collapsed and died at her feet.

At his memorial service at St Paul's Church, Knightsbridge, the Lazard clan gathered to pay tribute to a remarkable friend and colleague. David Verey delivered the eulogy; Adrian's younger daughter, distraught and willed on by us all, just managed to complete her reading, the crackling emotion in her voice echoing around the vaulted roof of the church. His memorial service also marked the end of the old Lazard era, as three houses became one and the leadership passed to Bruce Wasserstein, a Wall Street leader whose culture and style were very different from the old Lazard London.

I had also been asked to join the board of Lazard Asia, operating in Hong Kong, Singapore, Seoul and Beijing, by David Anderson, a clever mathematician and investment banker who had joined Lazard shortly after me. To invigorate the business, he had moved to Singapore and rather nobly wanted someone on board from

London to ensure that if anything happened to him, his business in the Far East would not be orphaned. I jumped at the opportunity to help and to return, four times a year at least, out East.

The South Koreans have never forgotten Britain's role in the Korean War, where in spite of exhaustion after the end of the Second World War Britain still spent its blood and treasure on their behalf. They could see for themselves across the border in North Korea what fate would have awaited them had America and Britain, amongst others, not intervened.

In the company of the defence attaché, I went to Panmunjom, the border village on the demilitarised zone. We travelled via a number of memorials to British forces who had fought and died there, including the Imjin River where in April 1951 the 1st Battalion Gloucestershire Regiment, the 'Glorious Glosters', for three days held off a massive Chinese infantry attack before being surrounded on Hill 235. When their ammunition ran out, they threw beer bottles at the advancing Chinese troops before fixing bayonets. They were totally encircled. Six hundred and twenty-two died and the rest were captured.

We went up to the main guard post on the border and I saw the famous hotline phone linking the two countries, which are technically still at war, and asked when it had last been used. 'Oh,' the American officer said, 'yesterday. The North Koreans rang to ask us to remove our key from our side of the door of the visitors' hut where the armistice ending the war had been signed so that their group of tourist visitors could come in!'

At that time the demilitarised zone on the Korean border was one of the most dangerous places in the world. On a visit to the American officers' mess nearby I noticed a large number of monks' habits hanging in an anteroom. To relieve pressure on what was an extremely stressful assignment, every few weeks all the off-duty officers would dress up as monks and have a hell of a party.

Frequent air-raid practices underlined the dangers for Seoul – a city of 9 million people just 30 miles from the border which military planners believed could be destroyed by North Korean guns, dug in and in range, within little more than an hour of the balloon going up and an attack being launched by the Communist North on South Korea and the huge American garrison billeted there.

*　　*　　*

We sold our home in Tithby in Nottinghamshire not long after the 1997 election. I went back to Gedling frequently, however. On one such visit, where we stayed in a bed and breakfast, Sharon and I saw how much Hannah and Rosie missed the countryside. They had both been upset about leaving Tithby. A few weeks later, a tumbledown, sprawling farmhouse in Screveton, on the edge of the Vale of Belvoir, which we had been offered the opportunity to buy in 1992 was offered to us again by its owner, who had incorporated most of the surrounding acres into his estate but did not want the house. Back in 1992 we had had no money. We were paying off our mortgage in London so although we thought it had huge potential as a wonderful family home, we were not in a position to proceed.

Now that I was earning my living, we could contemplate buying it – with its five acres and three paddocks (and of importance, if only to me, its cellar). Part of the house was very old, divided into two with extensive barns at the back, while the main part had been built in the early 1800s. Sharon drove up to have a look and called me from the village phone box. She said it would make a wonderful home – perfect if I went back to Gedling, or quit politics, and highly sellable if I were adopted for a constituency a long way away.

And so we bought it, determined to restore it and make it a family home for our children and their friends. Previously, planning permission had been secured to provide for more building there, and so we endeared ourselves to others in the village who had been up in arms about prospective development and could see that our plans would make such building impossible. With a great deal of love, an expanding mortgage and a very good and sympathetic builder, David West, we set about restoring and renovating Manor House Farm, replacing the steel barns, a relic from the days when it had been a working farm, with a large wildflower meadow. An avalanche of health and safety requests assailed us, along with paperwork on vacant possession, planning permissions, heritage permissions, bat surveys and coalmine surveys. For eight months there were never fewer than fifteen builders, craftsmen, electricians, plumbers and decorators as our project took shape. We incorporated some of the barns into an area for our guests and put the house back into one rambling entity.

We also refurbished the cellar. I'd drunk all my old clarets while a junior minister and I now set about, through friends in the wine trade, identifying and buying parcels of wine from Bordeaux with the aim of building a balanced selection of wines to last a lifetime. I procured some older wines – certain vintages from the 1980s – and subsequently bought en primeur 2000, 2002, 2003, 2005 and 2009, the last of which probably won't be drinking at its best for twenty years. My ambition is to consume the final bottles of my cellar with friends and family before passing away peacefully in my sleep – though preferably not for a while.

We set aside one part of the farmhouse for Hannah, aged twelve, and Rosie, aged nine, and built a vegetable garden, a winter garden, a drystone wall along the drive, and stables with a tack room. We moved in just in time for the Millennium New Year.

We would all leave London on Friday night after school and arrive in time to throw open the shutters in summer or light a huge fire in winter. We soon realised we had acquired our own bit of paradise, with views over the vale as far as Belvoir Castle. That summer I swallowed hard and told my various employers that I'd be around much less in London during the school holidays but would be 'available', and I decamped to Screveton. Both my daughters acquired ponies and lived a *Swallows and Amazons* existence with the children of our great friends from the other side of the political divide, Charlie and Marianna Falconer, who lived in the next village.

For several idyllic summers I bonded with my children. As a Member of Parliament, I had far too often been an absent father, so I tried hard to reboot our lives together now that I had more time and more income. I became their groom, helping with their horses, competitions and numerous Pony Club activities. Amongst these was the annual summer camp. This was run by an amazing assortment of parents and others, utterly dedicated to horse riding and the children. Many of them lived for little else. I would sometimes do guard duty from 11 p.m. to 7 a.m., walking around the stables, which contained nearly seventy horses, checking every half-hour that none had got out or got into trouble, and enjoying the solitude. I was always rewarded with an outstanding cooked breakfast once the dedicated mothers came in early in the morning. My duties also included hiding in the bushes near the back of the boys' dormitory armed with a powerful torch. I would hear the creak of the door hinges and a boy's head would peer out enquiringly before starting to tiptoe towards the girls' – only to be bathed suddenly in a very bright spotlight and sent back.

One particular pleasure in Screveton was walking across the fields and through Barleyholme Wood to neighbouring Flintham to see the Falconers. Over the years first he and then I served as Cabinet ministers. On one afternoon, dressed informally and gossiping over a bottle of chilled white wine, Charlie and I were lying on the grass when one of his ministerial team, David Lammy MP, hove into view en route to a ministerial engagement nearby. He stood looking at the two of us with raised eyebrows before declaring, 'This sight confirms my worst fears about the British political Establishment.'

On Christmas Eve 2000, I was tiptoeing through Rosie's bedroom on official Father Christmas duties when a little voice, half-asleep, whispered, 'Dad?'

'Yes?'

'I've got to have a dog; I've got to!'

Previously we had had two Burmese cats, each adopted by a daughter and each surprisingly relaxed about being dressed up in clothes and carted around on bicycles and in prams. When the day came that they were no more, I had vetoed the suggestion that we should get a dog because I thought it would be difficult with our peripatetic lifestyle between the Midlands and London. But Rosie's plea was too much to resist and so I gave way. The type of dog and a suitable name were determined by Mitchell 'democracy', with weighted votes (to teach my children about the democratic process!) whereby Sharon and I each had six votes and each daughter had three. This encouraged lively debate and training in the careful use of alliances and now resulted in our welcoming a Welsh Springer spaniel puppy named Molly. She was a wonderful success, with her gentle disposition and soulful eyes, and was perfectly happy travelling at her mistress's feet. She was very much Sharon's dog but a wonderful and loyal family pet. (We took her shooting once and on the last drive she chased all the birds away from the guns. We were not invited again.) She was also the proud winner of the Westminster Dog of the Year in 2008 – a competition organised by the Kennel Club to encourage responsible dog ownership. Her extremely photogenic picture appeared across much of the UK's local and regional press over the following weekend.

In early 2012, she became ill. She was only ten years old, but she deteriorated very fast until we knew she would have to be put to sleep. Sharon held her as she wagged her tail for a final time and then she was gone. It was a Wednesday morning and the only day in my entire time as DfID Secretary of State that I went home early. We took Molly to Screveton and buried her under the apple tree on the edge of the wildflower meadow with a piece of slate above her grave: 'Here lies much-loved Molly, beautiful and dutiful.' We buried her in her favourite basket with a note that Rosie wrote on behalf of us all. The next day in Sutton Coldfield, for the first time in a generation, we lost a council seat to the Labour Party. Although I worked flat-out with all our activists, I hardly noticed a thing. I was so upset about Molly, I found it hard to engage at all.

In the way that often happens, four months later Scarlet arrived in our lives. Almost identical to Molly, as a tiny puppy she received most of her early training from Rosie and had soon won our love and affection. She too has competed in the Westminster Dog of the Year competition, coming second in 2018 to a Labour retriever double act. For many years she boycotted the competition because on an earlier occasion she was beaten by a pug. This, she concluded, meant that the competition must be rigged.

Screveton has been a most important part of our family life. Quite apart from being home to our children, it has been a remarkable oasis of tranquillity. I have never left on a Sunday night without feeling sad, nor arrived back without my spirits lifting. We have had so many wonderful weekends there with friends, always with the same routine, and our daughters with their friends too. We have photographed an ancient weeping ash tree in each of the four seasons of the year. These four pictures adorning the walls of my ministerial office were a source of joy and solace in moments of tension or difficulty – a huge comfort knowing that Screveton would be there waiting for our next visit.

I considered carefully whether I should try to return to the political world. Bob Worcester, the well-known pollster, had kindly agreed to see whether there was any chance I could win Gedling back. His expert advice was that it simply wasn't going to happen – nor did it for nearly twenty-three years. I toyed with the idea of not going back at all, thinking seriously about carrying on with my various employments. But as William Hague pointed out, 'You really can't go on bicycling around London making money. You need to run something or come back into politics.' I have teased him about the fact that, having lured me back, he resigned as leader just as I was re-elected. Part of the reason I wanted to come back was to try to help him become Prime Minister!

Once I decided to try to return to Westminster, I told my many friends in the Gedling Conservatives, with a heavy heart, that I was not planning to fight the seat again. Mel Shepherd and Alan Bexon were understanding and supportive and I went with their blessing. We all understood how difficult it would be to win the seat back; it would be a while before the tide went out on New Labour.

Once I was on the seat-hunting trail, I hit trouble – well described in Simon Walters's book *Tory Wars*. A group on the Tory right briefed against me, mainly on the grounds that I had been pro-Maastricht and one of John Major's whips who had forced the legislation through. There were also vague smears about my City career, all of which were completely untrue. I kept on coming second in constituency selections, though I couldn't really argue that I was any better than the eventual winner. A pattern emerged. In three seats for which I was interviewed, I was in the lead after the first round in front of the selection committee, which sifted the CVs of the many candidates. By the time the selection process reached the final stage in front of the wider membership, it was clear that some sort of whispering campaign was causing doubts about my candidature. In one seat, a well-known local woman with strong links to the party's right suggested I had been involved in 'peculation', which she was then unable to specify.

Had I known this was going to happen and that William Hague was going to stand down from the leadership, I am not sure that I would have started down the long pathway back to Westminster.

I complained to the Chief Whip and the party chairman about what was happening. It felt quite wrong that the process of selection was being polluted in this way. Not unfairly, they said there was nothing they could do, and I would just have to suck it up and battle it out. After another couple of seats where I also came second, the seat of Witney in west Oxfordshire came up. I had friends in the constituency and it rapidly became clear that the same process was taking place. I was apparently in the lead at the end of the first round, but it was clear that one the party's brightest and freshest faces, David Cameron, was a very strong contender. I was tipped off that an organised group was allegedly busy ringing people up and briefing against me.

This selection process was always going to be turbulent. The seat had been represented by Douglas Hurd, who had run up against some trouble there over Europe, then by Shaun Woodward, who had defected to Labour. It was not, therefore, surprising that there was some tension, with strong views about the new candidate. At the final meeting, more than 400 people turned up. It was clear that the audience was divided. When it was my turn to face questions, I was asked to explain my involvement in some undefined City scandal. I responded that any such allegations were completely untrue and that they could rest assured that I would not be standing before them if there was even the faintest question of anything like that having happened. When the votes were counted, I came second, and David Cameron was ahead by seventy votes.

It is often the case in politics that Members of Parliament tend to end up in the right seat for them. There was also no doubt that David, quite apart from being much abler than me, was very well suited by background and nature to the beautiful seat of Witney.

Immediately thereafter, Norman Fowler announced that he was standing down as the MP for Sutton Coldfield, an ancient royal town with a distinct identity, community and heritage. The decision to axe the Sutton Coldfield Council in favour of joining the area to Birmingham, albeit only for local government purposes, had come about in 1974 under the Peter Walker local government reforms. The royal town had been outraged by this decision and Ted Heath, the Prime Minister at the time, once told me that his office had received more letters of complaint about this than all the other correspondence received by the PM's office from the UK and around the world in the preceding months.

Geoff Southall, one of my oldest friends, lived in Sutton Coldfield and together we explored the town and the issues which most affected the people who lived there. I immediately felt at home. Sutton Coldfield felt like a grown-up version of Gedling, and I noticed that it had always been represented by someone who had had experience of serving in Parliament before, and not by a novice.

The first round of the selection process took place at Moor Hall Hotel over two weekends. Forty people were interviewed. I found myself amongst a Conservative community that was steeped in business, community service and One Nation Conservative values. The process was well organised and run by an experienced agent, Martyn Punyer, and a self-effacing businessman, Paul Brown, the local party chairman.

Sure enough, after I'd cleared the first hurdle, the outside intervention began. But this time it backfired. Tessa Miller, one of Sutton Coldfield's best known Conservative activists and a long-standing opponent of our membership of the European Union (she once turned up at a Conservative conference dressed from head to toe in a Union Jack), was approached and warned that I'd been involved in 'City corruption'. However, as well as being anti-European Tessa is a stickler for fairness and probity. She concluded that if this was true it needed to be properly investigated and exposed, and she called the constituency agent to tell him what she had heard. She also said that if it was not true it was a disgraceful intervention. Martyn Punyer rang Norman Fowler, who had made clear that he would play no part in the selection of his successor. Martyn asked him to find out, chapter and verse, about these allegations so that he could give a full report to Tessa and the constituency chairman in charge of the selection. Shortly thereafter Norman Fowler rang Martyn to say that the allegations were without any foundation whatsoever.

The second round, in front the executive council, went well and the final – open to all paid-up members of the local Conservative Party – took place in Sutton Coldfield's royal town hall on a Saturday morning. This clashed with an important home game for the local side Aston Villa at Villa Park, a point noted by some slightly disgruntled attendees.

Three finalists, including my old friend and fellow whip Derek Conway and Sharon Buckle, whom I had briefly worked with at Boots and who had been the third candidate in the final with David and me at Witney, waited for the vote to be counted in the old royal town council chamber adjacent to the town hall. To my and my wife's great delight, I was the fortunate winner. Once I had been selected, Daniel Moylan – now Lord Moylan – wrote to me to say that Sutton Coldfield was the only parliamentary seat he had ever wanted to represent. He said that as a boy growing up in the city of Birmingham he never came across the border into the royal town without wearing a jacket and tie. My prospective new constituents would have appreciated this mark of respect.

I went back into the town hall to start getting to know members of this centrist, decent, loyal and energetic Conservative association. In a sea of surrounding Labour seats – including the whole of Birmingham – this was an oasis of blue and a bastion of Conservatism. Above all, at a time when smaller and less well organised and powerful Conservative associations were falling into ideological division and conflict over Europe, the Sutton Coldfield Conservatives declined to go down that path. The good sense and decency of Paul Brown, David Roy, Margaret Waddington, Kay Noone, Ewan Mackey and Malcolm Cornish, all of whom have led the association over the past twenty years, have seen to that.

Many years later when the Conservative Party was once again convulsed by Europe and seeing off the premierships of David Cameron and Theresa May in turn, the Sutton Coldfield Tory high command decided that in the European referendum the association would not take a fixed position. It declined to do so afterwards as well. Three of my association officers favoured staying and three leaving. While many members held strong views, I never felt pressured into doing anything other than making up my own mind.

In May 2000, finally selected for a constituency where I felt at home, Sharon and I found a terraced house right in the middle of the town and I started to get to know my new patch and all the different organisations and interests that made up the community as well as the issues, many of them environmental, that concern a predominantly well-heeled Middle England community.

Just as Norman Fowler had come to Sutton Coldfield from a Nottingham constituency, so history repeated itself and I started to dig in. When polling day arrived, I was elected with over 50 per cent of the vote and a majority in excess of 10,000. Westminster beckoned anew.

CHAPTER 6

TORY DECLINE AND RENEWAL

Arriving back in Westminster in 2001 was a cultural shock. It was Labour's House and Tony Blair was in his pomp. We Tories were without a leader, comparatively few in number and fizzing with divisions over Europe.

A leadership election acted as useful displacement therapy for the fact that we were flat on our back as a party. I decided I was too recently returned to take any active role in the campaign, though at the request of David Maclean, later to be Iain Duncan Smith's Chief Whip, I seconded David Davis's nomination. David fought a spirited campaign – running as 'the dark horse' candidate, with a wind-blown mane and flared nostrils, until he was eliminated. In the final round, Ken Clarke, Iain Duncan Smith and Michael Portillo battled it out, with Iain the ultimate victor. David was keen that his troops should support Iain but gave up when Jim Paice, Greg Knight and I styled ourselves 'Eurosceptics for Ken'. 'Getting you lot together is like herding cats' was David's verdict.

With hindsight I am even more convinced that Ken Clarke was the right candidate. The Tory Party was still convulsed by the trauma of Margaret Thatcher's departure and badly needed his experienced hand and direct connection to Middle England. But, as ever, Europe was exercising its grip on the party's collective sanity and if Ken was willing to trim his views a little to beguile the electorate, this would be stopped whenever he returned home to Nottingham, where his wife Gillian would step in to stiffen his sinews. While Ken would have given Tony Blair a run for his money, he'd have been deeply out of sorts with the tide of Euro-scepticism running increasingly strongly through our ranks.

Michael Portillo's politics had radically altered since he was one of Mrs Thatcher's youngest and most favoured ministers. But the parliamentary party thought the bell struck a false note and anyway, Michael had outgrown the constraints of opposition and old-fashioned Conservatism.

Once elected leader, Iain assembled his team. He asked me to serve as his shadow Financial Secretary. While I was flattered, I declined his offer, mainly because I'd just returned to a House of Commons which I barely recognised. I thought I should bed in. I also did not think this would end well, as the party retreated into its comfort zone. Prime Minister's Questions were not Iain's forte and you could see Tony Blair deliberately pulling his punches as our side sat dejected, worrying we were going nowhere.

Maybe Prime Minister's Questions didn't matter that much; after all, William Hague had been amusing and often outwitted Tony Blair at the Despatch Box, thereby raising morale and rallying his own troops. Much good did it do him or us. But we were not a happy bunch. Blair had a way with the Commons – an almost feline and flirtatious approach – treating the House with respect; always courteous, always prepared and always compelling.

As the country headed towards war over Iraq, most of the

opposition came from within the Labour Party. On the day of the critical vote, our Whips' Office had strongly encouraged the party to support the war. I told my whip I would listen to the debate before deciding and sat on the floor in the gangway that runs down between the opposition benches because they were so packed. I listened, spellbound, to Tony Blair as he made that extraordinary speech. With complete mastery of the Commons, he spelled out why Britain should go to war and risk the lives of our soldiers in the interests of collective security. Across the House, I watched the agony on the faces of Labour Members as they fought with their consciences. On our side we egged Blair on, slightly alarmed that his instincts were more bellicose than ours. Having heard the case he put, I was in no doubt how I would vote. If a British Prime Minister said that war was necessary, that was good enough for me.

After his speech, and as the debate continued, I went home to have dinner with my family in Islington and told them that I had decided to support the Prime Minister. They were horrified. Sharon, who subsequently marched against the war through the streets of London, strongly supported by our children, was extremely cross about my decision. Later that night after voting, I crept back very quietly into our home.

One of those on the Labour side who had abstained was my namesake, Austin Mitchell, who sadly recently died and was much liked and admired on our side of the House. I got to know Austin well, not least as we kept on receiving each other's mail – which we each treated honourably, returning it to each other confidentially – something which worked to his advantage as I often received his lucrative media fees. I would from time to time work with his wife, the television producer Linda McDougall, and later with

Hannah, their daughter. She ran the British–American Parliamentary Group, one of the most influential country caucuses at Westminster, with whom I worked, once I left government in 2012, as its vice-chairman. As she and my elder daughter shared the same name, on more than one occasion I had to apologise to her for inadvertently sending her emails starting with the word 'Darling'.

As a family we had also benefited from this prospective confusion. When we moved into our home in Gibson Square, we had required planning permission for the necessary renovation work. We were told that Islington, with its controversial and left-wing council (one of those who had flown the red flag over the town hall), would take at least six months to grant us the necessary approvals. Imagine our delight when, three weeks into this period, all the necessary permissions arrived back signed, sealed and delivered. Our neighbour, a Liberal Democrat councillor, who had assured us this process would take for ever, could not believe it. Some weeks later, following his enquiries, he told us that the planning officer, believing he was dealing with the long-serving Labour 'A. Mitchell', had waved it all through quickly. He was apparently disciplined. This may well be the only example ever of a local government official being rebuked for delivering results too quickly.

Quite early on following my return as a 'retread', my correspondence with David Willetts, our shadow Work and Pensions Secretary, was leaked and appeared on the front page of *The Guardian*. David was furious and demanded to know how it had got there, clearly suspecting me as the leaker. I had written to him suggesting that we look seriously at the argument for funded state pensions, with the younger generation enabled to save for long-term security later in their lives rather than having to rely on prevailing economic circumstances and the whim of politicians. It was an extension of the property-owning democracy – having your own pension pot. But it was obviously very controversial. Regardless of whether there was merit in the idea, it should not have leaked, and I was embarrassed.

Pursuing my own leak inquiry, I looked at the possibilities and asked Austin Mitchell whether the correspondence could have come into his office in error. He called me from New Zealand and said that his enquiries indicated that one of his office staff – a researcher – had indeed passed the correspondence to *The Guardian*. He said he was very sorry and had 'told him off'. I thought a sterner punishment was merited and said so, but Austin decided a reprimand would suffice and declined to sack him. I was very unhappy about this, but at least I could now explain to David Willetts that this had not been an attempt by one of his own to shaft him.

Literally three weeks later, an extraordinary letter arrived on my desk. Headed up with an address in Grimsby, Austin Mitchell's constituency, it purported to come from the Grimsby Naturist Society and was an invitation to 'A. Mitchell MP' to attend and speak at the annual general meeting of the assorted members of the town's nudist community. Smelling a rat, I sat and stared at the invitation, trying to work out the angle. In the end I got my secretary to ring them up and ask for a few more details, saying I was minded to accept. Listening into the call, I gleefully discovered that the invitation was entirely genuine, that a relation of Austin's was a prominent member and Grimsby enthusiast for naked cavorting, in spite of the chill east wind normally prevailing in that part of the world.

I rang Simon Walters, knowing that the *Mail on Sunday* would

definitely run with the story about an MP speaking to their constituency naturists, presumably in the buff. Mr Walters did not let
me down; it was a pleasure to be giving him a story – especially in
this case – rather than appearing in one of his. Sure enough, the
Mail on Sunday had a decent spread with a quote from me saying,
'It's bad enough gazing at Austin fully clothed; the idea of viewing
him in the nude is too horrifying a spectacle to contemplate.'

On the Monday morning as I arrived in the Commons, Simon
Walters was lurking near the Members' Entrance looking sheepish.
'Oh goodness, Andrew. Now you've got us into trouble. Austin has
rung the editor and is threatening to sue.'

'Well, he can't,' I said. 'The story is entirely accurate, with the
possible exception of my rather offensive remark about his phy-
sique. I'll go to see him.'

When we met, Austin was cross. I said he'd get no sympathy
from me; it was too good a free kick following the bad behaviour
of his office. After a short discussion he asked if we could revert to
our previous happy and harmonious relationship, returning each
other's mail privately as before. I agreed. In that rather English
way, he stuck out his arm and we shook hands, our old relationship
restored.

As the 2001 parliament continued, the Tory Party turned in on
itself, and Iain's leadership became increasingly beleaguered. He
apparently believed that the old Maastricht Whips' Office was
trying to do him in because he'd been troublesome in days gone by,
but this was untrue. While he had been a rebel from time to time,
he had always behaved honourably and told us what he planned
to do. We used to refer to him as 'the Major'. Besides, it was never
personal in the Whips' Office – just business. I had returned to the

Commons with four other 'retreads': Henry Bellingham, Alistair Burt, Greg Knight and Derek Conway. Re-entry was difficult, not least because we were out of government, the party was more fractious and the polls showed we were going nowhere. I spent much of that parliament in Sutton Coldfield. As a first-termer, there were so many local organisations to get to know and people to meet in my new constituency. It seemed a better use of time than languishing in the Commons, able to do little more than flick pellets at the Labour behemoth.

One of my most distinguished constituents was Doug Ellis, the owner of Aston Villa Football Club – heavily supported throughout the royal town – and an under-acclaimed but huge national and local philanthropist. He saved the NSPCC's Childline, giving its night service in Birmingham £1 million so it could continue coming to the aid of distressed and vulnerable children. I'd go at his kind invitation once a year to watch his beloved Villa playing at Villa Park. Travelling there in his blue Rolls-Royce was a terrifying experience as he veered all over the road while trying to acknowledge the waves and shouts of his royal town fans. Once at the Villa, his progress through the crowds in the hospitality area was akin to Noël Coward's experience in the film *The Italian Job* as he was clapped out by his fellow prisoners.

Doug was a superb and self-made businessman, having opened up package holidays for people across the Midlands and in the early days helped make the sandwiches the punters ate on their journey. He was also legendarily careful with money. Towards the end of his life, he was in Good Hope Hospital in my constituency, very sick but hanging on. Admittedly, if you are unwell enough to be in hospital, a visit from your MP may not necessarily be an aid to recovery. When I went to visit him, he was lying flat out with his eyes closed. I talked to him without any discernible reaction until I suggested he was about to move to the private hospital down the road, which he had been involved in founding. Suddenly he sat bolt upright in bed, eyes wide, and looking at me said, 'I most certainly am not moving there! They'd charge me nearly a thousand pounds a day.' He then slumped back on his pillows.

Back in Westminster, after a One Nation dinner Francis Maude said to me, 'I don't know what's happened to you, Andrew; you left Parliament in 1997 a compliant, loyal young officer, anxious to please, and you've returned as a surly, rebellious cynic.' I certainly thought the party was in deep trouble and going nowhere. Gradually the Conservative tribe decided Iain had to go. The long, drawn-out process to achieve this was by writing letters to the chairman of the 1922 Committee.

As early as November 2002 I had been fingered as a plotter. Each November at half-term, we would go as a family on holiday somewhere hot. As we returned after that half-term, George Jones, the political editor of the *Daily Telegraph*, called to say they were running a front-page story claiming that I and two others had been plotting the previous week to get rid of Iain as leader. It was not true – indeed, as I'd been abroad for the previous ten days I was able to send a holiday photograph to Iain's chief of staff, Owen Paterson, showing me being attacked by my children as I lay on a beach, which at least showed the specific accusation was wrong.

Over the next month I took soundings in Sutton Coldfield amongst the most senior members of my local party. There was a good deal of sympathy for Iain and a residual loyalty, but there was also a recognition that we could not go on like this. Throughout

2003 the forces gathered and on 1 May, Crispin Blunt resigned, with considerable courage, from the shadow team, demanding a vote of no confidence.

By this time, I was indeed plotting along with others, but I decided I would not sign a secret letter to the chairman of the 1922 Committee, as this felt a bit sneaky. I would go to see Iain and tell him what I thought. At a meeting witnessed by Alistair Burt, his PPS, in the shadow Cabinet Room, I told Iain I would not be signing any letters or saying publicly that he should go, but I urged him to quit. I said that remaining as leader 'will bring you neither success nor happiness' and that he was in a cul-de-sac. Meanwhile, I'd been one of those trying to persuade David Davis to stand. He had been badly treated by Iain and sacked as chairman of the Conservative Party on the ludicrous grounds that he was 'idle'. Whatever David Davis's faults, idleness and lack of energy are not amongst them. Had he become our leader, he would have expected the whole parliamentary party to be doing press-ups at 6.30 each weekday morning. David had been reasonably loyal to Iain in spite of this ill treatment, but he could now see that the game was up.

As the conference season approached and after the breathing space of the long recess since July, the party assembled in Blackpool. During his speech, Iain Duncan Smith received twenty standing ovations from the shadow Cabinet, sitting very publicly on the stage and rising to their feet whenever cued from off-stage, each of them looking as if they had swallowed a lemon. At this point it was clear that Iain's leadership was doomed. Camps were forming around Ken Clarke, Michael Howard and David Davis, and some liaison was taking place. On the long drive back from

Blackpool to London, I was travelling with Anthony Coombs and spoke to three key journalists who were taking a close interest in what was going on. Having tipped off a colleague in each of the other campaign teams, I suggested to the journalists that they talk to the other camps to take the temperature within the parliamentary party. That weekend the tone of the Sunday press was different. The Conservative tribe had decided it was over. As the days went by, Iain lost the support of his Whips' Office and subsequently a confidence vote of Conservative MPs. He behaved with considerable dignity and a further leadership election was avoided through a bloodless takeover by Michael Howard. David Davis considered running at that point and would have done well. But after a series of calls to his friends and supporters over the weekend, he concluded that he should not do so. In a statement to the press outside Westminster Hall, surrounded by his friends and some of his supporters, he explained why he was not running and urged the party to unite behind Michael Howard.

Under Michael's leadership the party started to recover. He'd brought in different people, both on his staff and into his shadow Cabinet, making it smaller and sharper. He asked me to join the shadow Economics team, and subsequently to work with David Davis as shadow Home Secretary, in a team which also included Dominic Grieve and Damian Green. In running his team, David took a leaf out of Nick Ridley's book. One of Margaret Thatcher's leading supporters and Cabinet ministers, Nick had resigned after making injudicious comments about the Germans, describing monetary union as 'a German racket to take over the whole of Europe', adding for good measure, 'I'm not against giving up sovereignty in principle, but not to this lot. You might just as well give it to Adolf Hitler, frankly.' Unlike almost all other ministers, Nick Ridley would give his juniors the good news to announce from the Despatch Box at the House of Commons while keeping the bad – announcing it himself and taking the inevitable brickbats that followed. David's approach was similarly generous to his team. Campaigns were led with military precision and efficiency: he despatched two Labour Home Secretaries, David Blunkett and Charles Clarke, without any apparent rancour on their part – they understood it was just business. A third, John Reid, had resigned by the time DD could take aim, but David took out Labour's Minister of State, Beverley Hughes, as compensation. It rapidly became clear that David would make an extremely effective Home Secretary were we to be elected. Trusted by the party's right as one of their own, he was also a strong civil libertarian, viscerally opposed to unnecessary state power.

David had also had to manage a serious disagreement on identity cards with Michael Howard – and indeed with Tony Blair – believing that they would be ineffective and unworkable and mark a profound change in the relations between the state and the individual without any commensurate benefits. Dominic Grieve and I agreed. It remains the only time I can remember where I would have resigned from the front bench rather than vote with the whip. Dominic Grieve and I went to see Michael Howard to explain why we could not support identity cards and that with great reluctance we would resign from his team if he insisted we did so. After resolutely defending his view that identity cards were right, he told us both to go off and do our Christmas shopping when the vote was to take place. David, however, was obliged to defend his leader's view in the House of Commons and did so in a way which left little doubt about his true feelings.

Sometime later, when shadow Home Secretary in Cameron's team, David resigned and fought a by-election over civil liberties. He had previously managed to inflict one of the very few defeats on the Blair government over the preposterous proposal, as I saw it, for people being kept in custody without charge for ninety days. In a by now rare all-night sitting, the House was kept up, while camp beds were set up in a dormitory for their Lordships down the corridor.

I was in my office when the news of David's departure broke. An apoplectic Cameron was entertaining party donors at his home in Notting Hill and phoned me to see if I could dissuade my old friend from resigning. George Osborne called for the same purpose during an interval from a performance at the Royal Opera House. I completely agreed with both of them and raced to the Terrace, where David Davis was sitting with his chief of staff, Dominic Raab, planning his campaign. As I sprinted across the Terrace to reach them, he grinned at me, saying, 'You're too late. The train has already left.' He told me he had not discussed it with me as 'it would have presented you with a conflict of loyalty'. I assured him that had he done so I would have implored him not to do it. Cameron never trusted him again and thus was the UK deprived of a very fine Home Secretary. I have always believed that it does not really matter so much which political party holds this very senior position in government as long as the incumbent has decent instincts. Looking back, this is surely a reasonable yardstick.

In 2005, Tony Blair secured his third successive election victory, a feat never previously achieved by a Labour leader. His majority was reduced by sixty-six seats. In the circumstances, Michael Howard had done as well as any Conservative leader could have done. Under Michael, the party had been re-established as a fighting force. He led a tight team and reimposed discipline within the ranks, and his Eurosceptic credentials were clear. He had also committed the party to supporting the pledge to spend 0.7 per cent of our gross national income on development overseas. As soon as the election was over, Michael announced that he would be standing down but not until after the party conference that October. This was to ensure that the Conservative Party had a good long chance to consider who his successor should be.

At that point David Davis was the runaway favourite. Sceptical on Europe, he was anchored on the right of the party but with a social conscience, a firm view on the importance of civil liberties and an understanding of the need for the party to change. He patented 'modern Conservatism' as his slogan. He was, however, not inclined to trim for popularity; indeed, he was neuralgic about it, preferring to steamroller through what he thought was right. By the time the summer recess arrived, he had asked me to run his campaign and over 100 Conservative colleagues had pledged their support. As the end of term approached, we had a party to which more than seventy of them came. By now Iain Dale had joined the team as David's perceptive chief of staff, and much of the thinking on what a Davis-led party would try to achieve was being done in conjunction with the successful new think tank Reform, under the leadership of Nick Herbert and Andrew Haldenby. Derek Conway kept tabs on the numbers; Damian Green and David Willetts helped with policy and press. At that summer party, standing on a chair, I urged everyone to head off for a good break, returning for what would be a big fight in the autumn. To catcalls and dismissive jeers, I remember saying, 'Don't forget, the favourite never wins Tory leadership elections.'

A month later, on 1 September, George Osborne came to spend the weekend at Screveton together with Hugo Swire and their families. George and Hugo were early supporters of David Cameron, but we hoped to peel them off and lure them into David Davis's camp. Michael Howard had wanted both Osborne and Cameron to run, knowing them both well and admiring their talents. Michael's view was said to be that George would make a better leader, but George had decided that he would support his close friend David. Indeed, at that stage, George and Hugo probably constituted 50 per cent of David Cameron's supporters. During the course of an amusing and enjoyable weekend, Screveton received enquiring calls from Davis and faintly anxious ones from Cameron. Greg Barker, another early supporter of Cameron, described the weekend as 'George's night in Transylvania'. All good friends of mine, none of them really understood why I was supporting David Davis rather than Cameron, whom they thought was more 'my type'. I remember the now famous diarist and skilled shorthand-taker for her husband, Sasha Swire shouting at me in the early hours of Sunday morning, 'You can't support Davis: you're one of us!'

I had decided long before that DD had what it took to be a fine Prime Minister. Clever, principled and self-made, above all he was a brilliant example of social mobility and could inspire people struggling and pinned down by the system. Coming from a difficult start in life, being brought up on a south London council estate by a single mother, he was now an example that anyone could make their way to the top in Britain. Children in Lozells in Birmingham or Hackney in London could see that he was someone to whom they could relate. His example could inspire and motivate them. I'd seen from our time together in the Whips' Office, too, his resilience under pressure and his strategic judgement. His general toughness was underlined by his military activity in the Special Air Service Territorials – meaning, as one wag put it, that he knew how to kill people in twenty different ways, but only at weekends.

By the beginning of August, DD was knackered. It had been an extremely exhausting year and he wanted to spend the month recovering with his family. I urged him to prepare his conference speech. I suggested that he set out what he would do as Prime Minister for our country, how it would change under his leadership, and how he would build on the Thatcher – and indeed the Blair – legacy.

When we returned to London in September, he had not written his speech at all. He had succumbed to invitations from colleagues to visit their constituencies in what should have been a restful month. We were now within weeks of the conference, so I asked the brightest wordsmiths in the party – Paul Goodman, the first of the new intake to sign up to DD's team, Damian Green, Nick Herbert, David Willetts and Iain Dale, with some assistance from Robin Harris, Mrs Thatcher's speechwriter – if they would meet and draft DD's offer to the party and the country so he would have a core text to work on. All knew him well and understood what he wanted to do. I assumed, like a papal election, that smoke would issue from a chimney and a speech would appear. As we got closer to the conference, they met. They argued. They could not agree. A couple flounced off and the result was a text which, though workmanlike, did not really measure up to what was required. It was my mistake to believe that such an important speech could be drafted by committee. At the same time, everyone wanted to see him, and I inserted far too many meetings into his conference diary.

On 29 September 2005, first David Davis and then David Cameron launched their leadership campaigns. We played it safe, in a wood-panelled room off Parliament Square. Many of David's old colleagues from the Whips' Office days were there, allowing journalists to take the mickey about the type of rough trade supporting him. Across London, David Cameron launched his campaign with a cast of people not intimately connected with politics, which had a freshness about it. Serving smoothies to a generally younger, more optimistic group caught the imagination of the media present.

Both the Davids had a very similar message. Cameron, under the slogan 'Change to Win', argued for an update of traditional Tory values to meet the challenge of 2005. Davis, under his banner 'Modern Conservatism', talked about 'opportunity for the many, not the few', better public services and the value of 'decency and tolerance'. Although it was soon fashionable to argue that Cameron represented the future and Davis the past, their language about change was not dissimilar. Davis certainly knew that the party had to be far more welcoming of modern social attitudes, including gay rights, and that the parliamentary party needed to be much more diverse in its composition. Both men understood that the party would have to change and look more like the country we aspired to govern.

Before the two launches, most of Cameron's supporters would have fitted into the back of a London taxi. After his launch, he had caught the interest and imagination of the political press. He was the 'new new thing'.

As we travelled up to Blackpool by helicopter, though, flying up the spine of England, Davis was still clearly the man to beat. Ken Clarke and Liam Fox had joined the fray and Michael Howard was determined that all four candidates should get the chance to be seen and put through their paces under the full glare of the media scrutiny the conference would provide. It soon became clear that I had committed DD to do far too much as we rushed from meeting to meeting. On the Monday morning as we entered the Blackpool Winter Gardens, I was horrified to see two girls surrounded by cameramen with 'DD for Me' emblazoned on T-shirts stretched tightly across their ample chests, organised by one of the younger members of our team. Neither of us had known about this stunt and we had to spend the next few hours explaining it away. Meanwhile, David Cameron was spreading sunshine and novelty around the conference, supported by a young cohort of good-looking, bright-eyed enthusiasts. Elsewhere, Iain Dale had pulled together the speech following a final input from our speechwriting team and we set about rehearsing an exhausted DD. He worked his way through the text, making sensible changes, but he needed to learn it so that it flowed better, and time was very short.

Under considerable pressure as he mounted the stage to deliver what needed to be the performance of his life, DD did a perfectly reasonable job, stressing the personal background that he would bring to the role of leader and what he viewed as the core parts of modern Conservatism. By contrast, David Cameron had learned his text in full and, brimming with optimism, he looked and spoke like the future. The truth is that David Cameron's speech was a great one but not to the extent lauded in the press, while David Davis's was not as bad as the media made out. But the image of the new boy on the block, the underdog surging ahead while the front runner looked old-fashioned and a representative of the past, gathered momentum amongst conference delegates and with journalists.

I stood at the back of the hall for DD's speech, willing him on, and afterwards went straight to the press office. I asked Trevor Kavanagh, the experienced *Sun* newspaper political editor, what he thought. 'Your boy's had it' was his considered opinion. We struggled on for the remaining twenty-four hours of the conference as David Cameron continued to pull ahead at our expense. His communications and literature were much better than ours. The final straw came as we left Blackpool and I headed off by train to London: at the station, a team of young people sporting Cameron fleeces and T-shirts with 'Change to Win' on them were handing out well-presented pamphlets on behalf of their candidate. DD had arrived in Blackpool as the heir apparent. We left as yesterday's news.

Back in the House of Commons we struggled on, but the tide was going out on our chances. Fundamental to our early plans had been that Nick Herbert would run the campaign. With his experience at Business for Sterling and the Countryside Alliance, coupled with his founding of Reform, he was a shoo-in for this role. But Nick was selected for the constituency of Arundel and South Downs when Howard Flight was defenestrated, and he was unwilling to continue to lead the campaign. I and others were a poor substitute for the skills Nick not only possessed but had used with such good effect elsewhere.

As ever, Europe played a huge part in the calculations of colleagues. DD was undoubtedly the more Eurosceptic of the two candidates. We had to decide what to do about the Conservative Party's membership of the EPP – the European People's Party. I felt very strongly that we should remain as members. It gave us real influence in the European Parliament when it came to the chairmanship of committees and decisions on legislation, which we would not have as members of a smaller group outside the main centre-right caucus. Thinking at the time that we were going to win and needed to be realistic, DD faced down the pleas from the party's Eurosceptic hardcore of MPs to leave the EPP. Cameron, however, agreed that under his leadership we would leave and team up with more like-minded allies elsewhere. It was a decision that would come back to haunt him once he was in No. 10 but which helped move the dial during the early stages of his leadership election.

After Blackpool there were recriminations within our team and our numbers shrank as our parliamentary colleagues made their excuses and left. Relations between the two Davids remained pretty civilised, although they were as different as chalk and cheese. There was a row about drug use, as Cameron declined to say whether he had ever tried Class A substances, but DD and I had made it clear to all our supporters that we were simply not going there, and we deliberately did not stoke it. The fact that George Osborne and I are old friends and sorted out issues privately over a drink certainly helped keep the contest civilised. Indeed, as it became clear we were not likely to win, George approached me to check we would not be throwing in the towel; they had no workable plan for taking over the party at that stage and needed the time the contest provided to sort themselves out. George and I also teamed up to stop an absurdly high number of hustings across the country that the chairman of the 1922 Committee, the returning officer, wanted to hold. We would also tease each other with salacious gossip about which of our colleagues was being the most disingenuous about their support. One of these, we agreed, was strung out on the Berlin Wall, being tugged from both sides. 'We're sick of him,' said George. 'We're throwing him over to you!'

One Thursday night I was leaving the Cambridge Union, where I had been speaking, and heading back to Sutton Coldfield when a chortling Osborne came on the phone. 'Do you know what your candidate has just said on television when they were both asked what job each would give the other if elected? Your man responded, "A very good one. Definitely better than overseas aid"' – which was just as well, since I was already shadow Development Secretary.

It was true that while DD had thought about British develop-ment policy and supported the promise on 0.7 per cent, he was not as enthusiastic or fluent on the subject as Cameron.

The result of the contest was announced on 6 December at the Royal Academy on Piccadilly. Cameron had secured 134,446 votes to DD's 64,398. Cameron's ascent to the leadership had been me-teoric. Still only four years into his Commons career, he had been at best the dark horse in this leadership contest all through the summer.

David Cameron immediately set about appointing his shadow Cabinet, and I was fortunate to be included as he sought to unite the party. Ed Llewellyn became his chief of staff. I had met Ed when visiting Hong Kong and spending time with Chris Patten, the last British Governor. Ed had been his chief adviser. Sharon,

Ed and I had travelled together to Macau, where we got to know each other over garlic prawns and lager at a beachside restaurant. He was a straight up and down adviser in the best British tradition, utterly loyal to his master and nearly always wise. I once said to him that as his master's voice, 'if instructed to put a bullet in the back of my head you would do it, however reluctantly'. 'Only if you deserved it' was his reply. Kate Fall added feminine intuition to an almost entirely male team. Steve Hilton was there, a creative if erratic genius who understood both the need to widen the brand and the importance of politicians as servants of the electorate. The linchpin, though, was George Osborne; loyal, cunning certainly, and with a streak of ruthlessness. He understood the parliamentary party and could be wickedly funny about his colleagues. As a result, he had devoted supporters, who valued his tactical judgement and humour, as well as detractors. When issues needed to be resolved, I noticed that David Cameron would take note of the voices around him and reflect before making up his mind; George's voice was invariably the decisive one. I liked and respected almost all of his team and they let me get on with the task I'd been allotted – crafting a centre-right international development policy for the party and helping the team effort from my experience in government in the 1990s. There weren't many left who'd been through that period. My friend Patrick McLoughlin was one of them and became the Chief Whip. Wise and generous, he held this role in opposition and in government for more than seven years under Cameron. Overall, he was a whip for seventeen years and used to say, 'You get put away for less for murder.' There were some colleagues who thought I transferred my loyalty to the new regime with unseemly haste, but my whips' mentality and David Davis's clear desire to put his shoulder to the wheel made this a very natural position for me, and the new team made me welcome.

As Cameron's shadow administration came together, the Labour Party was indulging in serious in-fighting. I marvelled that they should so easily wish to despatch Tony Blair, a leader who for the first time in Labour history had delivered continuous electoral success and who appeared to have an unerring hotline to Middle England, where the minutiae of day-to-day politics was generally regarded as tedious and uninteresting. As time went by, it began to look as if Cameron, rather than Gordon Brown, was the legitimate heir to Blair.

Once Gordon arrived in No. 10, my Labour friends were despatched, first Charlie Falconer and then Geoff Hoon, with a ferocity which suggested familiarity with the *Godfather* trilogy. Some of the old Blairites were lucky not to wake up with a horse's head in their bed.

During this time, I also became one of Cameron's 'shadow City ministers', with responsibility for Birmingham. Though it was very different from my other political work, where I spent much of my time trying to keep Sutton Coldfield separate from Birmingham, I learned a huge amount about what makes Britain's second city tick. Cameron spent time there too, staying with a Muslim family in Balsall Heath, as part of his preparation for governing a diverse and modern Britain. As the only Conservative MP in the Birmingham local government area, I was the political outsider as I got to know more about the huge and valuable role of Birmingham University and the other higher education establishments in the city. I met almost all the faith community leaders who had been at the heart of the extraordinarily good community relations for which this wonderful city is known. I also developed an understanding of the huge economic challenges across a region which had suffered great industrial decline as well as very high youth unemployment but which was now rising up the league tables of success.

I admired the way Cameron repositioned the party and the strength of the partnership between him and George Osborne. In shadow Cabinet he let everyone have their say and he led a good and united team. We started making significant progress. The election that never was came and went, derailed by a combination of Brown's indecisiveness and Osborne's bold announcements on inheritance tax. On 3 October 2007, at a time when an election would have been difficult for us and the pressure on him must have been immense, I watched with great admiration as David Cameron came on stage and made what truly was the speech of his life at the Conservative conference.

'So, Mr Brown, what's it going to be? Why don't you go ahead and call that election? We will fight and Britain will win.'

CHAPTER 7

PREPARING FOR GOVERNMENT

Back in 2005 after we had lost the general election, I had been summoned to Conservative Party headquarters, then on Victoria Street, and invited to become a member of the shadow Cabinet. Michael told me that he wanted me to become his shadow International Development Secretary. I accepted with relish, but I also said I would be campaigning for David Davis to be our new leader – a potential candidate unlikely to attract Michael's support – and I hoped that he would not feel the two roles were incompatible. Michael confirmed that they were not and that he would not be departing for some months.

I had little experience of my new brief. Like most Members of Parliament, I had good relationships with the representatives of Oxfam and other NGOs in my constituency and I supported several of their campaigns, but it was not one of those issues I had contributed to in the House of Commons.

At this time international development was a thoroughly Labour fiefdom. Tony Blair as Prime Minister had championed its importance and the UK was increasingly seen as a world leader with genuine impact and sincerity in our desire to tackle the egregious depths of poverty which disfigure our world.

To make matters worse for the Tories, his Development Secretary, Hilary Benn, was both extremely good at his job and utterly charming to deal with. On one occasion during International Development Questions in the House of Commons when Hilary and I were opposite each other at the Despatch Box, I looked up at the gallery and saw Tony Benn and my father sitting together watching their sons sparring below. Apparently they both suggested there was some room for improvement in their sons' performance.

Once I had assembled my team, I used to tell them we would find it very difficult to score any political runs against Hilary but we would learn a great deal from him. It is an uncontroversial point to make that the Labour Secretaries of State for International Development, Clare Short, Valerie Amos, Hilary Benn and Douglas Alexander, and particularly Clare, were dedicated and effective ministers.

Throughout the international development sector, the Tories were viewed with deep suspicion. Twice before, our party had abolished separate departments of state set up by Labour and put them back into the Foreign Office. When Mrs Thatcher had asked Neil Marten to be Minister of State for Overseas Development (ODA) he told her he 'did not believe in it'. This seemed to have added to her desire to give him the job.

I started to put out feelers to key organisations. I was later told that at least one meeting was held to discuss whether they should even bother to engage with Tories on this subject. At this point in their discussions, someone suggested that it was a theoretical possibility that the Tories could one day win an election again and the

Blair hegemony might come to an end. So, they nervously decided to respond positively to my suggestions that we might meet.

Just as I was appointed, big rallies in support of Make Poverty History were taking place. I got on a plane to attend the one in Edinburgh and met some of the organisers and some of my Labour parliamentary colleagues. They reacted with jovial hoots of derision at seeing (a) a Tory MP in Scotland and (b) one attending an international development rally. Others quite literally came up to prod me to see if I was a Conservative Party hologram. I returned to London fascinated by what I'd learned and with a diary full of people to talk to.

Chris Patten called me to offer help, as did Lynda Chalker, and it was invaluable to have the advice of two former Tory ministers who had been much respected for their work on international development. Chris told me that even on a bad day, to be DfID Secretary was a very good job indeed, and on a good day he thought it might be the best job in the world.

In New York for a Lazard board meeting, I took time to meet my old friend Mark Malloch-Brown, then deputy to the UN Secretary General, Kofi Annan. As well as being the senior Brit at the United Nations, he was undoubtedly our most knowledgeable expert in this policy area. He invited me to lunch. 'I have good news and bad news, Andrew. I have managed to get us a table in the UN Dining Room. However, each week a different nationality has responsibility for the cuisine, and this week... it is the Koreans.'

I soon assembled a comprehensive list of the greatest experts with the most experience of international development around the world. I was determined to go and sit at their feet and learn how

Britain could 'do' international development better and build on the admittedly firm foundations constructed by the Blair government.

To do this I needed to raise money to travel, to commission research, to pay staff and to raise the profile internally within the Conservative Party.

Mark Florman, a senior City figure and Conservative supporter, asked to see me to talk about development and questioned me closely. He listened as I explained what I intended to do and agreed to help me raise the necessary funds. I assumed I would hear little more (usually the case, in my experience). But sure enough, a week or so later he asked me to come and speak to a group of party supporters and put my case to secure their financial help. As a result, we raised enough money to keep us afloat and fully develop our plans without constantly having to take time off to raise funds.

Lord Ashcroft invited me to tea in the House of Lords. He had been a staunch supporter of the Tories at a time when our prospects were bleak and had helped keep the party afloat because he believed strongly in Conservative principles and policies. He also hugely respected William Hague. Lord Ashcroft said he was a sceptic on aid generally but had heard we were developing a new and different approach. He offered the use of his plane from time to time to enable us to travel to places not easily reached commercially, thus beginning the first of around fifteen visits with his Lordship to far-flung places to see at first hand the effects of poverty, conflict and misery and to develop policies which could counter these ills. Throughout all my time in receipt of Lord Ashcroft's help and support, he never once asked me for anything in return.

And so it was, as my eighteen-year-old daughter succinctly put it when she spoke memorably at my 50th birthday dinner, that I 'set about exploring international poverty from the comfort of a private jet'.

As part of my role, I inherited Richard Parr, a young and brilliant researcher within Conservative Central Office hired by my predecessor, Alan Duncan, and we set about constructing a five-year work plan. Our aim was to develop a centre-right policy, authentically Conservative. I started reading voraciously and was soon surrounded in my office in the shadow Cabinet block with piles of books and papers. One evening I picked up Paul Collier's seminal work *The Bottom Billion* and, utterly absorbed, finished it in one sitting.

When David Cameron became leader of the Conservative Party, it was by no means certain that my services in his shadow Cabinet would still be required. I had after all been the principal cheerleader for his main opponent. But he asked me to come and see him, and opened with the words, 'Mitch, I want to promote you; would you like to do Work and Pensions?' – the department in which I had previously served as a junior minister. I explained I would not see that as a promotion and would be very happy to be left at International Development. I was also by now aware that David and I shared a very similar passion and belief in its importance and that he wanted it to become far more central in a Cameron-led Conservative Party. So I stayed put.

Our first overseas visit was to Uganda, courtesy of Air Ashcroft. I wanted to see for myself how progress was being made on the ground in the fight against HIV/AIDS.

My predecessor as the MP for Sutton Coldfield, Norman Fowler, deserves eternal praise for having stopped HIV reaching epidemic proportions in the UK. He achieved this in part through the hard-hitting 'tombstone' public information campaign. Mrs Thatcher was not keen, as she felt it was in bad taste to discuss publicly 'risky sex', but Norman found a way to go around her. At the critical moment, Norman, as Secretary of State for Health, had gathered the leading experts to a meeting in his department to discuss prevention. During the meeting, one of the officials asked if HIV could be contracted through oral sex. Norman allegedly asked, 'What is oral sex?' Whereupon the Chief Medical Officer turned to the department's Permanent Secretary and said, 'Are you going to tell him, or am I?' I have never summoned up the courage to ask my distinguished predecessor whether this story is totally accurate.

Once we had landed in Entebbe, we went to see President Museveni, who delivered a discourse on the virtues of Adam Smith. We then headed off to Masaka and the general hospital there run by nuns from the Medical Missionaries of Mary, an inspirational Catholic charity which continues to do extraordinary work in difficult and dangerous parts of Africa. Once we'd arrived at our lodgings, I opened a window and heard a knocking sound echoing across the valley outside. I asked the receptionist what it was. Vividly underlining the scourge of HIV, she said, 'That is the sound of Uganda's fastest-growing industry, the making of coffins.' As we drove around, we saw stalls displaying these wares out front, including very small ones for children. It provided graphic evidence of what was now happening as HIV spread.

Next morning, we arrived at the main hospital and met the sister who ran it. Aged eighty, she had been there for fifty years, and two years earlier had received the OBE from the Queen. Before we started our discussions, I had managed to secure the 8.10 a.m. slot on the *Today* programme – no doubt as a result of BBC curiosity over what a Tory politician was doing in Uganda looking at the fight to contain HIV/AIDS. We found an outhouse where my old mobile could get a signal. With literally thirty seconds to 'on air' and my interview with Jim Naughtie, a squealing piglet chased by a sister was cornered close to me and carted off. Five seconds later and the listening British public would have been led to believe that the Tory subject of the interview was in his death throes.

The sisters took us to see their outreach work. We visited people dying of HIV and gave out antiretrovirals. It was my first experience of real poverty. Some of the shacks we visited had only sleeping mats, a few pots and pans, and quite often a picture of the President. The sisters' main priority was to ensure that the men and women they were supporting took their medicines at the right time.

Taking my courage in both hands, I asked the eighty-year-old sister her policy on condom distribution and education – so essential to progress. 'Oh,' she said, 'we give them out all the time.'

'What does the priest say?'

'Oh, he completely understands.'

'What about the bishop?'

'He doesn't want to know. He turns a blind eye.'

'And the cardinal?' I enquired.

'Ah,' she said. 'I'm afraid he burns them publicly and preaches against contraception.'

She had seen the epidemic unfold in Uganda during her fifty years there. In the early '80s just down the road in Kasensero, a new fatal illness, 'slim disease', was being seen, affecting women and men alike. She said, 'I used to look out over all the men and women in the square on Tuesday, market day – I could see that vast swathes of them were sick. We just did not know then what it was. Today we do.'

Shortly after this we travelled to Mali to see the plight of the cotton growers there. One of the poorest countries on earth, its cotton could be its route out of poverty. We travelled from Bamako for four hours on mud tracks to the heart of the cotton-growing belt. There we met villagers and their families and representatives from the Cotton Cooperative. They could not sell their cotton for a living wage because of the protectionist policies of the USA, which spent more than $4 billion subsidising cotton growers in the Deep South. I remember vividly how these dirt-poor farmers knew so clearly how the protectionist policies of the rich world – the EU then included – were depriving them of the ability to build their homes and educate their children.

The irony, too, is that the country subsequently fell into the hands of terrorists and the US taxpayers were obliged to pay twice over: first to their own cotton growers and secondly to counter a terrorist threat in Mali which threatened America's own security and which their economic policies had, at the least, inadvertently promoted. And just consider what has happened since in this poor benighted country, where Britain currently deploys 300 soldiers but has virtually eradicated its soft power and development programme.

Having looked at the fight against HIV and seen also the impressive scale of American support under George W. Bush and the work of PEPFAR, the President's Emergency Plan for AIDS Relief – as well as the impact on the cotton growers of protectionist policies – we went to Darfur in Sudan to learn about a conflict which President Bush had described as a 'genocide'. General Bashir, the head of state, had become an international pariah for his role in the slaughter of his own people by Arab–Sudanese military and their proxies in the Janjaweed. The conflict had been exacerbated by climate change, eroding the land for pasture and crops as a result of advancing desertification and the consequent competition for land between those who planted crops and those who grazed their animals. Oxfam and other NGOs, engaged in humanitarian work there, took us to meet people affected and see for ourselves what was happening on the ground. I was outraged by what I saw and asked why the international community could not impose a no-fly zone to stop the Sudanese attack helicopters from killing innocent civilians. I later discovered that Tony Blair as Prime Minister was asking the same questions of his military advisers.

Cameron, with his strong interest in international development, asked me to report on my visit at the shadow Cabinet meeting in Manchester and decided he also should visit. We went back, looked after by Oxfam in Al Fashir, where the road dividing two parts of their compound was too dangerous to cross at night for fear of snipers. Amongst our guides was a young humanitarian, Jo Cox, engaged in working with dispossessed women. We visited two huge refugee camps and saw the extraordinary work done by Oxfam, providing water for thousands of refugees in the arid desert. I learned from Darfur two fundamental lessons about international development: first, that it is impossible to understand what international development is and why it matters so much without seeing poverty through the eyes of girls and women who suffer so terribly from it, and secondly, that conflict is international development in reverse. No progress is possible until violence and disorder have been stopped.

So, our next visit was to Rwanda to try to understand how a country recovered from the extremes of conflict and the terrible genocide which took place there in 1994, when nearly one million Rwandans were killed. I went with Charles Moore, the former editor of the *Daily Telegraph* and an old friend who had a specific interest in supporting a school twinning project. On arrival we visited the memorials to the victims of the genocide against the Tutsi people. We met the President, Paul Kagame, and other senior figures in the regime. It was little more than ten years since the genocide had taken place and feelings were raw.

Charles and I visited a church where members of the local Tutsi population had been assured of safe haven by the Catholic priest and had subsequently been murdered by the Interahamwe, the murderous gang of Hutu government thugs. The skulls and bones and the faded garments worn by the victims still lay in the pews and side rooms where they had perished, a silent reproach to international visitors whose countries had done nothing while genocide, murder and mayhem took place. The Rwandans had for the most part forgiven the UK, who along with the other members of the UN Permanent Five had sat by while Rwanda burned. This was because afterwards Clare Short had visited Rwanda as Development Secretary and had agreed that the UK would help the country rebuild. Tony Blair too had given Rwanda special attention and support at a time when the French government had continued to make life difficult for the government there in international fora. Britain had opened an Embassy in Kigali, the capital, and DfID had become a key partner and supporter of Rwanda's recovery.

Once the genocide was over and the Rwandan Army under Paul Kagame had liberated Kigali, the lust for vengeance by the remaining Tutsi population as they came out of hiding had to be contained. The departing regime's leaders fled to Paris, with French assistance, and key leaders of the genocide escaped over the border to Goma in the Democratic Republic of the Congo. Back in Kigali, everything had been destroyed. The incoming government had nothing, not even a typewriter. Depending on the Tutsi diaspora in the US and Canada for funds, they had to work out how to hold a shattered society together and reinstate the rule of law and governance. Kagame disciplined those of his soldiers who took matters into their own hands. One, whose entire family had been murdered, found the killers and shot them before turning his weapon on himself. He left a note saying he was sparing his colleagues the agony of putting him in front of a firing squad. Twenty-one ringleaders were caught by the Rwandan Patriotic Front. In order to stop wholesale retribution, the new government decided to execute them publicly in the Nyamirambo Regional Stadium for what were incontrovertibly crimes against humanity, reviewed on appeal and reaffirmed by the appellate court.

As the day approached, the international community called for the executions to be stopped. The Pope phoned the President. The British Foreign Office issued a statement that it was 'not conducive to progress and good order'. But the new regime in Kigali knew that if it did not act, it would not be able to contain the powerful forces manoeuvring for vengeance, determined to take the law into their own hands.

On the day of the executions, the national stadium was full. No cameras were allowed in. The genocide perpetrators were led in and shot. Thereafter the stadium emptied in silence. As a result of that day, the rule of law in Rwanda held and calls for vengeance were muted. Indeed, not long after, the Rwandan government abolished the death penalty. Many very serious crimes were tried through village communities by the gacaca courts, where criminals were judged by their peers and, after a period of detention, released back into their communities. Hundreds and thousands of individuals have been processed by this Rwandan version of a truth and reconciliation process. So successful were they that the many individuals implicated who had fled across the border into the DRC slowly began to return and go through the gacaca process. Major criminals faced the international tribunal in Arusha in Tanzania, but the process was cumbersome and ineffective in terms of the numbers who received justice there.

In an unusual turning of the tables, it is the British system of justice, not Rwanda's, that today stands accused of ineffectiveness and indifference. Five alleged perpetrators of the genocide wander free in the UK in receipt of British taxpayers' benefits and legal aid running into millions of pounds. Eleven years of British legal obfuscation and delay have still not brought them to any form of account. Today, even the French government, to their credit, has arrested alleged perpetrators.

On our last day, we visited the genocide memorial at Murambi. Perched on the top of a hill, it is the site of a school to which more than 50,000 Tutsis from the surrounding area fled once the genocide started. Once again, the Tutsis were promised safe haven by the local bishop and mayor. The gangs of Hutu militia laid siege and attacked but, using bricks and their fists, the terrified Tutsi families fought back. So, the militia leaders turned off the water supply and waited several days for the people who had taken refuge there to become weakened and their food to run out. Thereafter, in an orgy of violence lasting two days, the killers murdered nearly every one of them. One of the survivors – with a bullet hole in the side of his head – told me that story outside the gates of the school. The local authority had laid on a barbeque and alcohol on the approach to Murambi on the first day of killing to keep the militia motivated. One of the leaders of that local authority is amongst the five alleged genocide perpetrators currently enjoying life, free, in the UK.

Once the French intervened, sending in troops to help the Hutus escape, they set up their headquarters at Murambi and, using bulldozers, moved many of the dead into a mass grave adjacent to the school. The French troops concreted it over and played volleyball on top of it. I have been told this story several times by senior Rwandan officials. It is when they relay the story of the French volleyball games that they are reduced to uncomprehending silence.

As we left, I looked down the valley and amidst the magnificent scenery I heard the sound of church music rippling across the intervening distance. I have never been anywhere so beautiful and yet so cursed. Throughout the long journey back to Kigali, I cried for one of the few times in my adult life.

I returned to the UK deeply moved by this visit. The palpable grief of an entire country is hard to describe, but in Rwanda you could feel it on the streets. The extraordinary beauty of the place, with its rolling green valleys and hills, and the determination of its leadership to forge a new and optimistic life in the years ahead, is hard to describe but easy to admire and respect.

By now we were beginning to see the outline of a centre-right

British international development policy. I realised it was going to be a waste of time attacking Labour, who had made a huge contribution to the fight against international poverty and were respected around the world for it. But if we had a criticism, it was that Labour often saw the best answer to all problems as throwing money at them. Under Michael Howard's leadership, the Conservative Party had signed up to honour the pledge to spend 0.7 per cent of gross national income on international development. This was a significant and important amount of taxpayers' money. Even more importantly, all parties agreed it must be governed by the clear international spending rules which set out what is and is not eligible aid expenditure. To have any chance of persuading sceptical taxpayers that such spending was right and in the national interest, we would need a far more rigorous approach to accounting for it. We would need to be able to show that for every hard-earned pound we spent on development, we were delivering 100 pence of value on the ground.

A much better quality of dialogue with the development sector and the NGOs started to emerge. They would come to see me in my House of Commons office in the shadow Cabinet block and I would explain our commitment to the 0.7 per cent expenditure, our commitment to the international rules under which development money would be spent, and our commitment to keeping DfID as a separate department of state. They would glance enquiringly at the latest pile of books on development on my table. We started to engage with the Institute of Development Studies at Brighton University under the clever academic Lawrence Haddad, and the Overseas Development Institute in London under its experienced and knowledgeable leader, Simon Maxwell.

This dialogue developed as we set out our thinking: it was conflict that had to be tackled if progress was to be made. The most important ingredient for development to take place was peace – bolstered by accountable government. So, policymakers should address how to stop conflict starting; how to stop conflict once it had started; and how to reconcile people once the conflict was over – the reason I had first visited Rwanda.

The key area was the building of prosperity: people who are poor escape poverty most easily by being economically active. Whether in the rich or the poor world, having a job is the most effective ladder out of poverty and destitution.

We went to Bangladesh and spent two days with Professor Muhammad Yunus, credited with inventing microfinance during the war with Pakistan, when as a young academic he determined to do something about the dire living conditions he saw all around him. We saw at first hand the way the Grameen Bank, which Yunus had founded, operated – lending money mainly to women in rural communities, where they were jointly liable for the debt (key to ensuring timely repayment), to start and grow their businesses.

The professor took us to see how effective he could be in helping the poorest of the poor – beggars on the street – escape their circumstances. By advancing money to buy a couple of hens, we saw for ourselves and heard many times over how the poorest had sold eggs, earning themselves out of the deepest poverty, defined as living on less than $1 a day.

In Dakar, we also visited a slum divided in two by a railway line where UK Aid had recently installed clean water. Drilling down into the figures carefully tabulated in a local clinic, I learned the extraordinary impact that clean water makes on perinatal mortality, death and waterborne diseases, which particularly target and kill children.

At the other end of the scale, we Tories started attending the high-level jamboree at Davos. On the first such visit, I joined David Cameron and George Osborne. The Tories had been absent from Davos for many years during our period of opposition. 'What are you lot doing here?' my former pair and old friend Peter Mandelson hissed at me at one of the many parties laid on for those who attended. I went to Davos several times in the ensuing years, normally facilitated by Mark Malloch-Brown, and found it useful but ghastly. It appeared to be above all a massive orgy of the great and the good wandering around assuring each other how great and good they all were. It was presided over by a Swiss national who referred to himself as 'President' and showed every sign of believing himself to be on equal terms with heads of state around the world, whom he had, admittedly, managed to persuade to attend.

As we travelled and absorbed the evidence – only available by seeing circumstances on the ground and meeting the experts who gave so generously of their time – we started making inroads into Labour's development fiefdom. Charities concerned with tackling conflict started taking an interest in what we were saying. Our credibility built as the Conservatives made progress under David Cameron and there was recognition that a future Conservative government could not be ruled out. It was also clear that David Cameron was fully supportive of what we were doing, in both head and heart. I sent him a note every fortnight explaining what we were up to, which was normally returned with a large number of ticks and the occasional helpful comment or interested enquiry.

Bob Geldof, whom I met at a dinner at a Wilton Park seminar

on the first day I was appointed shadow Development Minister – and who greeted me with the words 'Ah, you're the fucker who used to run the fucking Child Support Agency' – took an interest, as did Richard Curtis, concerned to find out whether we had a genuine determination to build on Britain's international work in this area.

With generous financial support, our shadow DfID team could employ more people, travel and commission more research. We managed to persuade Philippa Buckley to join Richard Parr and they became my brilliant and engaging core team. Richard was superbly analytical, ineffably cautious and questioned everything; Philippa, clever, astute and always up for a fight in support of what we wanted to do. Jessica Lever, an extraordinary bundle of energy who was later poached by David Cameron for the No. 10 team, joined up for her gap year and stayed on the team while at university in London. Mark Lancaster, later a senior minister in the Ministry of Defence, joined as one of the shadow spokesmen, as did Sir Geoffrey Clifton-Brown, Mark Simmonds and, from the Lords, Baroness (Patricia) Rawlings – all committed to the new direction on which we had embarked.

We persuaded Gilbert Greenall, an old development hand, to let us use his country house and extensive facilities each year for a two-day meeting. We'd invite experts from the UN, IMF, World Bank, specialist think tanks, academics, senior soldiers and the charity sector to join us for strategic discussions as we deepened our understanding of complex development issues followed by an excellent dinner, thanks to Gil's generous hospitality, where we'd be joined by other experts.

The next question was how to persuade Conservatives to buy

in to this new enthusiasm, understand and prioritise international development as a party. We were greatly assisted by our realisation that many a Conservative association branch officer would also likely be connected with charities like Oxfam, Save the Children and Christian Aid. I developed close relations with Islamic Relief.

We needed a central focus to attract MPs and activists and give them direct knowledge and experience in international development on the ground. As a result, they would feel a passion for the cause and gain an understanding of its importance. Steve Hilton had led the party into a good deal of 'social action', changing the way the party worked and was perceived.

I went to see David Cameron when I returned from Rwanda and told him I had the bones of an idea which he might conclude was crazy but if not would require his active blessing as our party leader. The UK had invested time and money in helping Rwanda – a country which for good reason tugged at our heart strings – and where Britain had no strategic interest. Our involvement there as a country was rightly seen as unselfish. Britain's engagement was simply the right thing to do. I thought the party should start a significant social action project in Rwanda, a country small enough for our project to be noticed, safe and at a suitable stage of its growth for us to learn about development at the sharp end.

The project would have three aims. First, we would hope to make an admittedly small but useful contribution to Rwanda's development; second, we would give those Conservatives who went on the project a life-changing experience; and third, and most important, we'd ensure that within Conservative Party ranks there would be a group of people who had been to a poor and underdeveloped country, got under its skin and seen at first hand what works and doesn't work at the coalface of development. Looking across the developing world, most other countries were either too big, too unsafe or too advanced in development terms for our purposes. We narrowed the list down to Rwanda and Sierra Leone. David Cameron was enthusiastic and told me to get on with it.

As usual, the party was skint, so it was clear we would need to raise a considerable amount of money if costs for individuals were not to be prohibitive. We called for volunteers from throughout the Conservative Party who might be interested in this unique experience: 'Bring your skills and help build something in a poor country; learn about local people's lives and what they need in order to develop, by cooperating in the teaching of English, helping and partnering in the practice of medicine, teaming up with local businesspeople to amplify skills and entrepreneurial activity, working within the judicial system to help develop capacity or, finally, helping relaunch and refurbish a school.'

Forty-eight people signed up for two weeks in Rwanda in late July 2007, including seven MPs, and after an induction meeting to ensure our volunteers understood the history and trauma of that country, we were ready to go. I had asked the dapper Rwandan Ambassador in London, Claver Gatete, what we should call the project. I wanted a name to signify partnership and cooperation rather than anything patronising or neocolonial. He said, 'You should call your project "Project Umubano" – the Kinyarwanda word for friendship.' The organisational and logistical effort by my team, Jessica, Richard and Philippa, was immense.

That first year before we set off, I was extremely nervous, lying awake at night, going through my checklist and imagining all the possible disasters that might befall us. I had in my back pocket a note of what to do if anyone was hurt or, worse, died in a hot African country. I did not have to wait long for something to go wrong. On arrival at Heathrow Airport with my forty-seven volunteers, we learned that Kenyan Airways had summarily cancelled our flight. One way or another, we managed to get everyone to Kigali within twenty-four hours, the six doctors travelling first class by way of compensation.

Welcomed by Jeremy Macadie, the British Ambassador, we all stayed in Solace Ministries, a Christian mission near the Novotel which we made our headquarters. Amongst our number were teachers of English as a foreign language and doctors, nurses and clinicians who mainly worked up country in Kirambi and at Butare Medical School, a remote community hospital run by the Medical Missionaries of Mary. In the following years, word would go out through the churches that the British doctors were coming. Patients would often make a journey by foot, taking twenty-four hours to reach the clinic. Under the leadership of David Mundell, my shadow Cabinet colleague and later Secretary of State for Scotland, we worked with the Ministry of Justice, and Suella Fernandes (later MP and Attorney General) helped set up a law library in Nyanza, the site of Rwanda's law college – generously supplied by Allen & Overy, the City of London lawyers. We renovated a school; Tobias Ellwood MP turned out to be a very good carpenter. Mark Lancaster, in the finest military tradition, could more or less get hold of anything we needed within twenty-four hours.

I spent an absorbing week shadowing the Rwandan Minister of Finance on the grounds that if you aspire to be a development minister, you should learn what it is like to be on the other side of the table. I discovered he spent half his time running his country's finances and the other half meeting and greeting foreign delegations who, if properly treated, might agree to help financially. This taught me that it is far more sensible in a developing country to have one lead donor acting on behalf of all state donors to minimise the bureaucracy dealing with them. Rwanda by then had nearly 100 officials, nearly all graduates, running the Ministry of Finance and at a moving town hall meeting with them all, I promised that if I ever became the British Development Secretary, I would come back to meet them as one of my first visits. At that point Rwanda was raising only about 15 per cent of its annual budget; it was dependent on foreign donors for the rest. In 2019, the country's own revenue was 70 per cent of its national spending, a huge increase and precisely what international development is all about.

We met the President – indeed, we took part with him in umuganda, a national effort held on the last Saturday of every month for the whole country to come together and engage in public works. I found myself with a pickaxe breaking stones and laying the foundations for a road with the Minister of Defence on one side of me and the Minister for Local Government on the other. The President was genuinely surprised at the extraordinary interest and activity from a Western political party and he gave considerable time to the seven MPs in our group to explain his vision for his country's future. On another occasion I spent my umuganda building a wall for a new school along with the Presidents of Rwanda and Uganda, the latter on a state visit at the time.

And we played cricket, challenging the newly formed national team. We played on the ground made famous by the John Hurt film *Shooting Dogs* – the site from which the UN withdrew during the genocide, precipitating a further massacre. We renovated the 'stadium', repairing the bullet holes in the sides and painting it out in Rwanda's national colours. There on the final Saturday in impossibly poignant circumstances (with UN equipment and indeed spent cartridges still in the undergrowth behind us) we played cricket against the Rwandans. We recruited the head of the Blair-led global governance group in Kigali, giving him sanctuary in the Conservative cricket team. He and Francis Maude were the highest scorers and the match was a draw. Afterwards at a party organised by the British Embassy we drank Primus beer and ate goat kebab with the Rwandan cricketers and our new friends. Our football project, led by my colleague Alistair Burt, was swamped by the many hundreds of children who wanted to take part. It was a triumph for Alistair's superb organisational skills.

David Cameron was keen to come and see what we were doing. Alas, his constituency was flooded at the time and he was under attack from the right wing of our party. Worse still, the royal corps of British journalists arrived early to cover his visit and were intent on writing a story about rich Tories living it up in a poor country. There was an obsession with Cameron's sleeping arrangements and a determination to photograph the bed he would be sleeping in – in a room opposite mine on the first floor of the Christian mission.

We put all the journalists and photographers up in the Serena Hotel, one of Rwanda's finest and a considerable contrast to our own living arrangements, in a bid to stymie their efforts to paint a portrait of the Tories living it up in the poorest of countries. We did not, however, manage to prevent lurid stories appearing later about Tory volunteers boozing at the bar of the Serena, surrounded by 'ladies of the night'. In conversation with the head of Rwanda's intelligence service and a good friend of the UK, Emmanuel

Ndahiro, I enquired, more or less in jest, whether he couldn't just lock up all the British journalists for a couple of days to teach them a lesson. 'I'm afraid, Andrew, we don't do that sort of thing any more,' he said.

Once in the country, David Cameron saw the work that we were doing. Dinner at the mission enabled him to hear for himself from the different volunteers about the breadth of our activities and the relationships being forged. It was clear the project would endure, and the press would be unable to write it off as a Tory decontamination exercise.

Along with Steve Hilton, David and I spent the afternoon writing the speech he would deliver the following day in the Rwandan Parliament, the main public event of his visit. Choreography for the event was taken over by Liz Sugg, his brilliant events organiser, and I enjoyed watching her arranging Rwandan parliamentarians, security officials and journalists into their appropriate places. All was going well as David began his address – until a power cut hit and the lights went out. My political career passed before my eyes and reporters' pens reached for the headline 'The Lights Go Out on David Cameron'. It was what we always referred to on the Project Umubano team as a TIA moment – 'This Is Africa'. Inevitably tempers frayed and later in the day David had to intervene physically to stop a fight breaking out between me and Steve Hilton, who has a ferocious temper. In spite of being nearly a foot shorter than me, he was poised to spring into a violent attack.

We published David's speech – the Kigali Declaration – setting out the Conservative Party's offer on international development under Cameron's leadership, which was widely read by the development community. In the words of Chris Mullin, the Labour

Development Minister, this signified a profound change in Conservative thinking.

Following the first year of Project Umubano, I set about its expansion. We established a small sister venture in Sierra Leone, taking about twenty volunteers there, run by David Mundell and Philippa Buckley. But the main effort went into Rwanda.

That next year, 2008, 100 Conservative activists descended on Rwanda. I was determined that younger Tories, often giving up their annual holiday, should not be deprived of this opportunity by the cost, and raised thousands of pounds from generous donors to subsidise air fares. The Christian mission remained our headquarters and our doctors continued up country in the hospital at Kirambi led by Dr Bennett, otherwise known as Sharon Mitchell, Dr David Tibbutt, Mayor of Worcester, and Dr Andrew Hardie, a Sutton Coldfield councillor, together with his wife Monica, a senior nurse. Sheo Tibrewal, an eminent Conservative-supporting orthopaedic consultant, had also joined our team. I recruited Christopher Shale to help run the work we did with the private sector, as well as Jeremy Sillem, the City financier. Some small private investment took place, including in a Kigali taxi company, as a result of this partnership. Harriett Baldwin, Wendy Morton, Maggie Throup and Vicky Ford, all now in the House of Commons, helped direct this effort, including setting up a Rwandan 'Dragon's Den', while Suella Fernandes and Robert Jenrick (later a senior minister) led the justice project, working with local lawyers.

On the night we arrived in Kigali, the government there generously held a reception to welcome us back. A large troop of Rwandan dancers entertained us, and the Ambassador, Jeremy Macadie, informed me that we would both be required to dance. This would be a gender-neutral occasion. The male Rwandan Finance Minister advanced towards me. There was nothing for it but to join in. I'll never forget catching out of the corner of my eye the look of horror on my seventeen-year-old daughter Rosie's face at witnessing a very public display of dad dancing.

For our education project we had taken over a girls' boarding school in Kigali and 500 Rwandan teachers of English had assembled to attend our two-week course. Although we had all done the obligatory English as a foreign language work before leaving the UK, it was a daunting challenge. At 6.30 on the morning of the first day, Francis Maude and I were nervously swotting on the bonnet of a Land Rover. Eight of us took on the task, with approximately seventy students of English aged between nineteen and fifty in each class. Apart from Francis, the other six included Pauline Latham, later MP for Mid Derbyshire, who rapidly secured a reputation as a strict disciplinarian which ensured the rapt attention of her class. Rob Halfon, now MP for Harlow and later – and appropriately – chairman of the Education Select Committee proved a skilful teacher, using old Beatles songs, and I often heard 'Can't Buy Me Love' floating out across the playground. David Mundell's daughter Eve and Rosie Mitchell also taught throughout the two weeks, much to their fathers' delight and pride – no easy task for two teenage girls.

Further south, in Butare, the major education project there was run by Geoffrey Clifton-Brown and Justine Greening, while Desmond Swayne ran the education project in Eastern Province. At the end of the project, Dezzy had an open-air haircut back in the main Kigali marketplace – an event which drew an audience of several hundred admiring locals as the mzungu underwent a Rwandan short back and sides.

Thanks to the generosity of Lord Ashcroft, we procured the construction (by local builders) of a community centre in Kinyinya. Organised by Mark Lancaster and Tobias Ellwood, our team embellished the new building by planting trees and laying out a football pitch and an extensive playground for the local children. What began as a shell was completed in a fortnight and opened by the President on the Saturday before we went back to Britain. By then we were all exhausted, elated and deeply moved by what we had seen and learned about this impossibly beautiful, tragic but uplifting country.

That year, the President of Rwanda came to speak at the Conservative Party conference in Blackpool. It was an important moment and an eloquent testimony to how far the party had moved under David Cameron in this area of policy. Project Umubano had helped change views amongst Conservatives and boosted the party's development DNA. Many of those who had been part of it have written about the experience. It changed our lives – it certainly changed mine. It has meant that within our parliamentary ranks more Conservative MPs are alumni of Project Umubano than there are Members sitting on the SNP and Liberal benches combined. These are knowledgeable Conservatives who care about international development and who would stand up for it when the inexorable pressure on public expenditure makes that difficult. It is true, as we often hear, that 'charity begins at home'. We learned in Rwanda that it does not end there.

Project Umubano continued for ten years. Rwanda is a country not without controversy and from time to time eyebrows were raised inside No. 10 which necessitated my visiting, clutching the smelling salts, to stiffen their backbones. I was unable to run the project while I was Secretary of State at DfID, for obvious reasons, but I went as a volunteer and Umubano was ably led by Stephen Crabb, Maggie Throup and Wendy Morton. I ran it again for its 10th anniversary in 2017 – again with nearly 100 Tories involved – and decided that this should be our final year. Once again the Conservative Party's volunteers taught hundreds of Rwandan teachers of English, distributing over 500 copies of Chimamanda Ngozi Adichie's book *We Should All Be Feminists*, generously donated by her publisher, as an aid to teaching English and life lessons, with its inspiring message, 'I would like today to ask that we begin to dream about and plan for a different world. A fairer world.' Christopher Shale, my deputy, had tragically died at Glastonbury of heart disease in 2011. We all missed him so much. To honour his name, and led by his family, who raised the money to do so, the national Rwanda Cricket Stadium was built; the best-equipped and most beautiful cricket ground in Africa north of the Limpopo River. On the final night in Kigali, we were joined by the President of Rwanda and many of his senior ministers with whom we had worked over the previous ten years. As the African night descended and the lights twinkled across Kigali, we reflected happily on the cooperation and friendship between our party and Rwanda.

* * *

Following the second year of Project Umubano, Conservative fortunes in Britain were again looking up. We were able to take on more people in the Conservative international development team as we spread our message about what we would do as a government to boost international development if we were fortunate enough to be elected. To join my team, you had to have read Collier's *The Bottom Billion* and Martin Meredith's *The Fate of Africa: A History of the Continent Since Independence*, the best impartial analysis of Africa's recent history. *An Imperfect Offering*, written by James Orbinski from Médecins Sans Frontières, was an optional but important third choice.

We travelled to Cambodia and Laos, both of which were roaring out of poverty, to learn lessons from them, and into Burma shortly before the Saffron Revolution, when the monks demonstrated and the house arrest of Aung San Suu Kyi began to look less permanent. The Burmese regime let me have a visa by mistake and its Ambassador to the UK, a brigadier, was subsequently sacked. We visited a refugee camp on the Burmese border by coming out and re-entering illegally by boat from Thailand. The pitiful and terrified refugees living there made a very deep impression on me and on the cynical world-weary journalist, Nick Wood, who accompanied us.

On our return I gave a lecture at RUSI on conflict prevention and we published a pamphlet, 'UN peacekeeping and the failure to protect', trying to bring together some new thinking and developing R2P (the responsibility to protect) – a UN-agreed policy brilliantly negotiated through the UN Security Council by the former Australian Foreign Minister Gareth Evans. Today, the bones of that policy survive but there is little flesh on them.

We visited the Democratic Republic of the Congo together with War Child, whose staff hitched a lift with us on Air Ashcroft to see one of the most dysfunctional countries in the world – where, paradoxically, some of the poorest people live on top of the richest

The author and his bear – brutally dismembered in the dormitory of the prep school where he and Boris Johnson were educated.

The Cambridge University Conservative Association committee, 1976.

Cambridge, 1977.

HRH Princess Anne addresses the Cambridge Union during my term as president.

Training with the
Royal Armoured Corps
in Bovington, Dorset.

Defending the convoys of Turkish Cypriots moving from the Greek zone to the north of Cyprus.

Campaigning in Sunderland South with my father
in the 1983 general election.

Elected! The Member for Gedling.

Emerging from a visit
to Gedling Colliery.

The night John Major won the leadership of the Conservative Party.

ABOVE The government Whips' Office 1993 –
probably the most effective team of whips since 1917.

LEFT Hannah and Rosie with the Prime Minister
at the whips' Christmas party 1992.

My children regarded ministerial red boxes as 'the enemy'.

Whale watching in Canada off Vancouver Island.

LEFT The Mitchell family.

BELOW Making the case for a centre-right international development policy, watched by my boss.

Project Umubano: teaching
English in Rwanda.

Building a new school
during umuganda in Kigali,
with eighty Conservative
Party Project Umubano
volunteers, President Kagame
of Rwanda and President
Museveni of Uganda,
who was on a state visit.

Representing the UK at the
UN, with Hillary Clinton.

Molly, the much-loved Mitchell Welsh springer spaniel, wins Westminster Dog of the Year.

The Royal Sutton Coldfield community games: tug of war between the town's elected politicians and the youth. The youth won.

Now, who's the candidate again?! An election planning meeting with Ewan Mackey and Alex Hall, respectively my brilliant campaign manager and election agent.

In the Horn of Africa, guarded by the British-trained Somaliland police force.

Protected by the Ugandan military on a visit to Villa Somalia, the government administrative centre in Mogadishu, the war-torn and largely destroyed capital of Somalia.

My brilliant team of officials, advisers and ministers at the Department for International Development – and Alan Duncan!

Together with Jeremy Corbyn, David Davis and Andy Slaughter in Washington to secure the release of Shaker Aamer, the last British detainee held in Guantánamo Bay. While in DC, we met with Senator Dianne Feinstein (*centre*).

On St Helena at Plantation House meeting Jonathan, the oldest known living land animal, born in 1832 not long after Napoleon died on the island.

Visiting the remains of Al Kubra Hall in Sana'a, capital of Yemen, where coalition aircraft attacked a funeral service, slaughtering 155 mourners and wounding 525. A second attack eight minutes later was presumably intended to finish off the wounded and the aid workers and medical personnel caring for them.

ABOVE With Jo Cox, meeting the Russian ambassador to complain about Russian war crimes in Aleppo and breaches of international law across Syria.

LEFT The Mitchell family at home, 2021.

real estate, with its kaleidoscope of rich and rare minerals. We called on President Kabila, who had recently 'won' an election in contested circumstances, and stayed with Britain's superb Ambassador, who had shortly beforehand been the subject of a neighbourly complaint that there were 'too many naked women in his swimming pool' (raising the question: how many were too many?).

We flew to an area close to President Mobutu's abandoned summer palace, landing on his runway in the jungle built to accommodate Concorde so that the former President's wives could go shopping in Paris. Plundered and destroyed, the palace still boasted one of the magnificent four stone lions lying on its side outside the old entrance – too heavy for the marauding militias to cart off. Though now derelict, the palace was guarded by a couple of local policemen. It stood on top of a hill with magnificent views over the rainforests in all directions for as far as you could see. It was an extraordinary place, a monument to the corruption and wealth of the previous ruler.

We returned to Kinshasa and as we prepared to leave from the airport, a fire truck was put across the runway to stop our departure. This was clearly a bid for a bribe, and I set off back to the tower to try to negotiate, deliberately taking no money with me. A call to the President eventually got the fire truck removed, but it was a fitting exit from a country whose government is little more than an organised kleptocracy. Hopes of redemption for that benighted country rest with the former Governor of Katanga, Moïse Katumbi, an honest and effective leader and administrator, banned by Kabila from taking part in the 2018 presidential elections.

Not long after our visit, Gordon Brown became Prime Minister and it looked as if there would be an early election. We were visiting Tanzania to learn about its fight against corruption, and Madagascar to see evidence on the ground of a highly success-ful World Bank programme. As we flew back, Richard Parr and I crafted the contribution that international development would make to our election manifesto. We had just finished as we landed in Tunis for dinner with the African Development Bank's pres-ident, Donald Kaberuka, and his team – in exile in Tunisia from the bank's headquarters in Abidjan, where civil war was raging. Kaberuka, a former Rwandan Minister of Finance and the elect-ed president of the AfDB, had introduced a series of notable and impressive reforms and we were determined that the UK under a Conservative government would back him and help make the bank a genuine force for private sector reform and development.

As the election got closer, we needed to complete our plans. I asked my deputy in the shadow team, Mark Lancaster, if he would agree to go to St Helena. We wanted to try to help the Overseas Territories stand on their own feet and develop their economies, as they had remained a charge on the UK taxpayer. For many years an airport for St Helena had been considered as a way of opening up the island, replete with its history from Napoleon's exile and amongst the remotest places on earth. Getting to St Helena took a minimum of a week. The boat, which ploughed its way between Cape Town and the island, needed to be replaced; this looked like a more expensive option than an airport in the longer term. But an airport would be a considerable feat of engineering and ex-tremely expensive in the short term. Having crunched the numbers as far as one can in opposition, I thought that the airport could be the answer. And so the intrepid Mark set off, returning three weeks later having been to the remotest place on earth and met the Governor of St Helena, its wonderful people, and Jonathan, St Helena's 188-year-old giant tortoise, still regularly having sex every morning after breakfast. On one recent occasion, owing to his failing eyesight, he – Jonathan, not Mark – attempted to mount a male tortoise, causing a great deal of harrumphing and disputation. During his visit, Mark was taken to the pub by more than 100 Saints, as the islanders are known, and ended up sleeping on a park bench outside the Governor's mansion.

In the weeks that remained before the election, I rapidly visited a number of key countries about which we would need to make decisions. I visited Bolivia, the last country in South America to receive UK aid, making a terrifying flight up through the mountains from Cochabamba to La Paz in a small aircraft to one of the highest airports in the world. We concluded that the programme should be ended.

India had, since the Second World War, always been the biggest recipient of British aid. Under the coalition government, we wound it down and changed the nature of our support into purely technical assistance and equity investment.

My visit to Pakistan, the recipient of large amounts of UK taxpayers' money, was particularly thought-provoking. Under the Tories it would be Pakistan that became the largest recipient of UK aid, but our approach needed to be refined. This nuclear state, with its loathing of India and difficult relations with the US, was somewhere Britain could make a difference, through our close historical relations. We decided we should use our taxpayers' funding to promote education – particularly amongst girls – while also helping the government to raise more tax. This would be the most effective use of our expertise and money. Too few wealthy

Pakistanis were paying any tax at all, and it clearly would not be acceptable for the British public to continue to support Pakistan's development unless the rich in Pakistan played a full and proper part in the raising of revenue.

My penultimate trip was to Zimbabwe. Ministers could not go there due to the EU ban on visiting but there was no prohibition on opposition spokesmen, so long as they didn't meet Mugabe. Mugabe's demise was always said to be imminent and DfID had sent one of its most senior and experienced officials, Dave Fish, in the expectation that the logjam would shortly break and this beautiful, tragic country would lose its international pariah status. I spent time with David Coltart, the last senior white minister in the government, Morgan Tsvangirai and Tendai Biti, the brave Minister of Finance who habitually received bullets sent through the post along with menacing messages.

We determined that if the impasse in Zimbabwe should end, the United Kingdom would help rebuild the education system, which, despite everything, had just about survived. We would also assist the economic revival of the private sector. Zimbabwe had been the breadbasket of southern Africa, with one of the continent's best education systems, but such was the scale of economic misman-agement that it was now dependent on food aid. How much it had changed since I first visited in 1982, two years after independence, when Mugabe had been hailed as a unifier and conciliator.

Back in the UK, as the election approached, David Cameron in-vited Barbara Stocking, the development specialist who headed up Oxfam, to come and speak to the shadow Cabinet. I had worked hard to try to build some mutual respect between the NGOs and the Conservative Party; we'd started from a low base. The NGOs could be sanctimonious and unattractive in their lust for taxpayers' support, sometimes giving the impression that they were doing God's work and should not be fully held to account. I felt this was not acceptable with our new priorities of openness and transparency, but I developed a respect for them – clever, passionate people who believed in a cause and gave up their time and money to support it. They in turn came to see Cameron's Conservative Party as less hostile to their interests, and the crusty old Tory he'd entrusted with that brief as at least devoid of the horns and forked tail they tended to associate with Conservatives. It was a big deal for them to attend a Conservative shadow Cabinet and showed how much had changed on both sides. The meeting was a success and the NGO leadership accepted now that DfID, the 0.7 per cent, and the international development rules were manifesto commitments and secure.

David Cameron and I launched our Conservative agenda for international development, 'One World Conservatism', in late 2009 at the headquarters of Save the Children in Clerkenwell. We'd spent several months on this document, which set out our Conservative offering, focusing on value for money, wealth creation, conflict stabilisation and peacekeeping, and reforming DfID as a yet more powerful department of state, rather than a well-upholstered NGO moored off the coast of Whitehall.

The day of our launch was, by coincidence, also close to the day the Labour government was launching its own DfID White Paper. But all the interest from the media and the sector was on what we were saying in Clerkenwell. More than 200 NGO leaders, academics and journalists turned up. I was told that our document was prominently displayed on screens throughout DfID, where officials were reading it with close attention.

As the election got closer, Labour announced that they would enshrine the 0.7 per cent in law if re-elected. This was clearly meant as one of Gordon Brown's famous dividing lines – set as a trap for the Conservative Party. We had to decide what to do. At this point I was against enshrining the pledge in law, arguing that declaratory legislation demeaned Parliament because it suggested we could not be trusted, and pointing out that Tony Blair had introduced legislation in respect of child poverty, which, in spite of his law, had then risen. Both David and George, however, thought that this would be used to undermine us in the eyes of the electorate and decided to match Labour's pledge.

The final visit to round off our policy development was to Afghanistan. Charles Moore joined me for this visit, along with Mark Lancaster and Richard Parr. We spent time with the British Army and received briefings from those in charge of the Afghanistan strategy. It was a humbling experience to see how Britain was expending blood and treasure for our own security as well as in an effort to make Afghanistan a better place for its citizens. Unfortunately, it was far from clear that any real progress was being made on either count. We had a policy without a strategy, and in due course we determined to increase our development spending but start to draw down our military assets and involvement there. The British Ambassador, Sherard Cowper-Coles, assembled virtually the entire Afghan Cabinet around his dining table to tell us how they saw things. Following the dinner, Sherard and I retired to his fortified accommodation within the Embassy residence and consumed the best part of a bottle of brandy as he set out the barriers that stood in the way of our success. In spite of the brandy, it was a sobering experience. I saw the severe limitations of hard power and the realities of asymmetric warfare: it was extraordinary how a couple of fighters in flowing robes and flip-flops armed with Kalashnikovs could pin down a company of heavily armed NATO infantry. And as the Taliban said, we may have the watches, but they have the time. Development and soft power – educating girls, building health structures and offering hope and jobs – were more likely to act as a brake on Taliban progress than trying to embed liberal western values from the back of an armoured car. From my own time in the Armed Forces, I wondered what any politician would say to my mother about the value to Britain's international policy of such a sacrifice had I lost my life in Afghanistan.

The next morning, Sherard took me to see Hamid Karzai, the President of Afghanistan. It was clear they had an extraordinarily close relationship, with the British Ambassador literally waking the President up in the morning with a cup of tea. He had pretty much open access to one of the most heavily defended presidential palaces in the world.

* * *

Back in the UK, the 2010 election campaign was upon us. Together with my team, I visited eighty-four marginal constituencies, sleeping for only four nights out of a four-week campaign back in Sutton Coldfield. CCHQ billeted us in Premier Inns whose bedrooms were all configured in precisely the same way throughout the country, with exactly the same framed pictures on the wall. Frequently when I woke up I hadn't a clue where I was.

On election night, the good people of Sutton Coldfield returned me to Parliament with an increased majority, suggesting that the less they saw of me, the more supportive they became.

It was clear the next day that we had fallen short of a majority. Labour attempted to hang on, followed by five days of negotiations with the Liberal Democrats which were an agony of waiting. At one point it looked all but lost. I called William Hague, but he was optimistic: 'One more turn of the wheel should do it.' And so it was that the coalition was born.

David Cameron started to assemble his Cabinet. After a sleepless night, I had concluded that if the Lib Dems were to have five Cabinet positions, one of those must surely be DfID.

I sat in my office with a clear desk; all our preparatory work for government had been completed. Five years of work. We were ready to hit the ground running, but would I get the chance? I sat watching the television screen with Richard Parr and Philippa Buckley, my two key long-serving staff members. The first two Liberal Cabinet ministers were appointed: Nick Clegg as Deputy Prime Minister, followed by David Laws as Chief Secretary to the Treasury. Then number 3, Vince Cable, to Business. Danny Alexander, Secretary of State for Scotland, number 4. We sat in silence, sure that number 5 would be DfID.

Shortly after 2 p.m., Chris Huhne, the senior Liberal Democrat who had so nearly beaten Nick Clegg for the leadership, was appointed to Energy and Climate Change. The phone rang and Laurence Mann, the new Prime Minister's political secretary, laughing down the line, asked me to come over to No. 10 at 3.30 p.m.

It is hard to describe the feeling of elation as I walked over Whitehall and up Downing Street to No. 10. The journalists and photographers shouted across genially (or asked each other who I was). The door opened and I walked down to the Cabinet Room. Jeremy Heywood, the Downing Street Permanent Secretary, and David Cameron were seated at the table. 'Andrew, I want you to be my Development Secretary – you've done a great job in opposition and now I want you to do it for real.' I felt the blood pounding in my head as my eyes started to water. 'Thank you, Prime Minister; I think I may be going to blub. I will give it everything I've got and do my very best to fulfil your confidence in me.'

And with that I walked out of the famous door, waved at the photographers, gathered up my two key staff (shortly to become my special advisers) and set off to take possession of my department.

CHAPTER 8

INTERNATIONAL DEVELOPMENT

With other members of the new Cabinet, we trooped off to the palace to receive our seals of office from Her Majesty and to be sworn of the Privy Council. In an elaborate ceremony, kneeling before the Sovereign, I enthusiastically kissed her hand. 'You're supposed to air-brush it, not give it a great smacker,' William Hague whispered as I rose from my knees. As we bowed and departed, I mentioned to the Queen that my new department was over the road from her palace. 'Well, you'd better get back over there,' Her Majesty said. 'You've got a great deal to be getting on with.'

Before the election, I had arranged to see the DfID Permanent Secretary, Minouche Shafik, now a peer, a distinguished economist from the World Bank and development expert in her own right as well as a senior UK civil servant. She came to my office in the House of Commons and after some small talk I suggested that I speak for twenty minutes about what we proposed to do if elected while she listened. I then suggested she return in a fortnight to tell me what she and her senior colleagues thought about our plans. As

I set out what we wanted to do, an occasional cautionary eyebrow would rise almost imperceptibly, indicating areas of doubt.

When Minouche returned two weeks later, she brought with her a heavily annotated copy of 'One World Conservatism' with its 120 policy proposals, all of which we intended to pursue. The upshot of her twenty minutes was that the department could deliver on all of it if we were elected to power and thought it could improve on some areas to help us achieve our aims. I mentioned that I was nervous that some of her colleagues had only ever known a Labour government – one which had set up DfID and might be resistant to Conservatives taking it over. She reassured me about the professionalism and impartiality of the civil service and its officials.

Now, as the new Secretary of State, I set out to the staff our commitment to the 0.7 per cent spending, to the OECD Development Assistance Committee rules, and to DfID remaining as a separate department of state. I said the fight with the Foreign Office, which had characterised previous years, was now at an end as everyone could see the Prime Minister meant what he said. I added that we would work closely with William Hague at the Foreign Office: 'The Foreign Secretary is my close friend; you cannot get a cigarette paper between his views and mine. We must now prioritise being a good Whitehall citizen.' Simultaneously the new Foreign Secretary, William Hague, was making the same point to the Foreign Office staff in the town hall meeting that he held on his arrival.

I was introduced to my private office and to Melanie Robinson, who was to be my principal private secretary and a rising star in the department. Those first few days passed in a delirium of happiness and sense of purpose.

On the evening of our first day, with all the politicians exhausted from the campaign and the excitement of forming a new government, the new National Security Council held its first ever meeting, under the skilful guidance of Sir Peter Ricketts, newly appointed National Security Adviser. Grey-faced but exhilarated, I could see immediately that this would be an even more exciting forum than Cabinet. It was Cabinet plus plus. Setting it up had been an important manifesto commitment, and a key change to the Whitehall architecture. It brought together the Secretaries of State for Defence, Development, Foreign Affairs and Climate Change, as well as the Home Office, under the chairmanship of the Prime Minister, along with the chiefs of GCHQ, MI5 and MI6, the head of the Metropolitan Police and the Chief of the Defence Staff. This new council knitted together all of Britain's foreign and security components. Above all, it brought coherence and strategic direction to the key Whitehall international-facing departments of state and the other paraphernalia of government responsible for defence, diplomacy and development. It wired them all together. Crucially, development was properly treated, with a seat at the top table.

Over the first few days, I arranged to meet the thirty key officials in DfID and to set out our priorities as a new government. In the Secretary of State's office there was no large table around which we could meet: 'Your predecessor did not hold with large meetings with officials,' I was told. So I had one shipped in. At the first meeting, I explained our general approach, inviting comments as I spoke. None was forthcoming. A little later, as I was setting out our case, I was interrupted by one of my two key staff who had been with me throughout the long march through opposition and who were now my special advisers. 'Actually, you are wrong about that,

Secretary of State,' she said, and proceeded to explain why. 'Ah yes,' I responded, 'thank you, you are right,' and from that moment on the officials pitched in as we discussed the new direction we would like to take, and how they could best help advise and craft the right policies to achieve our objectives. I was clear that we were no longer going to hide behind No. 10's support but would go out ourselves and explain to the sceptical right-wing press the reasons why these policies were in Britain's national interest.

The PM had given me Alan Duncan as my Minister of State and Stephen O'Brien as the Parliamentary Under-Secretary. Stephen knew Africa well and working with Henry Bellingham, the Minister for Africa in the Foreign Office, made a great team driving forward an agenda to promote disease control, especially amongst those less well-known illnesses prevalent in the developing world. Alan Duncan, with his Union Jack and picture of Mrs Thatcher (definitely a first for DfID) behind his desk, was probably more suited to the Foreign Office – to which he subsequently moved – than to DfID, not least because his knowledge of the Middle East was markedly greater than that of anyone else in government. He was, however, a very good development minister. It might seem strange that three grey-haired, dark-suited, middle-aged men were in charge of an area of government policy where girls and women are front and centre in almost everything we do. But I was conscious that that juxtaposition can of itself make the advocacy more powerful, as it's coming from people so different from those they are seeking to help.

Those early days at DfID were exhilarating, frenetic and exhausting as we put in place the pillars of our new strategy. Changes in the private office to take account of this significant increase in workload, occasioned by a new government with a clear idea of changes mapped out over a full five years in opposition, led to a doubling in the number of private secretaries as well as an increase in logistical staff. Throughout my time as their Secretary of State, I travelled for approximately four days a fortnight and would arrive in the office before 8.30 a.m., clutching a hot chocolate from the café across the road. Every week on a Friday, when I left for Sutton Coldfield, I would take with me all the work and submissions left from the week. My proud boast was that there was never a Monday when I did not return with all the boxes completed and decisions made. I had arrived in possession of a 'BOLLOCKS' stamp and ink pad to be used if confronted by bureaucratic obfuscation when the civil servants were devising policy, but DfID civil servants were generally so clever and knowledgeable that they'd have been more likely to use it on me than the reverse. In the event, I turned the stamp over in my fingers on a number of occasions but never felt the need to use it.

Working on the papers over the weekend was a very different experience from my time as a junior minister at the Social Security Department. Then I often had to read the tightly written policy papers twice over to understand them and I worried about the time away from my children that this required. Now, late at night I would devour the paperwork with relish, sometimes glancing up to find it was 3 a.m. I remembered what Chris Patten had told me about this job. I realised that every morning when I got up and arrived at the department, the decisions I made that day could affect the lives of hundreds of thousands of children living in poverty and misery in the poorest parts of the world. My responsibility was to put into action the best of Britain's desires to help the least well off and make the world a better place; to uphold the noble instincts that had led Britain to promise to dedicate 0.7 per cent of its gross national income to helping others become safer and more prosperous; and above all to ensure that the taxpayers' generosity was not taken for granted but delivered 100 pence of results on the ground for every hard-earned pound spent.

Our most important task now was to review all this. We set up the Bilateral Aid Review (BAR) and the Multilateral Aid Review (MAR) to look at all areas of spending and identify waste and less effective expenditure. We asked why it would cost more in one poor country to educate girls than in another, and whether we could justify this discrepancy to Parliament and the taxpayer. We ruthlessly subjected all our decisions to academic and peer review. We decided that all DfID's spending above £500 should be put into the public domain. We championed transparency in every way we could. Paddy Ashdown generously agreed to chair a review of how Britain carried out emergency humanitarian aid, bringing in more private sector skill and participation. This is the most visible aspect of what British aid does as far as the public is concerned and is strongly supported.

We set up the Independent Commission on Aid Impact (ICAI), designed to be the taxpayers' friend and ally. This new body reported not to ministers and the government – which might be able to sweep inconvenient truths under the carpet – but to Parliament and the International Development Select Committee. Its independence was underlined by the fact that the Chief Commissioner of the ICAI could not serve for a second term and would not therefore be susceptible to influence from those who appointed him. We recruited Graham Ward, then president of the Institute of Chartered Accountants in England and Wales, to be the first Chief Commissioner, along with John Githongo, the Kenyan anti-corruption czar. There was some unhappiness amongst the development sector at such a task being given to a 'bean counter' rather than someone steeped in development, but I explained that the development sector cheerfully accepted the praise when British leadership ensured that things went well; we must also immediately put up our hands when things went wrong and sort them out. The answer to the slings and arrows of the *Daily Mail* complaining about Britain's development spending was not to shut up shop but to offer total transparency and explain and justify what we did.

It was for the International Development Select Committee to decide what the ICAI should investigate, but the Secretary of State could make suggestions. I asked that in one of their first reports they look into corruption, the cancer in development, and advise us on whether DfID was doing all it could to protect our funds from abuse. When the report on corruption came in, the department breathed a sigh of relief as our systems and defences were found to be pretty successful. But there were some areas needing improvement. The senior official who came to see me to discuss the ICAI report said, 'Don't worry; we'll do some of what they are suggesting, but we won't need to do it all.'

'I'm afraid you've got the wrong end of the stick,' I said. 'We're going to do everything they have recommended and what's more, we will ask them back in six months' time to kitemark what we have done.'

I was determined to change the press and communications department, which I thought was unproductive and tended to go into hiding whenever a controversy hove into view. This was partly because they had always received such strong cover from Downing Street that they didn't feel they needed to defend themselves. Instead, they had got into the habit of taking press attacks on the chin and hoping they would go away. I was determined we would no longer hide under the table on such occasions but confront inaccuracies and expose them; otherwise our chances of persuading taxpayers that this spending was worthwhile and in their interests would be non-existent. To manage this more muscular environment, we secured the services of James Helm, whose forthright style reshaped a department with too many press officers and not enough oomph. Instead of announcing spending in cash terms, we began to detail what the money was actually buying. Rather than boasting, 'We are spending £20 million on relieving this disaster,' we were saying, 'Britain is providing 5,000 tents, 100,000 water purification tablets, and medicines that will vaccinate 10,000 people including 8,000 children.' I thought that Britain should be more assertive and prouder of our work in this area. So we arranged that – outside of conflict zones, where badging UK aid could put brave humanitarian workers in harm's way – a Union Jack would feature on all British aid along with the words 'aid from the British people'. I was determined to do this following a visit to a project emblazoned with the German and EU flags but where 80 per cent of the funding had come from the UK. James managed to get our logo redesigned by a Foreign Office designer in return for a bottle of Chardonnay – and it's still in extensive use ten years later.

Back in DfID, the work on the BAR and the MAR, which involved the whole department in a significant effort, was proceeding apace. We had inherited programmes in forty-three countries, which we now reduced to twenty-seven. On my first morning as Secretary of State, I froze all aid to China and made clear that unless legally due, all cheques should be cancelled. India was more complex. Home to 40 per cent of the world's malnourished children, India had been the largest recipient of British aid every year since the Second World War until 2011. Britain also has a close historical relationship with that country but a complicated one where British ministers who misspoke or got their tone wrong were habitually publicly eviscerated. So we made clear we were walking the last mile in our development partnership with India, a country which was powering out of poverty, and we changed its nature to providing technical assistance and investing in companies and pro-poor sectors which helped boost prosperity while also giving Britain a return on our investment.

For each country in the bilateral programme, we considered two key factors. Were we securing value for money for the British public? And were our historical links – through the Commonwealth, for example – and continuing interests such that Britain should be providing development support? In the past, increases or decreases in expenditure for specific programmes had usually been made according to changes in the overall budget. We tore that whole process up by its roots, deciding first on the justification for the programme's existence, and second what we were getting for our money and whether it could be spent better or more effectively elsewhere. Basically, we created an internal market for the British taxpayer to buy results.

When we came to informing countries about how we hoped to partner with them and in particular what we could afford, I made a point of calling the President or Prime Minister to explain our thinking. This usually worked well as a way of identifying and agreeing our mutual responsibilities to each other.

In the case of Tanzania, a meeting in Davos had been arranged with President Kikwete, but when we turned up, he was too busy to see us at the appointed hour. A subsequent meeting agreed by officials also failed to materialise. I rather felt that British funding was being taken for granted and told officials that the President would need to see us at the African Union meeting in Addis Ababa before any details – or money – for the programme could be released. To the horror of DfID officials, I said they should inform the President that we'd be grateful if this time he would come to the British Ambassador's residence in Addis for the meeting. We offered 6 p.m. The Ambassador and officials were sure he would not turn up, but at 5.55, with flashing blue lights at either end of his convoy, the President arrived, and we went through our partnership arrangements for the next three years.

The officials were amazed at my effrontery in summoning the President and astonished that he came. I took a very different view: that British support was not to be taken for granted and that as the representative of the British government and servant of the tax-payer, it was my duty subtly to make this point.

For the Multilateral Aid Review, it was soon clear that a highly political process had been unleashed. Many of the forty-three international agencies had never been assessed in this way before. We told them all that we were looking for value for money and whether they were pursuing policies that matched British interests. Several simply did not believe that we were serious.

We divided all the different agencies into three groups: first, there were those who scored highly on both criteria, providing very good value for money and proving extremely effective in pursuing policies relevant to Britain's interests – UNICEF, for example, whose core grant we doubled because we thought its work on behalf of children around the globe was outstanding. The second group were those whom we thought essential to Britain's interests but who were not providing particularly good value – such as the Commonwealth Secretariat. On this second group we imposed special measures, and some had their grants reduced. On the third and final group, those who neither provided value for money nor pursued policies relevant to British interests, we axed spending altogether, a grouping that amounted to 10 per cent of the multilateral agencies Britain had previously funded. I did not, however, cut off support for UNESCO, as previous Conservative governments had done, though it was a close-run thing. After an extremely difficult meeting with the agency in Paris, we expressed the view that some of their expenditure was simply ridiculous. But in the end, we remained so we could support important world heritage work. Last year, however, UNESCO came in for heavy criticism after announcing an international prize in the name of Equatorial Guinea's brutal dictator, Teodoro Obiang Nguema, who is rumoured to be a cannibal with a penchant for skinning enemies alive and eating their organs. The award was shelved after an international outcry.

Once we had completed the MAR, the United States, Canada and Australia all sent their officials to DfID to see how we'd done it. Subsequently, they all introduced similar processes into their own development calculations.

Achieving fair burden-sharing in our support for UN agencies was always an issue. I was nervous that Britain could be taken as 'funder of last resort'. This was important as the UK led by example, putting our money where our mouth was. But it was not always easy to get others to step up to the plate. I spent huge amounts of time trying to persuade other countries to share the funding burden appropriately with us; the Gulf countries, certainly, but also other countries in the EU.

At one UN meeting, Bob Geldof showed up and was extremely helpful to the UK. He had achieved international iconic status as a result of Live Aid, when he pricked the world's conscience and with his unique style tackled the horrendous famine in Ethiopia. His reputation was underlined when we entered a meeting together which was also attended by the German Chancellor, Angela Merkel. Surrounded by fawning flunkies, she spotted Geldof across the room and immediately rushed across, put her arms around his neck and kissed him. He had also become my friend and supporter.

At a UN meeting where we were seeking funding support from others, the senior Italian delegate was droning on about the importance of support when Geldof intervened: 'Come on, Fabio, never mind all this bollocks – how much is Italy going to give?' The Italian looked embarrassed and shuffled his papers. 'The answer is jack shit, isn't it?' said Geldof, exasperated. More paper shuffling. 'Here, Fabio, why don't you fuck off back to Italy and tell them to put up or fuck off?' And with that the hapless Italian shuffled out of the meeting. After that the countries seemed more willing to provide extra funds for the worthwhile cause.

I found determining our new priorities traumatic. I knew we would be ending some programmes upon which people depended. While officials could advise on the relative value for money, it was my task to decide what we should do and, critically, what we should not do. For example, in Sierra Leone, a country with deep historical links to us and where Britain had been heavily involved recently, should we promote clean water (I'd seen the children playing in the slums and drinking polluted water, as well as seeing with my own eyes the vulnerable pipe providing water into Freetown from the reservoir, leaking copiously)? Or the education of girls (I'd seen the new school that Britain had supported with the children in their uniforms, thirsting for knowledge and sitting in rapt attention to the teachers' words)? Or vaccinating the children whose lives would be saved as a result of support from Britain (statistically, many thousands of them)? I felt the weight and responsibility of these decisions.

When I'd received the professional advice from our officials on the basis of the criteria we had set, I discussed the conclusions with Alan and Stephen. I spoke to Cameron and Osborne and also to Sharon. I then shut myself away one Sunday evening and made the necessary choices, with tears pouring down my face at having to make the inevitable trade-offs.

Once we decided on our priorities – where we would focus Britain's development efforts and money and to what extent – we cleared our decisions with William Hague at the Foreign Office and started to look at the mechanisms involved.

Previously we had allocated very substantial sums to the World Bank in Washington DC – a key engine for development around the world but one where, extraordinarily, Britain was providing even more funding than the USA. I thought this was disproportionate but decided we should still give exceptional support, pegged at a level $25 million less than whatever figure the USA provided.

I was determined, as the British governor of the Bank and in view of our colossal investment in it, to take a more active role in deciding the Bank's direction. We did this in part through single-issue trust funds – highly targeted expenditure – designed to tackle key problems we'd identified in difficult places.

Early on in the new government's life, it was decided that departments would have non-executive directors. John Browne, the former head of BP, was lined up to mastermind the process and came to see me with a list of the great and the good whom he thought could help. Nearly all of them seemed to be his friends, but that is the nature of the great and the good. We managed to persuade the very experienced Vivienne Cox to chair the board, but I did not feel the department had need of the three others he suggested. What I wanted was an advisory board of the best professionals in Britain to fill three areas of expertise which I felt were lacking. And so we managed to persuade Mark Malloch-Brown, with his huge UN and international knowledge and connections; Alan Parker, Britain's leading communications and PR expert; and Jeremy Sillem, the senior City figure who was to be helpful in the reform of CDC, to sign on – with help also from Sir Paul Collier, the patron saint of centre-right development policy.

After a year or two, Minouche Shafik, my Permanent Secretary, said she had decided to take a new job as the No. 2 at the IMF. Her departure was a blow as we got on well and I very much valued her advice and institutional memory. But I also understood the umbilical link between DfID and the international multilateral system, and I thought both sides gained from her move. To replace her, a civil service selection process was duly convened, but in my mind there was never much doubt as to who it should be. I thought the department, faced with a restless, reforming Secretary of State who thought he knew it all, needed a reassuring figure at the helm, someone with strong civil service experience, steeped in the workings of government and respected in the development world, who really did know it all. Mark Lowcock, the long-serving and experienced DfID senior official, was duly appointed.

At about the same time, I persuaded the PM that Valerie Amos, the former Labour minister, should be Britain's most senior official at the UN, running OCHA, the agency coordinating global responses to emergency crises.

'Why can't we send David Davis there?' Cameron enquired one day.

'You cannot send your political enemies to do that sort of job in the international system,' I said.

'Huh,' said Cameron. 'What about the governorship of St Helena – that's coming up soon?'

'It's not far enough away, Prime Minister?' I suggested.

*   *   *

Every year in most departments, the Secretary of State will receive a list of proposed honours. It is right that civil servants, many of whom would be paid far more if they worked in the private sector, should receive these. Such awards cost nothing to the public purse, bring great happiness and are highly valued. Normally the list appears at the bottom of a weekend box in the hope that a tired minister will mark it with a tick and wave it through.

I remembered my father saying that when he was a Northern Ireland minister in the 1980s, he had sent back the list, suggesting that officials add the man he had met who had walked the railway line near Newry looking for improvised explosive devices. When

I saw the list, I thought it had great merit but included too many unexceptional names as well. So I sent it back with some names removed and a number of questions. The list went backwards and forwards between my office and the Permanent Secretary's with names added and deleted until the time came for Sir Humphrey to negotiate. I wanted two of the sisters from the Medical Missionaries of Mary, who had worked tirelessly in Africa for decades, to be considered, but they'd not made the original list. Sister Helen and Sister Bridget had served the cause of development in Africa with distinction, bringing credit to Britain, and I thought they richly merited an award. And so, a deal was done: two of his for two of mine, and I let the list proceed. In due course, both nuns were awarded the OBE, which they received in person from the Queen at Buckingham Palace.

One of the criticisms we were determined to address was that DfID did not do enough for small charities. Too many were ineligible for taxpayer support – literally because they were too small. DfID was not configured to disperse minor amounts of funding which then had to be monitored. I remember an official at DfID in an unguarded moment saying, 'We don't do goat charities.' Equally unguardedly, I suggested that this might be just about to change. I'd got to know Send a Cow, a wonderful British NGO which operated on classic Conservative principles: give a family a cow; its milk would nourish their children and the surplus could be sold, giving the family an income. When the cow subsequently gave birth, the family could repay the charity by giving the calf to another family and so the virtuous circle was complete. We were clear that British people would want us to support smaller charities in their work; individuals are the main backers of small NGOs.

But structuring this support was difficult. By their nature such grants, though small, must be properly policed to prevent fraud. To achieve this safeguarding would require many more hours of work by officials. So we set up the Poverty Impact Fund, open to small charities to help them increase the effect they were having by doubling their money proportionately. I saw this as a good deal, effectively a buy one, get one free. It continued our focus on results, but by this mechanism the public could see for themselves that they were buying specific results on the ground.

It was not an easy scheme to devise. I wanted Members of Parliament across the House to be able to have direct influence too, on behalf of the good international charities in their constituencies. My two special advisers, Richard and Philippa, did much of the consultation. Their considerable advantage was that the civil servants both liked and trusted them. They had been with me developing our approach for so long that they could literally complete my sentences, so they were invaluable to civil servants trying to craft policy and detailed change. They were also both humble in their style and approach to their work and did not seek to usurp the classic role of civil servants – or ministers; rather different from one of their predecessors, who was found one Friday, to the astonishment of officials, sitting in the Secretary of State's office while his boss was away, with his feet on the desk, announcing that he was in charge.

At the other end of the scale to the Poverty Impact Fund was the reform of CDC, formerly the Commonwealth Development Corporation, the development investor 100 per cent owned by the British taxpayer. Started after the Second World War, CDC had attracted classic civil service types, experts in putting together agricultural projects in developing countries – rubber plantations in Malaysia, for instance. These were their stock in trade. But over the years CDC had deteriorated, sometimes making a loss on its activities – the worst possible example for the private enterprise culture it was supposed to promote. The Blair government had considered privatisation, which fortunately Clare Short had dissuaded the Prime Minister from pursuing, and CDC had been left as a 'fund of funds' – little different from its classic City commercial equivalent. Separated from its development DNA, with senior staff deciding they were no longer development civil servants but now City slickers, they thought they needed to be paid twenty times what they had been earning before. The former CDC-owned subsidiary ACTIS had pulled the wool over the then Labour government's eyes and arranged for themselves an ownership structure which I thought legged over the British taxpayer.

We had spent much time in opposition working out what needed to be done to reform CDC. I had met the head of ACTIS at Davos who explained, as he had previously to Labour ministers who had agreed to sell 50 per cent to management, that ACTIS wasn't really worth anything to the taxpayer so we might as well flog the rest of the ownership to him for nothing. I had told him we would be willing to sell if we were in government but would need to ensure the British taxpayers received their fair pound of flesh.

Further enquiries back in the UK suggested that DfID had more or less washed its hands of CDC. Its senior official had been given a hard time when he appeared before the Public Accounts Committee to discuss the subject and at the least the department regarded it as something of a hot potato.

The back pages of *Private Eye* were continuously commenting negatively on CDC, and the more I learned, the more I thought they'd got a very good point. I approached Jeremy Sillem, a senior and experienced figure and old friend from Lazard days, to ask if he would help me work out how to restructure it to restore its development DNA. I wanted to be able to create over time the leading development finance institution in the world. My vision was that it would deploy 'pioneer' capital and 'patient' capital – leading the private sector to parts of the developing world where the benefits of capitalism and free enterprise had not yet taken root ('pioneer') but also able to take a much longer-term view about investment, requiring less than a commercial return on its investments for a longer period than the commercial market could provide ('patient').

The final evidence that we needed for this radical reform had appeared on a visit to Sierra Leone. We had arrived in the country and taken a terrifying flight in a Russian helicopter flown by Ukrainian pilots between the airport and Freetown, its capital. An empty vodka bottle was clearly visible in the cockpit. The week before, the pilots had ascended to fifty feet when jets of flame came shooting out of the engine. The helicopter had dropped to the ground with a thump and the pilot shouted to the passengers, 'Stay put! We try again!', causing panic and a mass exodus.

Having arrived safely, we had breakfast with the British High Commissioner, who introduced us to Tom Cairnes, a remarkable young entrepreneur running a fund called Manocap. He told us how he had set up the fund to invest in local enterprises as part of the rebuilding of Sierra Leone. Much of the country had been destroyed in the violence and mayhem caused by the West Side Boys which preceded Tony Blair's most successful and brilliantly executed (thanks to General David Richards) foreign intervention. As a result of this, thousands of lives were saved, and a nation put back on its feet. Indeed, children born in subsequent years were frequently called Richard or Tony.

Tom Cairnes was trying to do his bit to help, but his investments were not without significant difficulties. My first question over a plate of the High Commission's delicious local produce – mango followed by avocado and tomato – was what help had this British entrepreneur received from CDC? The answer was nothing. He had financed his business by raising money through friends and family. CDC was only willing to engage once the first fund had been completed. They were clearly not providing pioneer or patient capital.

Following that visit, we had developed in earnest our plans for reforming CDC in government. We now had the chance to put them into effect. Within CDC, however, there was strong resistance to the changes we wished to make. I decided to use a speech at the London School of Economics to set out what was going to happen. The speech made clear my view that the CDC had lost its way and that much of the comment on the back pages of *Private Eye* was justified. CDC's most senior management was affronted by the draft, which I sent them as a matter of courtesy, and spent the day on which the speech was to be made trying to use officials, unsuccessfully, to persuade me to draw the teeth of what I intended to say.

Jeremy Sillem played a pivotal role in massaging through the changes, first by giving free advice and interest and later by joining the board at my request. We brought in an advisory house, Hawkpoint, to implement the reforms Jeremy and I had crafted.

We wanted CDC to be able to use a whole range of financial instruments (other than investing in someone else's fund) to enable it to drive forward the development agenda through the use of direct investment, co-investment and debt. I explained that on the golf course of international development I wanted CDC to be able to use the full set of clubs and not just a putter.

Bringing ACTIS to heel had also been extremely difficult until I discovered that under their memorandum of articles, as Secretary of State I had the right to appoint the chairman and non-executive directors. I believed that ACTIS was refusing to give the taxpayer what I regarded as fair value in return for its public investment. It was also seeking to raise a new fund for its investment business. I told DfID to make clear to ACTIS that I would not reappoint the chairman or the non-executive directors until a fair deal had been agreed. This would have made it virtually impossible for ACTIS to go to the market to raise the new fund – leading to the chief executive, Paul Fletcher, complaining publicly that he had been 'shaken down' by the Secretary of State.

I remember one morning arriving at DfID after a particularly difficult series of meetings and being concerned that I was in a very exposed position on CDC. I was nervous that if anything went wrong, I'd be rightly blamed and entirely responsible. One of CDCs non-executive directors, Ian Goldin, the South African development economist whom President Mandela persuaded to run his development work, was in London and had asked to see me, but the department had informed him that I was too busy. I immediately told officials to ask him to come in for a meeting and he came straight away. During the meeting he said, 'Everyone will tell you that the reforms you are making are wrong – for a variety of reasons, many of them self-interested. I am here to tell you that what you are doing is right and you must persist.' At a moment of doubt, his encouragement was just what I needed.

To head up what was now a new and much improved piece of the development architecture, we managed to recruit Diana Noble, a brilliant chief executive with just the right mixed experience of finance and development to lead what was effectively a totally re-engineered organisation. The staff of forty-seven was reduced to seventeen. Under its chairman, Sir Graham Wrigley, a most impressive business leader who in mid-career left the City to embellish his development credentials at SOAS, the London development-focused university, CDC's results are impressive indeed. In 2019, CDC employed through investments directly or indirectly nearly 900,000 people in the developing world – thus feeding hundreds of thousands of families. They also paid tax into poor countries' treasuries of nearly $3.5 billion – and wages of $4.5 billion – an extraordinary achievement given where they were just eight years earlier. Its staff now number over 500. I do not think it an exaggeration to say that in thirty years' time it will be CDC which will be seen as the visible embodiment of Britain's international development contribution and leadership, raising living standards in some of the poorest parts of the world and helping build economic success.

We decided we should hold one key event every year that would show the British taxpayer how important their development spending is and underline our international leadership and example. In 2011, we decided Britain would host the Global Alliance for Vaccines (GAVI) in London to try to secure a real boost for the vaccination of children in the poorest parts of the world. By vaccinating kids, a virtuous circle is created, as mothers can work and not have to look after sick children. I remember spending two days living with a family in up-country Ethiopia in a *tukul*, a circular thatched-roofed wattle and mud building in the company of a mum and dad, five children and their grandmother, as well as six goats and two cows. I was accompanied by Tim Montgomerie, the senior journalist and blogger whose work on ConservativeHome had done so much to embed the case for international development into the Tory Party's soul. We learned how at least one of the children was always sick and Granny's role was to care for them while Mum and Dad grew crops and looked after the animals. At night-time we saw the children trying to do their homework in a smoky and badly lit hut. As Tim and I bedded down for the night, sleeping between the children and the goats, our equanimity was disturbed by a large rat which ran across our half-asleep chests! We saw clearly from this experience how vaccinating children against disease, amongst other development aid, could transform lives.

Vaccinations also cut child mortality markedly, so mothers have fewer children. In London I set about persuading other countries to follow our lead and invest in this terrific endeavour. We teamed up with Melinda Gates and the Gates Foundation and together we hit the phones and raised money. We even persuaded the Vatican to support this replenishment of GAVI's funds for the first time, to the tune of €5,000.

At the fundraising conference held in the shadows of St Paul's Cathedral and following a remarkable speech on development by the Prime Minister, we managed to raise $4.3 billion, exceeding an initial target of $3.7 billion, with a British contribution of £814 million. This British money meant that in the five years of that parliament, thanks to the British taxpayer, a child in the poor world was vaccinated every two seconds and a life saved every two minutes – from diseases which, thank goodness, children in our country no longer die. Polling showed that 83 per cent of the public strongly agreed with this British development decision.

For our second annual event, I decided that we should prioritise family planning and reproductive health. Once again we teamed up with Melinda Gates and the Gates Foundation. This was a trickier area, as contraception was controversial within the Catholic Church and on the right, and focusing only on family planning rather than the whole gamut of women's rights did not appeal to the political left. It would be necessary to steer a middle course, securing the passive acquiescence if not the active support of both parties.

In northern Uganda I had seen the impact of family planning, as well as the controversy. The President's wife, Janet Museveni, asked to see me and requested that we desist from this work. I saw for myself in the arid north a group of fifty women sitting under a tree learning about the possibility of family planning. At the end of the talk, they were asked to put up their hands if they would like a private consultation. I watched as every hand went up. I then saw all these women forming three orderly queues outside private cubicles where they could receive advice from a counsellor and secure contraceptive support.

In Rwanda, Project Umubano had built a health clinic at Cyahafi near Kirambi which was run by the sisters from the Medical Missionaries of Mary. With two friends, my wife had done the coast-to-coast walk in the UK to raise the money to build it and on 26 July 2011 I opened it with Sharon, the Rwandan Minister of Health and a large number of British Conservatives in attendance.

At one of their first clinics I saw for myself the empowerment that family planning brings. Through an interpreter I heard from a woman who thought she was pregnant and who already had four children. She feared that a fifth would destroy the structure of her family and that her husband would leave her. She was tested and told that she was not pregnant. She laughed, she cried, she ululated and started dancing with sheer joy and relief. She departed having received a contraception injection, her life and her future restored. We realised that if we could do for family planning what we had done for vaccination the previous year, we could truly move the dial.

In the run-up to the conference held at the QEII Centre in London, I went to see the Archbishop of Westminster, Cardinal Vincent Nichols, whom I knew from his time as Archbishop of Birmingham. I asked him to support what we were doing, or at least passively acquiesce in it, and he agreed to give us a fair run, subject to there being no attacks on the Catholic Church and their theological position.

The conference was facilitated by Sarah Montague from the BBC *Today* programme and opened by David Cameron, with another barnstorming development speech. President Kagame of Rwanda spoke, as did President Museveni of Uganda. I asked the latter to speak for no more than fifteen minutes, but as he got up, he grinned at me and said, 'I may speak for longer than you requested but I have flown halfway round the world to be here.' Thirty-five minutes later he sat down. The conference broadly achieved its aims without causing an opposite reaction and if all the pledges made that day are honoured – by countries, the corporate and pharmaceutical sectors and charities – the level of unmet need for family planning in the poorest parts of the world will have been halved. In some of the least-developed countries – suffering from economic and political insecurity as well as food scarcity – the population increases each year by more than the level of economic growth yet contraceptive prevalence is extremely low. Providing family planning for women who want it but cannot obtain it is a world-changing event. In my view, allowing women to decide for themselves whether and when they have children is a basic human right.

Had I remained at DfID, I would have looked at two other areas for an annual event which demonstrated British leadership and which would have had a powerful impact. Britain has been a leader in getting children into school. Under the last Labour government this received a significant boost; Gordon Brown especially has championed it. And with a rising global population, the number of children who do not go to school today has fallen markedly. I set up the Girls' Education Challenge Fund, designed to ensure that 1 million additional girls attend school. The fund operated through a bidding process – corporates, charities and NGOs could bid and if they were found to deliver value for money, their bid would be accepted. The fund was designed to operate above all where there was no state education structure to be supported and where other money from UK taxpayers was not being used for the same purpose.

As I got to understand international development, I came to believe that educating girls is the most effective way to change the world. Educated, a girl is more likely to get married later rather than earlier in life. She will have fewer children. She is more likely to take a leading role in her family and community and, evidence suggests, increasingly in local and national government, as we have seen for example in Afghanistan prior to the Taliban seizing control. And she is more likely to ensure her own children go to school. Working with organisations like CAMFED (the Campaign for Female Education), the charity formed around a kitchen table and which initially raised its funds by selling jam in the local market, great progress has been made. CAMFED is now a world leader in ensuring that girls go to school but also in demonstrating value added. Going to school is not just about providing a school place; it is also about grades attained, courses taken and completed and jobs secured, as CAMFED has shown, using the example of success to inspire others to attend, to teach and to build education structures.

The other area where Britain and America have done much to help is in tackling starvation and malnutrition. It is obscene that in this world of plenty there are children dying of starvation. In Dadaab in northern Kenya, site of the largest refugee camp in the world, I met refugees from Somalia, many of whom had walked for weeks to escape the fighting, with their starving and dying children, to be helped by British international charities like Save the Children. It is another occasion seared into my memory.

Up in Karamoja in northern Uganda I saw the work being done to help tackle systemic starvation. Children would be lined up and, through measuring the circumference of their forearms, the degree of their malnutrition would be detected. A child with severe acute malnutrition can quite quickly recover through eating Plumpy'Nut – a peanut-based paste which costs just a few pence to manufacture. Within an hour or so a child would be up and running around as a result. But if their severe malnutrition tips beyond that point, then they need to be admitted to a clinic and receive intensive treatment, usually including being put on a drip. This requires days of medical attention. Some of the saddest sights I have witnessed are in the malnutrition wards of developing world hospitals – often supported by the British taxpayer – where a mother sits on a bed with her emaciated child, their wide, frightened eyes haunting you for weeks afterwards.

In Karamoja, Britain teamed up with the World Food Programme (WFP) – usually a highly effective organisation which is an ever-present feature of the international development system, acting at times of crisis and need. For some years, spending $25 a head, the WFP had fed 1.2 million people who otherwise would have starved in northern Uganda. We decided that for an additional $5 dollars a head over a period of three years – the extra money to be provided by the British taxpayer – we should be able to float most of the 1.2 million off aid and into self-sufficiency. The additional $5 would enable irrigation to take place and water to be reservoired. People would be taught how to plant and cultivate crops and husband their animals. Cold storage could be developed, markets encouraged and some feeder roads built so goods could get to market. Three years later, the record showed that nearly 1 million of the 1.2 million had been floated off food aid. It is a living example of the old adage 'give a man a fish and you feed him for a day; teach a man to fish and you feed him for a lifetime'.

Of all the countries in Africa, it was Somalia and Libya which most preoccupied me. Somalia was not only ungoverned space – a source of constant misery to its citizens – it was also an exporter of terrorism. At one point there were more British passport holders training in Somali terrorist camps than in Afghanistan or

Pakistan. We were worried about the risks to our own security and we thought we could do something to help. Although we had no staff based in Somalia, we tried to help from neighbouring Kenya and Ethiopia.

Ethiopia, like Rwanda, was a 'development darling'. In both countries we knew that the government could be trusted to do precisely as we agreed with our taxpayers' money. Ethiopia had strong government but no entrepreneurial spirit, having for so long been governed by an anti-capitalist regime. Somalia was the polar opposite – hugely entrepreneurial but with no government to speak of. Since the Americans had ignominiously withdrawn after Black Hawk Down, the country had been an irritant with its disorder and piracy, controlling which had occupied most of the world's navies patrolling off the Horn of Africa.

In 2011, for the first time Ethiopia became our biggest development programme anywhere. This was a partnership which yielded spectacular results, elevating the social condition of its people and hugely increasing the number of girls in school and the quality of its education system. In fighting terrorism and Al-Shabaab, they were also our partners. Indeed, Ethiopia was doing much of the heavy lifting. I had met their Prime Minister, Meles Zenawi, who had been a good and supportive friend of the then Labour government when I was the Tory opposition spokesman, and we had disagreed over his incarceration of the leader of his opposition in Ethiopia, Birtukan Mideksa. I had urged him to release her – which he eventually did. We got on better once I was in government, and he was the first person to call me when I was appointed to DfID.

Having the African Union (AU) headquartered in Addis Ababa

meant that I was a frequent visitor and Meles was helpful on wider British interests and foreign policy issues. I spent much time working with the AU and the Gabonese chair of the AU Commission, Jean Ping. We became closer too because I used to defend Meles when the British media was going through one of its phases of moral indignation about human rights. As with Rwanda, there was always a slow drumbeat of human rights concerns. It was a shock to many when Meles died in 2012, as he'd kept his illness largely under wraps, although there were rumours that he was secretly receiving treatment in Belgium.

Spending time in Addis Ababa meant staying at the beautiful British Ambassador's residence there, built on land given to Britain by Emperor Menelik II. The British thought the gift of this land in Addis Ababa was so generous that, uniquely, Ethiopia has been exempted ever since from paying rates on its residence in London. At one time the compound had a leopard as a resident who could be heard traversing the Ambassador's roof in the early hours of the morning. It was seen by his deputy late at night outside his window, looking in. Immediately the Foreign Office official responsible for health and safety issued instructions that the leopard must be apprehended and moved. An operation involving a tethered goat and a man with a tranquiliser was arranged, but night after night the leopard failed to appear. After a month, the Ambassador asked the health and safety official if he could stand down the goat and the tranquiliser and this was agreed. But the health and safety official decided to fly out to Addis to review matters. When he arrived at the compound, his driver suddenly stopped, turned off the engine and signalled to his passenger to remain silent. And there, strolling along the pathway, was the leopard, looking up enquiringly at the fellow who had ordered his capture as if thumbing his nose at him.

I went into Somalia on three occasions – the first British minister to have visited for more than twenty years. Travelling across from the Ethiopian side, we drove past Ethiopian Army units and military hardware deployed inside Somalia. In Puntland I visited a jail where even the *Sun* journalist who was with me was shocked by the conditions in which prisoners were held, and met with clan elders to hear what they thought was needed to build their country and defeat Al-Shabaab.

I also went to Somaliland, the former British protectorate, which was an oasis of peace. Indeed, at about this time a presidential election was won by the opposition with a slim majority of just 40,000 and power was transferred peacefully. I met the President and his Cabinet, many of whom seemed to have flats in London. Every August the President was sent by his wife to clean theirs, in Putney. Britain helped train their police, build up the quality of their government and accountability and raise the standards of their education and health systems.

In Mogadishu, the capital of Somalia, the few Brits working there lived within the airport perimeter. I negotiated for the commander of the Ugandan contingent to provide us transport in his armoured cars and to guard us as we drove through the city to Villa Somalia, which passed for the administrative headquarters of the government there. Driving through Mogadishu was extraordinary; concrete and rubbish were everywhere. There wasn't a single building that had not been partly destroyed or damaged. Kate Allen of the BBC joined us and I gave her an interview from amongst the devastated buildings. At a meeting with the President in Villa Somalia, our discussions were interrupted by a burst of machine-gun fire. It happened quite often, they said, and no one seemed particularly animated by it. Following the meeting in Villa Somalia, I visited a feeding centre which brought home succinctly the tragedy affecting so many women and children.

Back in Britain we agreed to do more to help. We decided to hold an international Somalia conference in London, chaired by David Cameron. My task was to deliver some meaningful development results and ensure that other countries contributed financially. The Deputy National Security Adviser, Olly Robbins, played an effective part in pulling it all together. Our aim was to beef up the AU forces – not least by adding some British defence and planning expertise to assist with fighting the terrorists and to ensure they worked better with Ethiopia, whose fighting troops were the most effective. We wanted to set up a development fund that would reward those areas which had accountable structures of governance, to set up a new constitution which was acceptable to all parts of Somalia – no easy task – and to ensure that public funds were no longer routinely pilfered when revenue was raised at the ports and customs.

When the conference was held in London, the UN and major powers, along with the regional ones, were represented, as were the different and disputatious representatives from Somalia itself. At Spencer House, I hosted a dinner for the Somali contingent, many of whom were routinely at loggerheads. Having them all under one roof was quite a challenge. I sat between the President of Somalia and the President of Somaliland, both of whom detested each other. Small talk – through interpreters – over dinner was challenging. At one point the President of Somalia pointed across to another guest and said, 'That man is an impostor; he is not, as he says, the Chief Minister of Galmudug; he lives in Manchester!'

Later that night there was a fight in the London hotel where we had put them all up and the police were called – something which mercifully escaped the British press. Some years later there was a follow-up conference in London and (whisper it quietly) Somalia is making progress.

Some months later I was brought up short while reading a note from covert sources. Such material was always brought into my office in a locked and battered brown box. This report addressed a meeting in central Somalia involving Ahmed Godane, the Emir of Al-Shabaab, and other senior figures. Mr Godane had complained, rather alarmingly from my point of view, that 'no effort had been made to kill the British development minister on his recent visit to Mogadishu'. Paradoxically, the Americans killed Mr Godane in southern Somalia in a drone attack in September 2014.

The Libya campaign has been extensively written about elsewhere. It should not be forgotten that this was a humanitarian intervention designed to stop what would undoubtedly have been a bloody massacre of thousands of innocent civilians. When Gaddafi said that his troops had halted their advance on Benghazi, we could see from satellite observation that he was not telling the truth and that his forces were indeed heading there – clearly with murderous intent.

My role throughout the campaign was to ensure we considered the humanitarian consequences of everything we did. Once military action was imminent, the full legal advice was given to the Cabinet. Following Iraq, this was an important innovation. After that meeting I asked the department to pull together all relevant lessons on humanitarian consequences learned from Iraq. During our engagement, extraordinary care was taken by Liam Fox and the MoD not to allow civilian casualties as a result of our actions. Throughout it all I sat on the War Cabinet that organised Britain's effort. We met fifty-four times throughout the campaign and I travelled with William Hague to Benghazi to meet the interim government and see what was happening on the ground.

Early on, rebel forces captured what were said to be two MI6 types and six SAS soldiers. They'd been sent in to liaise with the rebel leaders, who thought they were mercenaries for the other side. They were released after a couple of days.

At one of our meetings on a Saturday morning, we needed to approve the evacuation of British oil workers by RAF Hercules aircraft from the desert in southern Libya. When Cameron asked the Chief of the Defence Staff, General David Richards, about the timings of RAF aircraft leaving and returning to Valletta in Malta, Richards was very precise that flights would be back on the ground by 1500 hours.

'How can you be so sure?' asked the PM.

'Because the lads will want to watch the second half of the match,' he replied, referring to the rugby that afternoon.

My involvement with the Libya campaign started earlier, when the Prime Minister asked me to go to the African Union conference in Equatorial Guinea to rally support amongst African leaders for our military action. He also mentioned that the President of Equatorial Guinea had imprisoned his constituent, Simon Mann, not entirely unreasonably, for attempting to overthrow his government by force.

'He's threatening to eat his brains,' the PM told me.

Once at the conference, I set about my task – made rather easier by the fact that Richard Parr, my special adviser, managed to penetrate the coffee lounge where all the heads of state would retire to relax. This enabled me to nobble nearly all of them. In a written note to the PM when I returned, I was able to say that I had spoken to 'eleven Presidents, two Prime Ministers, four Vice-Presidents, one King and a cannibal'. The last three words were repeatedly struck out by nervous civil servants on the grounds that the memo would leak, but I reinstated them. There was also some discussion about whether Gaddafi might go into exile there.

Equatorial Guinea, judged by per capita income, is one of the richest countries in Africa. But unfortunately most of that income goes to the President and his family, meaning that its citizens live in dire poverty. I pointed this sad fact out in the House of Commons when I returned, which led to a note of protest and denunciation by the government of that country.

A delegation of AU leaders was meeting in Mauritania before setting out for Libya. I was asked to call Jean Ping, who was leading the delegation, on the Saturday to warn him against travelling to Tripoli on the next day as military action was imminent. I was also asked to persuade President Museveni, who was allegedly warehousing Gaddafi money through Ugandan interests, to desist.

I had a friendly but sparky relationship with the President, who regarded me as a white, middle-aged colonial throwback with redeeming features. There was a difficult moment when his Parliament appeared minded to pass a Bill legalising the execution of gay people. I had sent Stephen O'Brien to see him to try to dissuade him from doing so, but he had refused to meet him.

On a subsequent visit to the region I asked to call on him and the meeting was set for one o'clock in the morning. We were received in Government House, where he sat high on a throne while we assembled at his feet. He asked what we would like to drink and I suggested that in view of the hour a cup of cocoa might be appropriate. Following a short meeting with officials, he said, 'I know why you've come to see me. Let's go for a walk in the garden.'

As we walked around under the floodlights, he said, 'You've come to protest, haven't you, about our laws on buggery? It's absolutely disgusting.'

'Well, Mr President, it may not be your way or mine, but we believe it's a fundamental human right that people should be able to love whom they like.'

'I don't know why you're complaining. We are only using the colonial laws we inherited from you.'

'Nevertheless, Mr President, they were wrong and we all know it, and if you persist, Parliament in London will insist that all British aid to your country is ended.'

After some further teasing, the President said to me, 'Well, you can go back and tell your Parliament I am not going to sign this Bill.'

From the outset of the Libyan campaign, we prepared for stabilisation afterwards. Under nominal UN leadership, Britain put together an international team bringing in experts from all over the world, across a wide range of areas, ready to engage the moment peace was achieved. The problem was that in the end there was never a peace to stabilise in Libya; there still isn't.

During the course of the campaign, we managed to get food and medicines to remote and cut-off communities. When the clean water system failed in Tripoli, working with the UN, Britain managed to get it up and running again in forty-eight hours. Instead of dismantling the police, as happened in Iraq, we arranged that Libyan police officers would receive a text message making it clear that they still had a job so long as they had not been engaged in breaches of humanitarian law. And Alan Duncan, through his expertise in the oil industry, got Libya's key export restarted.

As the days went by, hundreds of refugees and migrant workers started to assemble in Misrata in the hope of escape. The port city became a battleground between the two sides and to my horror we realised that nearly 5,000 people were dangerously exposed on the quayside. We appealed to the International Labour Organization to send in vessels to rescue them and take them to safety further along the coast. We agreed to meet all the costs of them doing so. After several attempts, some of which took place under gunfire, the ILO vessels managed to rescue all of them from the quayside, to our huge relief.

One particularly dangerous moment occurred when a group of international journalists were holed up in a hotel between the lines in Tripoli. Snipers on both sides were engaging and the journalists were extraordinarily vulnerable. I was asked by a worried BBC in London if I could help get them rescued. Meanwhile, the MoD was considering its options, including deploying Special Forces from HMS *Ocean*, then lying offshore in the Mediterranean. I asked No. 10 to give us twenty-four hours to see what we could do to avoid what could have become a dangerous firefight. Sometime later, after my negotiations with the International Committee of the Red Cross (ICRC) and a reconnaissance by humanitarian assets, the ICRC were able to send in their vehicles, which they backed up to the hotel doors, evacuating all the journalists safely and without a shot being fired.

On the other side of the world, Burma was opening up and the regime had released Aung San Suu Kyi. It was agreed that I would go there, in view of Britain's strong historical links, to look at what we could do to help. Then, if it all worked out, more senior figures could follow, as William Hague, David Cameron and Hillary Clinton did, all of whom I briefed in detail after I returned.

As Burma opened up, we were determined that everyone should help and ensure that potential new commercial contracts were shared with those who were supporting the country's overall development. I was nervous that Britain could end up providing our taxpayer funding while the Italians went after the commercial contracts. There was also a clear role for the World Bank to hold the ring on all of this. I went up to the new capital, Naypyidaw, built in the heart of the jungle as a redoubt by the superstitious regime who feared they were vulnerable to attack in Rangoon. It was the most extraordinary place, reached by a four-lane motorway with no traffic at all to be seen, save for the odd ox-drawn cart. I visited the high-vaulted Parliament and met the Speaker, who was said to be a reformer, and members of Aung San Suu Kyi's party.

I spent a day with Aung San Suu Kyi. I had known her husband, Michael Aris, whom I'd met for tea on the House of Commons Terrace prior to an adjournment debate in which I spoke at 2.39 in the morning on 24 June 1991 about the mistreatment of his wife. On this visit we met at her house, where she had been incarcerated by the Burmese military regime. Following discreet enquiries, I brought her as a present three DVDs: *Downton Abbey, Yes, Prime*

Minister and, at her specific request, a ghastly 1970s sitcom called *It Ain't Half Hot Mum*, about the Burma campaign, starring Windsor Davies as a battery sergeant in a British unit during the Second World War. She said it made her howl out loud with laughter.

We went together to her constituency for a campaigning visit where thousands of her constituents turned out to see her. I was asked to go out and introduce her. In front of the largest audience I had ever seen, I did my best, and she then addressed her adoring public. Afterwards, as we walked through the crowds, who eagerly reached forward to touch her, it was clear she was venerated. She had no security; the crowds were her protection. Alas, her status has changed since then.

On the way back she took a call from what was clearly a troublesome member of her party. 'Andrew, you have been a whip – what do you do with irritating party members?' she asked. I saw shades of Mrs Thatcher in her comment that day, delivered in her cut-glass 1950s Oxford accent.

Not far away geographically was Pakistan, which absorbed a great deal of my time in government. It soon became the biggest recipient of British aid, replacing India. We knew we could make a difference there through our close connections and historical relationship and, in particular, could help to smooth the difficult relations with America by acting as a go-between. We had decided that the difference we could make was above all getting girls into school, not so much with our money but with our expertise – and through the leadership of Michael Barber, who had been Tony Blair's head of delivery and worked well with the Chief Minister of the Punjab, Shehbaz Sharif, to deliver better schooling. I persuaded

McKinsey to let the government have Michael's services for almost no fee. We also worked with the Pakistani revenue service to increase its ability to tax its citizens.

One of my earliest visits there in government was to organise help over the disastrous flooding in 2010 which caused such devastation and prompted deep concern in the UK Pakistani community. Afterwards I flew straight from Islamabad to the UN in New York to speak to the General Assembly, urging the international community to intensify efforts to help.

It was on a later visit that we ran into potentially serious trouble. Pakistan was going through a period of unrest, with rioting over a significant rise in energy costs. I had been in Peshawar, talking to the Governor in his magnificent home festooned with portraits of British generals from the Raj and the campaign in the frontier provinces. It was judged too dangerous to stay overnight, and we were to drive to Islamabad and back, starting early in the morning. On our return journey we found the motorway was closed by demonstrators complaining about the increased electricity prices, so the police shut a portion of the opposite carriageway so we could speed past the obstructing cars and get back. Unfortunately, the crowd of demonstrators had seen what was happening and congregated at the point we were to cross back over to the correct side of the road, blocking our passage. As we arrived, cars were attacked with rocks and staves, and several demonstrators moved to pour petrol onto the vehicles. I was in the back of the second car with our High Commissioner. Our convoy reversed and sped back the way we had come and into an Army base – the headquarters of the Pakistani Armoured Corps – from where we were all taken back to Islamabad by military helicopter. I realise with hindsight that this was probably the most dangerous situation I encountered while at DfID, but at the time everything happened so quickly that there was little time to process it all.

Another area of conflict that preoccupied me at DfID was Israel/Palestine. I was concerned that as the chances of the two-state solution diminished, the whole basis of what was a £90 million a year programme might be invalidated. Indeed, if it was seen to be based on a false premise, the accounting officer might not have signed it off as valid. We were committed to spending £30 million a year helping to build the structures, governance and sinews of a future Palestinian state and had DfID-paid staff attached to the office of President Mahmoud Abbas. We also spent around £30 million a year trying to boost the private sector and ensure that the agricultural and other goods which grew on the West Bank could reach international markets. The final £30 million a year was spent on UNRWA, the UN body which basically kept Gaza going.

On a visit to Israel, I saw the effect of the settlement programme and the closing ring which would effectively scupper the long-standing two-state solution. I spent time with Chairman Abbas, the head of the Palestinian authority in Ramallah, and with Benny Begin, a prominent member of the Likud Party and a leading Conservative, who referred to locations by their ancient biblical names. I spent a day in Gaza, visiting a clothing factory which had a significant contract with Marks & Spencer in the UK, as well as meeting with community leaders (the Hamas government being off limits) and seeing for myself the dire conditions in which people lived. Taking in the Commonwealth War Graves cemetery, which I always did on any visit, I paid my respects amongst the immaculately kept graves. I went to one of the secondary schools run by UNRWA and saw the extraordinary range of work carried out by this international agency, which is so often unfairly pilloried as being biased in the work it does.

The bigger question seemed to me to be whether the British taxpayer wasn't simply subsidising a humanitarian situation for which Israel was really responsible. But with the complexities of this intractable struggle, which continues to pollute the well of goodwill throughout the region, it does not seem unreasonable, given our ancient involvement, that we should play our part through UNRWA in supporting an essentially humanitarian situation.

Rwanda continued, as it had been during my period in opposition, to be a significant programme, as Britain supported its development work. It is a partnership which shows extremely good results. Crossing into Rwanda from the DRC at Goma is a salutary experience. The difference between chaos and corruption on the one hand and the steady building of an effectively governed society recovering from utter devastation on the other is very clear indeed. Throughout my time at DfID I continued to visit Rwanda, careful to separate out party activities such as Project Umubano, which I joined every year, and government work. Project Umubano built a school under the management of APIE, otherwise known as A Partner in Education, a charity set up by the then MP Brooks Newmark and his wife Lucy, which the President and I opened together. Today that school is a beacon of excellence in the Rwandan education system.

There were difficulties and tensions created both by Rwanda's actions in the DRC and by the fact that the Rwandan regime was surrounded by enemies. We strongly encouraged links between our two countries' intelligence services, not least because as intelligence priorities in the UK changed, Rwanda was in a position to help us out in areas of east Africa which are of great importance to us commercially and politically, with our significant interests there. We understood Rwanda's nervousness about remnants of the FNLR, the genocidal regime, living in the Kivus in eastern DRC and making money from the mineral wealth there, which they used to equip their forces and evade any efforts by the host government to bring them under their control. But we did not agree with their military interventions, and particularly their relationship with the M23, an armed group with which Rwanda had close links.

I raised difficult issues with the Rwandan government as required and a sensible dialogue took place. In 2012, having consulted with the Foreign Office, we decided we should suspend direct budget support until the position improved. Later that year, and before I left DfID, I restored our support, having secured agreement across government that this was the right thing to do given the progress which had been made on addressing the issues in the DRC. I did it also to help my successor by taking this decision just before I left, as I knew it would be controversial and thought that I'd be better placed to counter the inevitable questions raised by the *Daily Mail*. I also completed negotiating the delicate final winding down of our programme with India, rather generously, I thought, leaving it to my successor to announce. However, no good deed ever goes unpunished and, in the fracas when I was hanging on as Chief Whip, the Rwandan issue got used by the press against me. Aid was again suspended, then reinstated. A select committee hearing on the back of it did not particularly find fault with the decision.

Since that time the relationship with Rwanda has deteriorated. On 19 June 2015, I had a meeting with Emmanuel Karenzi Karake – KK – at the House of Commons. He was the head of Rwandan intelligence, a service friendly to the UK, and had come to Britain – though not on a diplomatic passport – to brief MI6 about events in east Africa. He generously offered me a private briefing. When I heard what he had to say, I urged him to pass it all on to MI6.

'I intended to,' he said, 'but mysteriously my meeting has been postponed and no reason has been given.'

I called the Foreign Office to alert them but, unusually, received no response. Twenty-four hours later, I was called by a Foreign Office minister to say that KK had been arrested. He had been boarding a plane at Heathrow when he had been taken off by four armed police and driven to prison, where his belt and shoelaces had been removed. This had been done as a result of a Spanish arrest warrant alleging his involvement in events in Rwanda at the time of the genocide. Similar arrest warrants had been issued before by both Spain and France and had a reputation for being used as anti-Tutsi devices, often on behalf of their enemies, rather than being credible legal instruments. Foreign Office lawyers had apparently advised the Foreign Secretary that if he did not execute this warrant and arrest KK, he would be liable to prosecution.

When the Foreign Office told me what had happened, I was aghast. 'Have you told Mr Blair?' I asked.

'We are just about to.'

I called Tony Blair later that day and he was as horrified as I. In due course, KK appeared at Westminster Magistrates' Court and was released to a London address and curfewed. Months later, he was released when no evidence was offered to the courts by the

Spanish government. A few days after his release and return to Rwanda, I was at Glastonbury with Sharon when my phone rang. It was KK, who thanked me for my help. I told him I was horrified at the way he'd been treated by the British authorities. 'Andrew, these things happen. They shouldn't happen, but they do, and we just have to move on.' I admired his capacity for forgiveness. To imprison and then leave under house arrest the head of a friendly service, here to help our country, was an extraordinary act and a self-inflicted wound. It nearly led to the closure of the UK diplomatic mission in Kigali. In Rwandan eyes, this offence has been compounded by the failure to extradite or even prosecute the five alleged Rwandan genocide perpetrators living freely in the UK for more than a decade. These events should stand as a textbook model in how to shoot yourself in both feet simultaneously and destroy diplomatic goodwill.

Early in 2012, at a meeting with senior officials at my home in Screveton, we worked on a plan for Britain to co-chair the UN body responsible for deciding what should replace the UN's Millennium Development Goals, which were due to come to an end in 2015. To do so would underline Britain's leadership in the international development field as well as steer the world in the right direction. Ellen Johnson Sirleaf, the President of Liberia, agreed to co-chair and I went to see her in Freetown to brief her on the UK's ideas. We also strongly supported the other co-chair, Susilo Bambang Yudhoyono, the President of Indonesia. At a meeting in No. 10, I persuaded the Prime Minister to lead the co-chairs for this crucial international purpose. He was obviously worried that such a task would take up an immense amount of his time, but with the superb civil servants at DfID to support him, backed up by the reach of Britain's outstanding diplomatic service, Cameron, together with his co-chairs, set about developing the Sustainable Development Goals. He was aided by Richard Parr, who, once I was no longer at DfID, went to be Cameron's adviser on international development at No. 10. Although I believe there were times subsequently during the negotiations when David Cameron cursed me for persuading him to do this, I know he is now very glad that he undertook this vital and successful role. I believe that during his premiership Britain did indeed build on the achievements of the previous Labour government, remaining a development superpower greatly bolstered by Britain's leading academic institutions, NGOs, charities and think tanks. Above all, the Department for International Development had become a proper citizen of Whitehall and widely regarded as the most effective engine for promoting development anywhere in the world.

Looking back over my time at DfID, I am proud of all the work achieved by the team I had the privilege of leading. I am certain that Britain saved lives and improved the conditions of countless people mired in abject poverty with none of the opportunities we in the developed world take for granted. Above all, we arrived in government in 2010 with a clear set of objectives. Most of these we were able to implement in full.

We commissioned some polling about public attitudes in Britain to this work. This clearly showed that if you stand up for international development and explain why it is in Britain's interests as well as the right thing to do, the public respond positively. In spite of the austerity policies pursued by the coalition government after 2010, support for the 0.7 per cent commitment and international development actually went up, from 46 per cent to 50 per cent.

These encouraging figures disguise the fact that support amongst women was greater still, and those under the age of thirty were overwhelmingly in favour. I think this shows that when the Prime Minister takes a real interest and is supportive – as was the case under Tony Blair, Gordon Brown, David Cameron and Theresa May – and the department is championed by a Cabinet minister who believes in its importance, the public respect and follow that lead.

Unfortunately, over recent years that has not been the case, leading to a general diminution in respect amongst the British public for Britain's critical work and international leadership in this role.

Which brings us to Boris Johnson.

CHAPTER 9

BORIS: MY PART
IN HIS ASCENT

In 1992, John Major appointed me to a fascinating job – one of the most secretive and influential roles within the Tory Party, with the power to advance political careers. I was made vice-chairman of the Conservative Party with responsibility for our Candidates Department at Conservative Central Office.

Norman Fowler was chairman of the party and I had recently seconded the Loyal Address to Her Majesty in the debate on the Queen's Speech in the House of Commons – a task normally given to a young MP who has narrowly missed out in a recent reshuffle. The motion was proposed, by tradition, by a senior ex-minister who was toward the end of their Commons career. Conscious that I was seen as an over-ambitious young arriviste by my colleagues, I had taken the advice of a seasoned older Member to take the mickey out of myself, describing the proposer, Kenneth Baker (somewhat to his irritation), as 'a genial old buffer on the way out' and myself as an 'oily young man on the make'. The House was suitably amused and my brashness, at least temporarily, forgiven. I was a party officer shortly thereafter.

My task was to recruit potential candidates and new MEPs and MPs for the Conservatives, but also gently to remove from the candidates list the deadwood and those whose time was up.

I inherited an office with two clever and able assistants with elephantine memories about candidates' misbehaviour. There were voluminous files with personal details and observations – many of them potentially libellous – including files on Margaret Thatcher and John Major from their early days as aspiring Conservative MPs. Once the Data Protection Act was ushered in by the Blair government, the Conservative Party organised a massive bonfire in the then chairman's back garden.

Removing people from the list – it then numbered nearly 600 – is the most difficult aspect of the job. Any fool can kick people off, but we then lose their affection for the party and potentially their support. I managed to remove nearly 200 and fortunately only a couple were notably vexed.

Recruiting new candidates, however, was the key task. We wanted more women and more representatives from minority communities. There was also a strong feeling that too many 'professional politicians' populated the list. There were of course many outstanding examples from the past – Rab Butler, Chris Patten and Michael Portillo amongst them – but also a feeling that the party's candidates should reflect the widest cross-section of society; people who would bring outside experience into the House of Commons.

There was a perceived supply line of (mainly) men who left university, worked as party researchers and became special advisers or think-tankers. They then secured selection having known with unerring accuracy from their political incubation how to handle a selection committee of local worthies – pressing their hot buttons in the speech they delivered and in the answers to their questions. Broadening the DNA of future colleagues was my instruction.

The process of selection for those wishing to enter Parliament started with an interview, followed by a parliamentary selection board (PSB). These took place at a suburban hotel, normally near Heathrow, where forty-eight hopefuls would assemble. Senior figures from the voluntary side of the Conservative Party would be joined by industrial assessors, Members of Parliament and Members of the European Parliament, who would consider the would-be candidates. The whole process was similar to the Army's Regular Commissions Board held at Westbury for aspiring officers but without having to climb ropes and physically exert yourself.

Starting on Friday morning, the aspirants would be divided into groups of six and put through their paces. The dinner on Friday evening was designed to check that our candidates would not let the side down by eating their peas with a knife and had the stomach for consuming copious dinners of coronation chicken at Conservative Party events. Written tests, debates, group discussions and speaking tasks took place over the next twenty-four hours, followed by an intensive assessment process on Saturday afternoon for the directing staff. Usually about two-thirds would be successful – a process ratified the following week by the great and the good, presided over by Lord (Basil) Feldman, the genial and decent president of the voluntary party. My role was to chair these proceedings.

It was in June 1993 that Boris applied to become a Conservative candidate. His application was in the first instance to be an MEP rather than a Member of the House of Commons – following in the footsteps of his father, Stanley. In the interview and pre-meeting at 32 Smith Square, my only advice to him was to take the process deadly seriously and remember that the judges included hard-working local party members who needed to be wooed with care. This was for them their moment of power.

As we settled into the PSB, it rapidly became clear that Boris was controversial. Richard Simmonds was the senior MEP assessor at the selection board. He had already complained that I had renewed Stanley Johnson's ticket to be a Conservative candidate even though Stanley had resigned as an MEP. Simmonds had inherited Johnson Sr's Isle of Wight and Hampshire East seat in the European Parliament in 1984 and regarded his predecessor as unreliable. Richard made it clear at the outset that Boris would join the Conservative Party's list of candidates 'over my dead body'.

Throughout the 24-hour process Boris behaved impeccably. The external business and industrial assessor deputed to monitor his performance was Ned Dawnay, a Norfolk landowner who had played a key part in the privatisation of British Airways and whom I had known from our Lazard days. In the group session, where each candidate chose a subject on which to opine to fellow contenders, Boris chose the subject of bananas, with particular reference to EEC lunacies, about which he had written copiously, amusingly and inaccurately in the *Daily Telegraph* – much to the irritation of John Major, against whom his mischievous humour was directed. From time to time, Boris would suggest that the Prime Minister was supporting a Commission proposal that only straight bananas and cucumbers could be sold to the citizens of the European Union.

Just before the final session, Richard Simmonds informed me that the MEPs intended to block Boris's application and hoped that I would agree. If I did not, he said, the MEPs intended to have the matter addressed by 'higher authority'. I suggested he put his reservations to the meeting of the assessors that afternoon. I opened the meeting to decide on the prospective candidates by saying that we would discuss Boris's application last. We went through the other forty-seven relatively quickly, but in the event nearly half the meeting was spent discussing the pros and cons of putting Boris on the list. Ned Dawnay was firm: Boris was a most impressive applicant; he was clearly a proper Conservative; his intellect, knowledge and energy marked him out; he must be admitted. Richard Simmonds, supported by the other five MEPs, was adamant: Boris was a cynical journalist, a chancer, a brand not a politician, a less than honest political thorn in Prime Minister Major's side; taking him onto the party's candidates list would be embarrassing for the Conservative group in the European Parliament. Were he to be elected as an MEP it would be a nightmare.

The voluntary party assessors were divided, though the MP Richard Ottaway was clear that Boris's application should definitely proceed. I secured agreement by majority at the meeting that Boris would be included on the list, but it was clear that the matter was far from over. That evening I called Boris and told him that it would be helpful if he would agree in the first instance only to seek selection for a seat that was unlikely to be won by the Conservatives. This accorded with his current plans as he had set them out to me at our earlier meeting, and he readily agreed. I then called Basil Feldman to alert him to the fact that there was a significant difference of opinion over one of our PSB applicants.

Meanwhile, Richard Simmonds phoned the Foreign Secretary, Douglas Hurd, and asked for an urgent meeting, which took place the following Monday. At the meeting he made clear that he spoke for all the MEPs who had been present on Saturday and said that they were adamant that Boris's candidature should not proceed. Subsequently, Douglas Hurd called Norman Fowler to alert him to the strong MEP reaction – a reaction which Douglas made clear he more or less supported. Norman, however, was having none of it, and said it was a matter for the party's normal procedures. Norman said he would not intervene and that he would stand by my decision. That decision was subsequently approved by Basil's committee.

That was not the end of the affair, however. After the vote the following Tuesday at 10 p.m., Norman waved me over to the corner of the Members' Lobby. 'Andrew, I am afraid you need to go and see John Major; he is very concerned that you put Boris on the candidates list. Apparently Boris has enraged him by writing rude copy from Brussels. He takes these things personally.' I told Norman that I did not think I could continue as his vice-chairman if the decision was reversed, as it would destroy any authority that I had in this area of our party's activities if I was over-ruled from on high. Not for the last time I found myself working for a superb boss: Norman made clear that he had backed my decision to admit Boris.

The following evening, I went to see the Prime Minister in his office behind the Speaker's chair in the House of Commons. It was the first time I had seen him on his own since he had been elected and I had been part of his leadership team back in 1990. The meeting did not start well. As I entered his office, he was standing by the fireplace. 'Ah, Andrew, thanks for coming: what the fuck do you mean by putting Boris Johnson on the candidates list?' I explained that he satisfied all the criteria for membership, had duly passed through the system and been selected and that it was not my job to make windows into people's ideological souls but to decide if they were suitable to be commended to constituency parties as selectable. To start discriminating in this way would undermine the list and could lead to constituency associations losing confidence in the way the central party list was put together. I also mentioned that I had extracted an agreement from Boris that he would not seek to stand in a winnable European constituency. I left the Prime Minister irritated and not much mollified but disinclined to intervene further.

Some weeks later, I was working at Conservative Central Office and reviewing the list of applications for a plum Conservative European seat where the sitting MEP had announced his retirement. There, halfway down the lengthy list of applicants, was Boris Johnson's name. There had clearly been some confusion given our earlier discussion (and, importantly, my conversation with John Major). I rang Boris and said I was sure there had been an inadvertent error as his name was down to seek selection for a strongly Tory European seat. There was a considerable amount of harrumphing at his end of the phone followed by him agreeing to withdraw his application. Subsequently, he was translated onto both parliamentary lists and fought the seat of Clwyd, where he duly – and unsurprisingly – lost to the Labour candidate in the 1997 general election.

While Boris was contesting Clwyd, I was fighting for my political life in Gedling and after ten years in the House of Commons I was unceremoniously despatched in the Blair landslide. I picked myself up and after a period of doubt about returning to the House of Commons was lucky enough to find myself selected for Sutton Coldfield. I had bumped into Boris on and off during the 1990s and we had both ended up living in Islington off the Liverpool Road. Our wives became friends too. The Mitchells had gone to Gibson Square and the Johnsons were a few hundred yards away in Furlong Road, living opposite an old Methodist chapel which had been converted into the headquarters of the Islington North Conservative association. Shortly after my good fortune in Sutton Coldfield, Boris invited me round for a chat. His eye had alighted on the vacancy in Henley occasioned by the retirement of Michael Heseltine, possibly concluding that if another tall, hirsute blond were to take over the seat, few people would notice. He asked me about my own experiences doing the rounds of seats, where I had encountered some difficulties in getting selected on account of my having been a 'Maastricht whip' at a time when being seen as moderate on Europe was not an advantage when up before selection committees. (I had come second five times.) I remember Boris questioned me closely about money. 'What does one get paid?' I told him. His eyes widened. 'Goodness, I can't possibly live on that. I've a family to feed.'

In 2001, we were both elected – or in my case re-elected – to the House of Commons. From time to time, we would cycle back to Islington together, puffing up the hill, and for my part enjoying shouted conversation as every now and then Boris would be recognised by a passing pedestrian or we would both come perilously close to being mown down by a lorry.

When William Hague resigned, I backed David Davis for the party leadership until he withdrew and then I backed Ken Clarke.

Boris also backed Ken. Once the Iain Duncan Smith interregnum was over, the party was firmly gripped by Michael Howard and following the 2005 election and Michael's resignation as leader, I ran David Davis's campaign for the leadership, while Boris was one of the first five supporters of David Cameron's bid.

I strongly supported Boris's attempt to become the Conservative mayoral candidate for London and although an MP in the Midlands I helped with his campaign in Islington, where some years before I had been chairman of the local Conservatives. Once he was elected, we came across each other occasionally in Islington. I asked him to speak at an event at a livery hall in the City of London in support of Alexandra Rose Charity, which John Wakeham and I ran together, to raise money for 'kitchen table charities' which lacked the fundraising infrastructure and which Alexandra Rose was able to back.

On the night of the dinner, with nearly 200 high-paying guests assembled, Boris was not there. As we moved from pre-dinner drinks into the great dining hall, I was desperately trying to track Boris down. I finally got him on his mobile. 'Boris – where are you? We are sitting down to dinner.' 'Never fear, I will be there – crack on.' And sure enough, as the main course was being served the Mayor of London arrived on his bicycle and rushed through the entrance, saying, 'I am so sorry, Andrew – just remind me, who are these people and what am I talking about?' I said it did not matter what he said but I hoped he would make them laugh and feel happy about coughing up considerable sums of money for a good cause. And that is exactly what he did: a piece of paper by his side, a couple of scribbled notes, charming to his neighbours, up he stood, wowed the audience, was suitably rude at my expense and sent everyone home well entertained and relieved of their money. As a result of Boris's support that night we raised more money than we had ever done before.

Some years later, he generously agreed to speak at my annual dinner in Sutton Coldfield. This is the flagship event for my local Tories – always well attended, much enjoyed and a terrific fundraiser. As the day grew closer, I nervously remembered my experience of Boris's time-keeping. As my wife was returning from London that afternoon after completing her doctor's surgery, the obvious answer was for her to chauffeur him up to the royal town.

Which duly happened: he arrived; no notes, no speech, a couple of questions to the association chairman, 'What would your lot like?' to me, and then he stood up, said very little, scratched his head, mumbled amusingly and had them all roaring with laughter from the start. He got into his stride with some London mayoral stories; why 'Dave' was such a good PM; onward the Tories; and then back to London, driven by my agent. Boris slept all the way. The Sutton Tories talked about it for weeks after and we made a fortune for the party. Boris's gold dust was sprinkled and charisma deployed; it paid good dividends when he subsequently stood for the leadership.

Back in London, Boris duly won a second term as mayor against the odds. In 2012, just after I had taken over as Chief Whip, I recall a conversation with David Cameron about Boris and his second term as mayor. 'You do realise, don't you,' said David, 'that Boris is going to be Prime Minister?' I expressed some surprise – not least because Boris was not even in the House of Commons then. I enquired how he felt so sure and queried whether he thought the UK was ready for Boris's finger to be anywhere near the nuclear trigger. I remember clearly Cameron's absolute certainty that, all objections aside, Boris would be Prime Minister.

His mayoralty (nearly) completed, Boris returned to the Commons in 2015 in good time for the European referendum. I was clear that he would choose to have a run at the leadership and having myself been involved in three leadership campaigns – not, it has to be said, entirely successfully – we naturally talked.

I had been the 'bookkeeper' for John Major's leadership campaign in November 1990. Our campaign headquarters was in Alan Duncan's house in Gayfere Street, around the corner from the House of Commons. Every day from 7 a.m. to around midnight I would sit in a corner keeping a note of intelligence coming in about the voting intentions of my parliamentary colleagues. This was a salutary experience for a young and relatively new MP. I had a ring binder with an individual sheet of paper for each of my parliamentary colleagues. (I have still got it.) The entry for one colleague in the course of a three-day period read as follows:

- Tuesday 9.30 a.m. – X told Alan Clark that he is definitely voting for John Major.
- Tuesday 4 p.m. report from the Tearoom – X is working hard for the Douglas Hurd campaign.
- Thursday 7 p.m. – during a vote in the Lobby X sidled up to James Arbuthnot and urged him to vote for Michael Heseltine. He said he was one of the whips for the Hezza campaign.

This was an extremely useful introduction to the workings of the most sophisticated and duplicitous electorate in the world. The price of calling it right can be instant elevation and the reward of a red box. Getting it wrong is more likely to lead to a one-way ticket to Siberia.

I emerged some weeks later from that victorious campaign – and the over-flowing ashtrays, empty milk cartons and fast-food wrappers festooned around Alan's house – wiser and chastened. (We bought Alan new carpets to replace those which had been worn out from pacing up and down during the contest.)

Once the campaign was over, the three 'bookkeepers' from the three different camps met for dinner. During the course of the evening, we each revealed how many pledges our candidate had received. On totting them up we realised that the total number was just short of 410. At the time there were only 372 Conservative MPs.

My second campaign contribution was on behalf of William Hague. We had become close friends as soon as he won his by-election in Richmond and entered the House of Commons. It was clear he was a rising star and at thirty-five the youngest member of the Cabinet as Secretary of State for Wales. As the storm clouds gathered ahead of the 1997 election, I was one of those who urged William to consider standing. He was resolutely loyal to John Major, but we started meeting for tea either in my junior ministerial office in Richmond House in the Social Security Department (where he had his first ministerial job) or in his rooms at the Welsh Office on the other side of the Ministry of Defence. Officials in both places were intrigued as to why a meeting was necessary between the Secretary of State for Wales and a junior Social Security Minister. William's private office included a clever and engaging official called Ffion who employed increasingly ingenious methods to identify what these meetings were for and was dissatisfied with the explanation that they were for 'internal party political matters'. This did not put her off marrying William sometime later. The meetings were held on a 'what if' basis, and we developed the plan for his campaign.

Once the 1997 general election was over and the votes counted, over half the parliamentary party had lost their seats – including me. That Friday morning I had just arrived home in Nottingham-shire at 3.30 a.m. when William called from the Conservative headquarters in London, where he had spent the night, as his own count in Richmond did not take place until the next day. 'I've just heard,' he said. 'Thank goodness you are safe.' Conservative Central Office was in meltdown and he had been wrongly informed that I had won. 'I am sorry to say I am out,' I said. 'You will need a new campaign manager and Chief Whip – I recommend James Arbu-thnot.' And that was that: I was out – and there is nothing more ex than an ex-MP.

I took little part in William's campaign thereafter – a few phone calls, a dinner and a key meeting as the contest drew to a close. The latter was the only visit I made to the Palace of Westminster until I was re-elected four years later. During the early stages of Wil-liam's campaign, the key piece of advice I offered him was wrong: should he team up with Michael Howard or go for it himself? On the night he made his decision, I urged him not to withdraw. 'The postman only knocks once,' I said.

With Tony Blair in power, even the Archangel Gabriel would not have been able to lead the Tories back into government. Over the next four years while I was earning my living and William was leading the party we would meet once a year for dinner at Rules in London and laugh a great deal over copious amounts of red wine and meat rounded off (as was permitted in those days) by a large cigar. We were together on the night of a particularly important and tricky by-election, and with reports coming in from the front from the party chairman, Michael Ancram, I watched William Hague cool under fire in extraordinarily challenging circumstances and witnessed the qualities which make him the best Prime Minister we have never had.

My third leadership campaign and by far the most consuming role I took on was the support for my old friend David Davis in 2005. It has to be said that when he invited me to be his campaign manager he was considerably ahead of the field. Alas, when we finished the campaign, he was second!

So, as I considered the political landscape in 2016, I was clear on two points. First, Boris's natural instincts and ideological beliefs were genuinely Eurosceptic. He was an internationalist and social liberal as well as being liberal on immigration. Thinking back to the early 1990s, there was no doubt that he was deeply sceptical about Britain's place in the European Union.

Second, I was clear in my own mind that the next leader of the party ought to come from the Leave side of the argument. Once the result of the referendum had been declared, I believed it would be incredibly difficult for a Remainer to lead what had become a strongly Eurosceptic party. This was at the heart of Theresa May's difficulties.

I urged Boris to stand once David had decided he could not continue. I had not declared my position as a Remainer until late in the campaign, as I was organising and chairing a debate on Europe which was held at the magnificent town hall in Sutton Coldfield. Once the debate was over, as I had promised David Cameron, I wrote an op-ed published in the *Sunday Times* arguing that while the European Union needed massive reform, we would be unwise to leave the biggest free trading bloc in the world. All the major problems facing the next generation needed more and not less international cooperation. On balance we should stay.

During the campaign, in a telephone conversation Boris had urged me to vote Leave. I had teased him that while I was voting to Remain, he should vote Leave so as to place himself in pole position to lead the party when David retired.

In the run-up to the leadership campaign, Boris and I met several times. At dinner at Côte's restaurant on Islington Green, I declined to join his leadership team but promised to help in any way that he wished. I did point out that he appeared to have assembled a bunch of rugged individuals who were not working well together and the parliamentary party sensed a degree of confusion. We subsequently met one evening after a vote, at his home on Colebrooke Row. A delivery of red wine had recently arrived from the Wine Society and we sampled most of the first bottle in about twenty minutes. I gave him some further thoughts. By this time, however, Michael Gove supported by Nick Boles, both friends of mine, had taken things over. They were an unlikely political coupling (Nick is a One Nation lefty), but their union only emphasises the eternal truth that it is friendship not ideology that influences how people vote in leadership elections.

As the date for the official launch of Boris's campaign approached, I became aware of tension developing. Boris appeared to be taking a very laid-back approach. When Nick told me this, I found it hard to fathom: lack of attention in planning meetings, failure to carry out agreed tasks and a seeming inability to draft a launch speech.

On the day of Boris's launch, Michael performed a notable piece of political theatre and assassinated his candidate. I was horrified at the falling out of friends and the disintegration of an incredibly powerful and attractive alliance for the leadership of our party. Boris's launch was set for 11 a.m. and I tried to contact him by phone to check he was OK and resolute for the fight ahead, which I was certain he would still win.

Once I arrived at St Ermin's Hotel in the company of David Davis, who was also supporting Boris, I was immensely relieved to see he was there and apparently going ahead. I did not then know that Lynton Crosby, his shrewd and experienced consigliere, upon whom Boris depended, had allegedly declared, 'You're fecked, mate' following the Gove *coup de théâtre* and persuaded him to withdraw after delivering the last rites for his campaign.

As Boris appeared to the tumultuous roar of applause from his supporters, I found myself shouting, 'Winner!' and clapping enthusiastically. David and I stood at the side.

Boris's speech started well and zoomed through the gears. Suddenly it veered off and disappeared into a ditch: '… and so, my friends, that is not to be me' – he was off, throwing in the sponge, deflated, dismayed and holed below the water line by Michael's actions overnight.

I was furious and said so on the BBC's *World at One* and to the other media camped outside the launch room. 'This is not an Oxford Union presidential election [both Boris and Michael were ex-presidents]; it is about who will be the next Prime Minister of the United Kingdom.' David Davis went off to see Theresa May and point out that he'd make a very good Brexit Secretary. I was furious with Michael and went to see him a few hours later. After vigorously complaining for three or four minutes about what he had done, I signed up to support him. I had come to believe ever more strongly that our next leader had to be one who had voted to leave the EU. Of the heavyweights still in the game, that left only Michael Gove. So, in the end I was one of his supporters in both rounds of the ensuing contest. Despite the result, I have no doubt I made the right decision.

When it was all over, Boris wrote to me to thank me for my support. It was back to the drawing board for him, and he ended his letter with his version of our preparatory school motto: 'Floreat Ashdowniensis'.

But politics is nothing if not a game of snakes and ladders and a few days later Boris joined the Cabinet. While he was at the Foreign Office we had dealings on three very different issues: Yemen, the Department for International Development, and money laundering.

I have always been strongly opposed to Britain's involvement in the Saudi-led war in Yemen, of which more later. Because of our relationship with Saudi Arabia we have been core members of the Saudi coalition. The judgement made in Whitehall appeared to be that our security and economic relationship with the Saudis trumped everything else. I disagreed: in my view, this has been an extraordinary and historic misjudgement. Our involvement will lead to short-term economic success but massive long-term damage, while our long-term security will be imperilled by the night after night bombings and killing of civilians who know all too well about British and American involvement. Our intervention has radicalised tens of thousands of young Yemenis and been an extraordinary recruiting sergeant for terrorism.

On this issue, Boris was not wholly unsympathetic. At the time of writing, I am still the only European politician who has been into North Yemen over the past six years. It was not a comfortable visit and when I reported back to Boris about it, he helped facilitate meetings in Riyadh for me 'so that the Saudis can at least hear the views of our Parliament'.

On DfID, Boris believed that the department was usurping the role of the Foreign Office in some parts of the world and had far too much money, which would be better spent under his control. He was amused when I described him on the BBC as 'acting like a medieval pirate whose eye had alighted on a plump Spanish galleon loaded with bullion which he wanted to board and plunder'.

On money laundering, he was strongly opposed – as this stage – to the plans Margaret Hodge, the distinguished Labour MP and former chair of the Public Accounts Committee, and I had for helping clean up dirty money. We sought to impose on the Overseas Territories in the Caribbean – principally the Cayman and British Virgin Islands (BVI) – open registers of beneficial ownership. The Foreign Office is the sponsoring department for all Britain's Overseas Territories (relics of our imperial past) and I think Boris's opposition arose because this seemed an unnecessary embuggerance, rather than because he took a principled stance against it. I went to see him in the Foreign Secretary's grand office in Whitehall, and as I was leaving he put an arm on my shoulder and said, 'When you have been to see the Saudis in Riyadh perhaps you will go to the BVI and explain why you want to destroy their economy.'

It cannot have been easy to resign as Foreign Secretary – even from Mrs May's administration – but he did so in the summer of 2018, shortly after David Davis had stepped down as Brexit

Secretary – in David's case, handing in his resignation on a Sunday evening in our garden in Islington, washed down with the last bottle of 1982 burgundy left to me from the cellar of my late father. Unlike most Conservative MPs, David is wholly disinterested in holding high office for its own sake.

Once Boris had resigned, the leadership issue was clearly afoot. Together with his magnificent bust of Pericles, he moved into an office next to mine on the third floor of 1 Parliament Street. I was a frequent visitor, and a bit of a flirt. I explained that I was sure he would understand that I was worried about his piratical views about DfID. As our Prime Minister he would lose significant kudos by putting DfID into the Foreign Office, quite apart from the damage caused to Britain's reputation by dismantling the internationally recognised and most respected engine for international development in the world. Boris was serious: 'Look, Andrew, I love DfID: I just think it should be more integrated with the FCO.'

'Ah well, yes, it is pretty well integrated, Boris; it's got joint ministers and it is part of the National Security Council. What have you in mind?'

The flirtation continued. I was also about to let down a close friend, Jeremy Hunt, and indeed Michael Gove, the cleverest man in the government as well as the one I had ended up supporting last time. If I was going to be of any real help to the campaign, it was time to make up my mind. Boris's head appeared around my office door. 'Andrew, are you in? Got a moment? Can we chat?'

I said I was almost ready to come on board and would definitely confirm within the next twenty-four hours: 'Just tell me again absolutely clearly where you are on my old department.'

Boris said, 'Listen, Andrew, I want your support, I have a really good team this time. James Wharton is chairing the campaign and Gavin Williamson is involved. It will be a professional show. You were an outstanding DfID Secretary and you will be my key adviser on international development. I am not offering any specific jobs to anyone, but I am going to put right the terrible wrong that was done to you when you resigned from the government when I was mayor – I need you on the team.'

'Thanks, Boris; I am very touched. And you'll be keeping DfID as a separate department?'

Boris said, 'DfID is safe.'

'And no question of going back on the 0.7 per cent promise?'

'Absolutely,' he replied.

Twenty-four hours later, and departing from the chicanery traditional in a Tory leadership election, I told Jeremy and Michael and called Boris to say that in view of our chat I would support him and do anything I could to help. He said, 'I want you with me *cent pour cent*' and I confirmed that I was. He asked me to attend his morning meetings in his office (by now in Portcullis House) and I joined his inner team from then on – mostly, as I put it, in case my experience of what went wrong in earlier campaigns could help him avoid similar mistakes.

I immediately saw that the campaign was very well run by James Wharton and Gavin Williamson, with an extraordinary electronic charting of the voting intentions of colleagues, conducted by Grant Shapps. It was a far cry from the pencil and paper exercise nearly thirty years earlier on John Major's campaign. I did my bit to help with colleagues who had yet to decide how to vote and as the secretary of the One Nation group of MPs (a fine group of men and women who were almost all opposed to Boris's candidature) I was employed from time to time on the media.

I was touched to be invited to do Jonathan Dimbleby's penultimate *Any Questions?* programme in the West Country – a hot bed of liberalism. As the rest of the panel grinned and salivated, I was invited by Jonathan to explain my choice of leadership candidate. I did my best. I set out Boris's considerable virtues and qualifications for the job as I believed them to be, including what I thought was his social liberalism and ability, like Heineken, to refresh the parts that others could not reach. The roof nearly came off the hall as the audience vented their disagreement. Most of my other outings were more successful, but one, on a very difficult day for Boris, went badly when I agreed to help by doing *Newsnight* and defended him to a particularly hostile interviewer bent on dipping their fingers into his admittedly convoluted private life.

I was genuinely surprised and dismayed at the incredibly strong and angry reaction of many of my closest friends who regarded my support for Boris as simply unconscionable. The reaction of my children was unprintable. At a Robert Harris book launch attended by many of my old friends from Cambridge days I was literally put up against a wall, interrogated and denounced. My delinquency was mostly put down to careerism, but I had genuinely decided that given our Brexit problems Boris was the right candidate. Sharon was furious with me.

Once the parliamentary vote had been delivered, the campaign moved to the party in the country. A series of hustings took place – the first of which was to be at Birmingham's NEC, close to my constituency. Unfortunately, the night before there had been a spot of bother when a row broke out between Boris and his girlfriend, Carrie Symonds, which led to the police being called and a tape of the alleged incident being sent to (naturally) *The Guardian*.

The front row of the hustings was occupied by Jeremy Hunt's supporters, including a spitting, snarling, snorting Alan Duncan, whose antipathy to Boris was well known. Boris was clearly tired and to my surprise I saw him unwisely looking at his watch as Iain Dale, the expert interviewer, conducted the meeting in front of a large audience. Inevitable questions, respectfully put, on the issue of his private life were batted aside. They would quite simply have sunk any other politician. When Jeremy came on for his turn, there was a feeling of anti-climax. The caravan had moved on. The audience had seen what they had come for.

The team had also decided that a hustings should be held in Sutton Coldfield, where our large membership would soon be casting their vote. With just forty-eight hours' notice the event was agreed and was held in the beautiful garden of Tessa Miller, one of our local and much-loved grandees. As Boris departed Birmingham, nearly 400 of the Conservative Party's members gathered in Sutton Coldfield for the meeting. Both Tessa and I had been praying that the weather would be fine, or the event would have been a disaster. Mercifully, it was a lovely evening. Boris arrived looking shattered, but the warmth of his reception transformed him as he worked the crowd. When he came to speak, he was in his element, drawing strength from the self-evident support. To much laughter and enthusiasm, he wowed the crowd with his unique style and charisma – including suggesting the imminent return to front-line politics of the town's MP.

Some days later, just before the result was announced, I met

Boris in his campaign headquarters in College Street, principally to offer some advice on who should be his Chief Whip – an appointment of particular importance for him. He said he was aware that neither I nor Gavin Williamson would wish to return to this role if asked, and I confirmed that I did not think I could do it well enough for him. I suggested that there were five key criteria he would want to consider (the first and most important being someone who would be willing to take a bullet for him) and that in my view no one in the parliamentary party met all five but there were several colleagues who had the skills that could serve him well. Boris, unsurprisingly, had never been a whip but had clearly already thought about the matter in some detail.

At the end of the meeting, he told me that he knew I wanted to return to DfID and repeated that he was not allocating any jobs in his team but asked if not DfID, what else? I said I thought I could serve him well in Defence – a job David Cameron had offered me when Liam Fox resigned but which I turned down as I was halfway through the DfID reforms. I wished him luck and left. The cameras and journalistic circus were already camped outside the front door.

The result of the contest was announced in the QEII Centre across the road from the Houses of Parliament, the two inner teams clustering in front of the stage, and Stanley Johnson entertaining the crowd, as ever. I remembered so well how Jeremy Hunt's team would be feeling from my own experience when David Davis lost in 2005. Then, as now, there was little doubt about the result.

The reshuffle came shortly after. I had heard nothing from Downing Street so after staring lugubriously at my mobile phone, I went back to Sutton Coldfield.

The general election followed five months later and I spent my time in Sutton Coldfield and in six marginal seats – especially Birmingham Northfield – which we hoped to win. I thought Boris would win it for us but not by such a significant majority. And it was Boris who was swinging it: in the marginals where I was campaigning it was noticeable that switching voters declared their support for him and not for the party.

Through the course of the campaign, Boris and I exchanged WhatsApp messages from time to time, discussing how it was going in the Midlands. He said it was 'a cause of national indignation and scandal' that I was not yet in his government.

And this, he said, 'will be addressed in due course'.

CHAPTER 10

WHIPPING, LIKE STRIPPING, IS BEST DONE IN PRIVATE

I can only lift the veil on whipping activity, normally covered by lifelong confidentiality, because the nature of the Whips' Office has changed so much in the past quarter of a century. In the government Whips' Office in 1987 there were still senior members who had had a good war: Colonel Bob Boscawen MC, awarded his Military Cross for his role in the relief of Arnhem, his face later disfigured by burns when in April 1945 he was seriously wounded as a shell pierced his tank. He was Comptroller of HM Household – No. 3 in the Whips' Office. Also there was Colonel Carol Mather MC, awarded the Military Cross for a successful reconnaissance mission to Nijmegen in 1944. He was badly injured in January 1945 when shot down in an Auster. He was hit by four bullets, suffering thirteen serious wounds and losing a kidney. These two former war heroes would sit in the Whips' Office just off the Members' Lobby, surveying the parliamentary party with a leery military eye. When Carol Mather was dined out by the Whips' Office on his retirement, he memorably observed, 'I may not have been a brilliant party whip, but at least I can spot a shit at 100 paces.'

On one occasion Douglas Hurd wandered into the Whips' Office wearing his green Loden coat (a style of attire common in pre-war Germany). When he left, one of the colonels turned to the other and observed, 'Huh! Last time I saw a man wearing a coat like that, I shot him.' I was in awe of both colonels and instinctively sprang to attention whenever they passed by me in one of the House's many corridors.

In those days, the Labour Whips' Office was a nest of skilful trade unionists, good negotiators whose aim was to deliver for the lads. The Conservatives tended to have a mix of 'old colonels' (literally, in 1987), who stayed in the office for many years, and 'young officers' learning their trade and passing through. The old colonels had seen it all before and provided ballast, judgement and experience. The office presented itself to the parliamentary party as a cross between representatives of the secret police and public school prefects. We assumed the whips knew everything about everything and, above all, that the office's view was key to any chance of preferment.

For the Tories in those days, membership of the office had the trappings of a fine officers' mess with a tremendous *esprit de corps*. The whips' *esprit* trounced party allegiance, too: there was a freemasonry, a fellow feeling amongst whips of different parties having to deal with the gadflies, ideologues and shits in their 'flock' – the group of twenty or so colleagues for which each whip was responsible.

On one occasion, shortly after an election, Labour Chief Whip Michael Cocks entered the government Whips' Office looking for his Conservative counterpart. The office was completely deserted, so he sat himself in the Tory deputy's chair and planted his feet on the desk. A new Conservative MP timidly knocked on the door and came in to ask if he might take the evening off on account of it being his wife's birthday. 'Certainly not,' said the 'deputy', drawing himself up to his full height. 'You've only just arrived here and now all you want to do is go home. There are hundreds of candidates out there who would give their eye teeth to be standing where you are now. They wouldn't bunk off. You are an absolute disgrace. Now bugger off!'

It was a day later that the shell-shocked newcomer, having stayed to vote, discovered that he had not been addressed, as he thought, by his own deputy but by the Labour Chief Whip.

The principal task of the government's Whips' Office is to ensure that the government 'gets its business through'. The Whips' Office will always be consulted, but once Cabinet has made its decision to proceed, the role of the whips is clear: they must ensure their flock votes the right way. A whip is not moral or immoral but amoral. If the government decides to proceed with the Slaughter of the First-Borns Bill, it is the whips' job to secure the necessary votes by explaining that there are too many first-borns around, fettering the chances of the second- and third-born children. So the public good is clearly served by their removal. 'It will go down particularly well in your constituency; have you not studied your own demo-graphic statistics?'

Not long after I arrived in the House of Commons, my wife was due to give birth to our first daughter. As the date got closer, I approached my whip to enquire whether I might miss a three-line whip to be present at the birth. He looked surprised and said he'd let me know. A few days later he came back to me. 'We've dis-cussed your request at a full whips' meeting. The view of the office is that your request would be understandable if it were you that was having the baby.' I had to explain that I was the subject of a spousal four-line whip.

And so it was that on 1 December 1987, on the night of the third reading of Education Secretary Kenneth Baker's Great Education Reform Bill, Hannah Katherine Mitchell, at 8 pounds 10 ounces, was born, with her father nervously and proudly standing by.

One of the roles of the whip on duty is to attend the weekly meeting of the 1922 Committee on Wednesday afternoon in Com-mittee Room 14 in order to announce the parliamentary business for the following week. Some care was taken in preparing for this each week, since, in a moment of potential terror for the whip on duty, he could be asked questions, not necessarily out of a desire to elicit information but to show up the whip's lack of knowledge. On one occasion when questions were called for by the chair of the 1922, a senior backbencher rose to his feet and asked a supple-mentary question about a Statutory Instrument to be placed before the House the following week of such an abstruse and arcane nature that the committee assumed the hapless whip would stutter incomprehensibly to a sudden halt. Not a bit of it! In fluent and mellifluous tones, the duty whip answered the question expertly and in considerable detail, much to the admiration of his parlia-mentary colleagues, who rewarded him with a round of vigorous desk-banging when he completed his virtuoso response. It was some weeks later that word filtered out that the whip had in fact placed the question with one of his close friends, thereby allowing him to display to his colleagues his general brilliance.

I aspired to join this brotherhood as soon as I got to understand what it did. To my surprise and delight, a vacancy occurred in December 1992 and I was summoned to the Chief Whip's office and invited to join as the junior whip. In those days, unlike now, when a vacancy arose the government Whips' Office chose who was to fill it, subject to a prime ministerial veto. Any serving whip could use a blackball if they did not think that the proposed newcomer was suitable. So on joining you knew you had already received a vote of confidence from your fellow whips.

The role of the junior whip included organising the social side of the office's activities. Amongst other things, this meant serving the champagne traditionally taken at the end of the Wednesday morning meeting during which the office considered the business for the week ahead and the parliamentary traps and opportunities that would arise. The meeting was chaired by the Deputy Chief Whip and took place in 12 Downing Street. Once Tony Blair took over in 1997 this was transformed into the communications centre for government under the iron rule of Alastair Campbell, but in 1992 it was the headquarters of the government Whips' Office. In the main ground floor room, we would sit in preordained places with a silver tankard in front of each of us, usually engraved with our name, mine marked 'The Junior Whip'. The office was run by a wonderful mother hen called Doris who looked after us all, and by the Chief Whip's special adviser, Shana Hole, as strict as she was charming.

Not long before I joined, the Chief Whip had come into the office meeting flourishing a piece of paper. 'I have received a communication from the British Ambassador in Germany,' he said. 'Apparently last night there was a raid on a gay nightclub in Berlin by the police. A Labour MP was found to be hanging in chains from a wall in the nightclub, dressed entirely in rubber. The police have him in custody.'

There was a general clamour amongst the whips, each keen to demonstrate that, by his hard work and energy, he had earned the privilege of telephoning the Labour Chief Whip, a devout Methodist and teetotaller, to advise him of this so he could quietly retrieve his errant member from German custody.

A cynical black humour overlaid our discussions. I remember the Deputy Chief Whip, David Heathcoat-Amory, opening one meeting with the words, 'Good morning, gentlemen. Today is National No-Smoking Day. Would anyone like a cigarette?' A box was passed round, with everyone lighting up, including the non-smokers.

Later that December, the pleasant annual event of the Whips' Christmas party took place at No. 12. This was a rare occasion when wives and partners were invited, to say thank you for their tolerance of the very long hours the whips tended to work. Even rarer, on this occasion our children were invited, and Hannah (aged five) and Rosie (aged two) attended. I have a photo of John Major, the Prime Minister, cuddling them both. Each year a senior whip dressed up as Father Christmas and with a 'yo-ho-ho' and a sackfull of presents would distribute largesse to our children. In that era – it certainly wouldn't happen now – pink wrapping paper denoted those presents for girls, blue for the boys. The obvious choice for this role was David Lightbown, the burly office 'enforcer'. But having performed the duty before, he was reluctant to carry out an encore.

To induce him to relent, the office presented him with a bottle of whisky beforehand. This proved to be a mistake, for when the time came he had somewhat over-refreshed himself and muddled up the wrapping paper so that various plastic firearms destined for boys were wrapped in pink while some of the dolls and other girls' toys were festooned in blue. As a somewhat unsteady Father Christmas made his way into the room, he bestowed a kind word and a present on each child in front of their parents and the Prime Minister. Loud exclamations of disgust and fighting broke out as the boys discovered they'd been presented with Barbie dolls, and mystified girls unwrapped an array of military-grade weaponry. Prior to the party, the pairing whip had established that the opposition were not opposing the government business that evening, so we were all in a relaxed state, none more so than Father Christmas, who had nearly emptied his bottle. However, the left-wing Labour MP for Bolsover, Dennis Skinner, discovered that senior Tories were partying in Downing Street and decided to divide the House. So all the whips had to scurry back to the Commons. David Light-bown, however, had no time to change his attire. So an astonished House was treated to the spectacle of Father Christmas lumbering through the lobby – a sight that almost caused the division to be suspended by Deputy Speaker Geoffrey Lofthouse.

David's sheer physical bulk made him an intimidating figure, particularly if you were one of his flock contemplating rebellious activity and he was tramping the corridors looking for you. He was once asked during a Blackpool party conference by a BBC reporter to explain the secret of his whipping success. Leaning over the BBC man in his most menacing way, he explained, 'My tactics are to love them back on to the straight and narrow.'

On another occasion he petrified a young provincial journalist who had asked him some impertinent questions about his whipping methods. 'Look, sonny, one of my ancestors helped finish off King Edward II by shoving a red-hot poker up his arse. Those skills have been passed down the generations.'

Sadly, some years later, David died, while still a Member of the House, leaving a rugby match. By tradition, the most squeamish member of the Whips' Office was sent to identify the body of an MP, if necessary. Although on that occasion the most squeamish member of the office was undoubtedly me, I had fortunately managed to avoid being identified and given the task.

*   *   *

In late 1992, the Maastricht Treaty engulfed the Conservative Party. I had been at a meeting of the One Nation dining club of Tory MPs when John Major had outlined his Maastricht strategy. At this particular dinner the Prime Minister had clearly understood the concerns of the parliamentary party superbly well, not least because of his time as a whip. He successfully negotiated the necessary opt-outs, meaning that Britain did not have to accept European monetary union nor the interference in our internal workings that the Social Chapter would have imposed. As I saw it, he had effectively filleted the treaty of the bits that the Conservative Party would not accept while ensuring that we would remain part of the biggest free trade area in the world. I thought he had done a brilliant job for his country and his party.

Older and wiser heads, however, saw massive trouble ahead. With a relatively small majority, the Eurosceptic minority had serious cards they could play. Nor were the dissenters all on the right of the Conservative Party. Peter Tapsell, the grandest of the grandees, was an old-fashioned One Nation Tory who was profoundly opposed to Maastricht. While Major's deal had indeed won the support of the vast majority of Tory MPs, it was clear in the Whips' Office that we had a fight on our hands. Amongst my flock, I had some of the treaty's most trenchant opponents. Photographs taken before and after Maastricht suggest that the experience turned my hair grey.

Night after night we fought our way through the Bill, clause by clause. In those days the House sat late, sometimes through the whole night and into the next day. I remember Ken Clarke fortifying himself in the Tearoom with an enormous plate of bacon and eggs, coffee and a cigar at 5.30 in the morning before winding up the case for the government between six and seven o'clock as if he had just risen from a good night's sleep.

Sharon was then a junior hospital doctor at Whipps Cross, working similar hours. We'd often talk at 3 a.m. as I drove back from the Commons and she was between patients, in order to deal with life's basics. With two small children, we were utterly dependent on our brilliant nanny, Liz, known as 'SizBiz', who came from Wales. She stayed with us for many years as a much-loved member of the family. On one occasion when I got home at 4 a.m. there was a note outside my bedroom door from her. It said, 'Andrew, you have some very strange friends. I had a call from someone who knows you and was looking for you at 2 a.m. He started talking about whipping, so I hung up.'

As the Bill progressed, we had to work out when we could win votes. John Smith, the Labour leader, was far more in favour of this legislation than the Conservative Party, but he cunningly waited for the fissures to present themselves and he exploited them brilliantly, luring Tories into his voting lobby. He was assisted by a newly arrived Labour lawyer, Geoff Hoon, who had served as an MEP and who, through clever parliamentary drafting, knew precisely how to exploit our party's political differences. Old friends from university days, we would pass in the corridors – me exhausted and Geoff grinning mischievously as he worked out his next amendment.

Our job as whips was to keep our colleagues in the House and win the votes. We'd scour the bars and the lavatories to make sure our own flock were there, and to establish whether our Unionist colleagues had made the journey over the sea from Belfast. We had a helpful spy at Aldergrove Airport. I became Ian Paisley's informal whip, mainly because he had taken a liking to my father when he had been a minister in the Northern Ireland Office. Whenever I hove into view to ask a favour, he'd beam at me and say, 'Ah, David's boy! What can I do for you?' He would tell me how he would vote and whether he'd be in Westminster. He always stuck by his word. Others may have seen a different Ian, but in my experience he was charming, amusing and completely dependable. I used to remind him of a wonderful exchange with a new Tory colleague who sat down beside him on the green benches and expressed surprise at seeing him on our side of the House. 'Never confuse sitting on your side with being on your side,' he had said.

Keeping our people there was just as important as making sure they turned up. A tricky moment could come when, after a number of votes, some on our side might assume the business was finished. On such occasions, whips would be allocated to man the doors to prevent colleagues from leaving too soon. An unfortunate incident took place one night when a new and extremely zealous whip confronted a man leaving the House. 'You can't leave. There are two more votes.' The man replied, 'But I'm on my way home; I need to leave now.' Whereupon the whip spun the fellow round and pushed him back up the stairs towards the Members' Lobby. The following morning the Foreign Office received an official complaint that the Belgian Ambassador, while making his way home from a dinner in the House of Commons, had been manhandled by a government whip.

On a much earlier occasion the damage had been more dramatic. The Labour Whips' Office had been having trouble getting Maurice Edelman, a novelist and Labour toff, to turn up to vote. His Chief Whip had finally had enough and one Thursday sent Peter Snape, the young and urbane whip and MP for West Bromwich East, to remonstrate with Edelman for non-attendance. His angry Chief Whip said to Snape, 'You're to get hold of Maurice and tell him if I don't see him in our lobby next week, voting in every division, he is for the high jump.' Dutifully, Peter Snape detoured on his way back to Birmingham to visit Maurice's house in Belgravia, where he was received and shown into the library. Shortly after, Edelman attended wearing a maroon smoking jacket with a cigarette dangling from a long, ornate holder. 'What can I do for you, dear boy?' Snape did as bidden and admonished Edelman for his non-attendance. He then drove back to Birmingham. As he reached the A38, he turned on the six o'clock news and was startled to hear that Maurice Edelman had died of a heart attack. As Snape entered his home, the phone rang and he picked up the receiver to hear the voice of his Chief Whip saying, 'Overkill, Snape, overkill.'

On the whole, incidents of violence were relatively rare. Jack Straw recalls having his balls squeezed by a senior whip to assist him in changing his mind, and I myself witnessed David Light-bown's imposing figure bearing down on Jerry Hayes, a likeable and independent-minded MP, whom David subsequently lifted off the ground by his tie and collar.

There were other ways of securing votes too. When a particularly difficult colleague was being obdurate, it was decided that the best way to obtain his support was for his best friend in the Whips' Office to approach him. The whip in question burst into tears, saying, 'The office regard me as completely ineffective and if you don't vote with us tonight, I am going to be sacked.' His friend duly gave us his support.

Once colleagues were within the precincts and not more than the customary eight minutes from the voting lobby (the time be-tween the division being called and the doors to the lobby being locked), the whips would be focused on any incipient rebellion. The cardinal sin has always been not to tell your whip that you were intending to vote against your own party. Various methods were available to deter colleagues from rebelling: the promise of promotion ('The PM has noticed your eloquent contribution to the debate; she has a meteoric career path already mapped out for you; she'll be so disappointed if you do not support her on this; she'll take it personally, you know'); the lure of an honour ('Do come in. How are the children? And how is the future Lady Mitchell?'); or flattery ('The Prime Minister is looking for good people – exactly like you – to help out in the Lords; but she needs to know you are constant of purpose and reliable').

In the early days of Maastricht, one of my flock who fan-cied himself as a bit of an intellectual (not something that went down well – particularly amongst senior members of the 1922

Committee) was taking to the airwaves and threatening trouble. Deputy Chief Whip David Heathcoat-Amory, Maastricht Whip Greg Knight and I convened a meeting to discuss what approach was most likely to be successful in reining him in. Eventually the deputy said, 'I've got it. I was at school with him; I know exactly what lever to pull. Andrew, get him into the office and stand by the door so he can't get out. Greg and I will shout at him.'

So off I set to find him and inform him in menacing tones that the Deputy Chief Whip wanted to speak to him. As he entered the office, I stood by the door, as agreed, to block his exit. The deputy's opening salvo was to express the view that our colleague had turned himself into 'just an intellectual masturbator'. Why did he not deploy his vast academic abilities to support his government and his party as his constituents expected? Greg piled in, heaping further humiliation upon him. He was allowed to leave after ten minutes of this. I found him an hour or so later in the Tearoom, staring miserably into a mug of coffee. 'I've not been spoken to like that since I was at prep school,' he confided in me. But in the following months, at no point did he ever vote against the government.

Nicky Fairbairn was another character who went off the reservation over Maastricht. Amongst the most amusing and idiosyncratic Members of the House, he was famous for his love of alcohol, described by a colleague when speaking in the Chamber after dinner as 'swaying in the non-existent breeze'. He also used to design and make his own Scottish trews. He got on particularly well with his whip, Timothy Kirkhope, whom he christened 'Mothy' – later a leading light in the European Parliament and now a senior figure in the House of Lords. The office decided that the best way to secure Nicky's support in the vote was for Mothy to accompany him on a prolonged evening of drinking and to steer him into the right lobby at 10 p.m. The plan worked well and just before ten o'clock the two were seen arm in arm making their way somewhat unsteadily across the Members' Lobby and into the vote. When he passed down the lobby, I noticed that Mothy's eyes had glazed over. As the two of them staggered past the clerks on the desk and out the door, their votes triumphantly chalked up by the whips counting the numbers, Mothy leant against the wall, slid down onto the floor and passed out. Two other members of the Whips' Office carried him off to recuperate.

Some exchanges were sadder. Peter Tapsell was a member of my flock. When I was first appointed as his whip, I'd gone off to tell him the news. He looked me up and down and in his aristocratic drawl said, 'One really feels one's age when the son of one's first whip becomes one's new whip.' Our regular exchanges usually involved me meekly meeting him with my hands behind my back asking his voting intentions. Most started with the words 'The trouble with you, young Mitchell...' as my various arguments were dissected and dismissed. One evening, Peter appeared to have misled us and the government only very narrowly won the division. The Chief Whip was incandescent. 'Go and find Tapsell and give him a bollocking.' The proposition was, of course, impossible for me to fulfil. So I decided I would find Peter after the last vote as we were leaving the House in the early hours of the morning and walk silently at his side down the stairs through the Members' Lobby and out through the cloakroom at the Members' Entrance. I hoped he would feel the reproach of a younger colleague through my silence. As we left the Members' Entrance, he turned to me and said, 'You see, Andrew, there is nothing I want from your office. I am rich – very rich – I advise central bankers around the world; I am already a knight and I certainly have no wish whatsoever to be a member of this benighted government. The only thing I want is to have my dead son back and there is nothing you can do about that.' And with that he stalked off into the night, leaving me about three inches tall in his wake.

Peter was an extraordinary presence in the House of Commons. Many years later, I was one of those who had persuaded him to stay on for one last parliament as Father of the House (earning a concise four-letter rebuke from the then Chief Whip). He was wise, and one of the few whose warnings on Iraq and Libya were pitch-perfect. Often, together with my two children, I would bump into him on a Sunday night at Grantham railway station as Peter, dressed in a cape, and his wife took the train down to London, as did my family and I. This tall, imposing figure would look my children up and down and say, 'Your father is my whip and tries to bully me.' They rightly regarded this observation as clearly preposterous.

The youngest member of my flock was Bernard Jenkin, who, together with his wife Anne, was an old friend of ours. Bernard was showing some courage in resisting the blandishments of the Whips' Office, whose strong-arm tactics and menacing threats on Maastricht had not been successful. I was deployed to be nice to him. One night I rang him and the phone was answered by Anne. I managed to resist the temptation to threaten to bring the attention of the press to her husband's unusual taste for swimming naked in Scottish lochs and instead enquired whether there was any briefing or help I could provide to assist him on this particularly difficult issue. Anne promptly burst into tears and said, 'I can handle the nasty ones. It's the nice ones that get me going.' I wasn't quite sure what this said about my skills as a whip, but we did not secure his vote.

Thirty years later, in a debate on Brexit, I arrived in the Chamber to hear Bernard deliver a message completely unchanged down the intervening years. The sense of déjà vu was so overpowering that my head started to spin and I reeled out of the Chamber.

It was late one night that I simply could not locate one of my flock ahead of a pivotal vote. I looked everywhere, but he was no-where to be found. I thought he might have gone home so I rang him at 2 a.m. to be greeted by his half-asleep wife: 'No, no, he's not here, he's at the House of Commons.' I apologised profusely for waking her and said I'd go and be sure to find him. The next day, somewhat sheepishly, he came to see me saying that he was sorry for missing the vote and he thanked me for not blowing his cover with his wife. I smiled and said I was sure that from now on we could absolutely rely on his vote – in every division, without qualification. He quickly assured me that we could.

In those days there was a lower Whips' Office and a larger upper one where whips' meetings took place. The lower office was occu-pied by the five most junior whips (assistant whips) and we joined the upper office (household officers and the Lords Commissioner of HM Treasury) for the regular meetings. During Maastricht we would meet several times a day, summoned through our pagers, so as to refine calculations about the numbers to decide if we could risk a vote. The meetings were tense and exciting, enlivened by the dark, cynical humour which makes the whips' fraternity so memo-rable. During Maastricht I saw far more of my brothers in arms in the Whips' Office than I did of my wife and children.

The two key members of the office pivotal to the government's success were Greg Knight and David Davis. Greg Knight was a most unusual colleague with a superb understanding of parliamentary procedure. A cynically accurate judge of human nature who had hollow legs, he possessed an ability to consume quite remarkable amounts of white wine with no visible side effects whatsoever. When I first knew him he owned two monkeys. He is now the drummer in the parliamentary rock band and owns more than twenty classic cars. His wife, Janet, once told me that in the depths of winter he would put on the heating in their voluminous garage for the cars but not in their home.

David Davis, along with Greg and Richard Ryder, designed and honed the Whips' Office strategy. He was the senior whip in the lower office and ran our affairs with military efficiency and a huge emphasis on work rate and productivity. His calculations were seldom wrong. He also had an extraordinary ability to see round corners. Always full of himself, with a ready answer on any issue, he was irritatingly almost always correct. These were the early days for computers and David was way ahead of his peers in harnessing the technological advances they engendered. James Arbuthnot was also ahead of his time on technology and I remember a moment of particular drama during one of the harassed meetings at which we were wondering whether we had enough numbers to win a vote when suddenly his computer sprang into life, playing the Ghanaian national anthem, to considerable amusement. Derek Conway, with a wry eye for the rougher end of politics and human weakness, was seldom wrong in his judgement of his fellow MPs.

I think it is a reasonable proposition that this Whips' Office, run by Richard Ryder as Chief Whip, was the most successful example of whipping since the end of the First World War. Night after night the Whips' Office kept John Major's government in power. We called votes at two or three in the morning, winning by a handful of votes each time. As we did the calculations, searching out colleagues, checking on the Unionists, we were never better than minus one on our numbers, but we always squeezed home. We lost only a single vote and we reversed that the next day in a vote of confidence.

I was always terrified of miscounting and used to shout out the numbers as colleagues exited the lobby. On each door there is a government and an opposition whip, and it was an old trick for the opposition whip to try to put off his counterpart so he loses count. I always kept a pencil and paper handy so I could record the tally if there were any delays.

The Whips' Office, running to David Davis's rigorous military efficiency and attention to detail and Greg Knight's mordant humour, barely had time to draw breath. What colleagues did not realise was that Richard Ryder, for all his brilliance as Chief Whip, was for much of this time in incredible pain. He spent many hours walking around London often late at night to try to sort out significant problems with his back. On many occasions, critical meetings in the Chief Whip's office would be held with Richard lying on the floor in agony.

During this period, the one serious error we made was to take away the whip from a number of hard-line Eurosceptics, thus denuding the government of its theoretical majority. The issue was hotly debated amongst us whips, who felt it was a mistake at the time, but the Prime Minister was adamant.

It was a remarkable effort: we band of brothers, supported by the

Chief Whip's private secretary, Murdo Maclean (the 'usual channels'), delivered on the Prime Minister's instructions and kept the party together. But it also foreshadowed one of the Conservative Party's worst defeats and exposed the fault lines on Europe which have destroyed the premiership of four Conservative Prime Ministers (so far). We will see what price the Tory Party pays once all the bills for Brexit (in their many forms) are in.

Once Maastricht was over and the treaty passed into law, whipping resumed its more normal drumbeat. However, I was soon embroiled in further trouble: the Members' Interests Committee was presided over by a decent former television journalist with matinee-idol looks, Sir Geoffrey Johnson Smith, who we always joked was Parliament's Dorian Gray, with his picture in the attic. Sir Geoffrey had been taken in hand by able Labour Members who were running rings around him and using the committee, as we saw it in the Whips' Office, as a whipping boy for Conservative Members. This coincided with sleaze allegations set out in the media and amplified by Labour – sadly with an element of truth. A tired Conservative administration was tottering, and we saw defeat looming ahead. None of us foresaw that half the parliamentary party would be wiped out, but we were learning fast that Tony Blair was a very different type of Labour leader, and we knew Labour was heading for a significant victory.

I realised how different it was when my pair Peter Mandelson clapped me on the back one evening and hissed, 'I want you to know I used the word "socialist" twice through gritted teeth last week.'

In the Whips' Office we decided someone needed to join the Members' Interests Committee to make sure it got back some balance and prioritised natural justice rather than party advantage. I was asked to do so and reluctantly agreed.

The small number of allegations of petty corruption were seized upon by Tony Blair, who later attacked the government at Prime Minister's Questions as being 'mired in sleaze'. I was sitting next to John Major on the front bench at the time and felt him flinch as if hit by a bullet. It is said that Tony Blair subsequently regretted this phrase, as in the eyes of the public it spattered all MPs with political mud, but as the election approached the temperature was hotting up.

On the Members' Interests Committee I genuinely tried to take a balanced view, leaving my whip outside the door and behaving as the Member of Parliament for Gedling. But it was clear that Labour Members thought I was effectively whipping the committee and cried foul.

Elsewhere a serious problem had arisen from the discovery in a Downing Street basement of 'whips' notes'. These were short notes, principally of gossip, which members of the Whips' Office would write up in duplicate and which would then be gone through at the daily whips' meeting. Often it would be 'X expressed doubts about the Finance Bill in the Tearoom today' or 'Y is fed up with not being promoted and is heading off the reservation' or 'Z needs looking after; his wife has left him'. The top copy was then destroyed but a duplicate was kept by the Chief Whip in the original notebook. If the note had an 'X' on the top right-hand corner, that note would be sent privately to John Major in his flat at No. 10. John Major had been a whip and knew all about 'The Book'. When Richard Ryder became his Chief Whip, he agreed to John Major's request that he be shown the more interesting amongst the notes.

This was a mistake. I remember that most skilful of Mrs Thatcher's Chief Whips, John Wakeham, expressing astonishment that Richard had ever agreed to do this. 'I regarded it as a key part of my job to tell Mrs Thatcher what she needed to know – but I'd never have shown her the whips' notes.' He didn't think Mrs Thatcher should be troubled too much with the gossip about the sex lives of her junior colleagues – which she might not have understood in any case. It also meant that some whips stopped putting notes in The Book. David Davis never wrote another one.

The duplicate copies of the notes, once discovered by the civil servants, became a significant problem. To whom did they belong? If they were 'state papers' belonging to the civil service, they had to be stored in the normal manner. If they were the property of the Chief Whip, then he needed to collect and destroy them – something we whips assumed he had done. Richard Ryder took legal advice and decided he could not go and collect and burn them. In due course these notes came into the public domain and the solids hit the fan. A note from me, on this occasion typed up, as well as a note from David Willetts (who was one of the government's most talented intellectuals and had served briefly in the Whips' Office), came to light. My note set out the Members' Interests Committee clerk's advice in respect of the Neil Hamilton inquiry. Neil Hamilton, a Tory colleague, was alleged to have received undeclared payments. While what I said was perfectly proper, I nevertheless was sharing with the Whips' Office details of the workings of the committee. David Willetts, while not on the committee, was recording a conversation about its work with its chairman, Sir Geoffrey.

In one of those hurricanes which occasionally hit Westminster but which mean almost nothing outside, a huge row broke out and the matter was referred to the Committee of Privileges (the parliamentary equivalent of the Supreme Court) to investigate in a series of tense sessions presided over by Tony Newton, the Leader of the House and a man whom everyone accepted had unimpeachable integrity. My father also sat on that committee but took leave of absence where I was involved.

David Willetts made the fatal mistake of trying to be too clever and ended up having to resign as a minister after the committee found that he had been less than accurate in his evidence. From then on, Members giving evidence to the Privileges Committee did so under oath. In his evidence to the committee on my role, the clerk, Jim Hastings, went out of his way to make clear that I was telling the truth. Clerks don't usually allow themselves to be dragged into such matters and I was extremely grateful to him for his evidence.

By the time the verdict on me was delivered, I was a junior Social Security Minister and on a visit to Northern Ireland. The Privileges Committee suggested it was a mistake for a whip to have served on a House committee, particularly that one, but found that I had behaved honourably. Had they decided otherwise I would have had to resign.

Throughout the time I was cross-examined I knew there was one issue that could have lit the touch paper and roared into a front-page story. My note had an 'X' on the top. Had the committee asked me what that meant I would have had to tell them. That would have drawn No. 10 directly into the whole sleaze row. My evidence session was watched discreetly by those in the know. One Labour Member's cross-examination got very close, but for some reason she veered off. (My session was interrupted by two votes in the Chamber.) So that dog never barked.

In my day job as a whip, I was responsible for the committee stage of the Pensions Bill. Pensions legislation is by tradition dealt with on a cross-party basis in as collegiate a way as possible, because it involves issues that have a long tail. For the government, William Hague took the Bill through. Donald Dewar led for the Labour opposition. The Bill was a nightmare to whip. It had a large committee of MPs on which the government had a majority of just one. Donald Dewar would never make up his mind how his side would vote until he had teased out all the arguments from the government side. This meant no one could ever be released from the committee to do other things as I had to maintain a majority. It was also a big Bill with huge numbers of clauses and probing amendments.

Throughout this time, I practically lived with George Mudie, the Labour whip and former leader of Leeds City Council whom Denis Healey had relied upon to keep order back home in Leeds when he was being vigorously assaulted by the Labour left. George was an extremely astute whip and a shrewd and able organiser. On one occasion he had promised me a pair on a contentious vote and, knowing that one of the Members on our side had a child sick at home, I had paired and released him. When the vote came, it was clear that if George did not stick to our agreement the government would lose a crucial division. As the clerk read out the names and the committee voted, everyone could see what was likely to happen. But George stuck to his word. When his name was called, instead of saying 'No' as all the other Labour members were whipped to do, George shouted, 'NO VOTE.' We won the division on the committee chair's casting vote. I bought George a half-pint of bitter after that.

A particularly unhappy experience occurred in 1994 when Stephen Milligan, a bright and clever new colleague, died of self-asphyxiation in lurid circumstances. I have never forgotten being an usher at his memorial service in St Margaret's Westminster when I escorted his grieving mother and father to their seats. On the day that his body was discovered and identified (by a whip), rumour and speculation spread rapidly. The matter was made even worse by the fact that the BBC announced at 6.25 during their evening bulletin that Stephen had died before we were able to tell his family. An investigation later found that a national newspaper reporter had called Mrs Milligan before she had been informed and asked her, 'How do you feel about your son being strangled?' That sort of journalism is fortunately much less common these days.

* * *

Seventeen years after I left the Whips' Office, in 2012, as the summer recess was drawing to an end, I got a call from Ed Llewellyn, the Prime Minister's chief of staff, to say the PM wanted to see me at ten o'clock the following morning. Rather alarmed, I asked what it was about. 'Don't worry, it's good news,' he said – with hindsight, somewhat disingenuously.

I made my way to No. 10 and met David Cameron in his study. After some flattering remarks about my two and a half years as Secretary of State for International Development, he said he'd like me to be his Chief Whip. Patrick McLoughlin, a friend of us both, had done a great job but something different was now required. The system needed shaking up; I was the man. There had been hints in the past both from David and from George Osborne that I might be needed as Chief Whip and, being rather flattered, I had not said anything to deter them. After all, a Prime Minister needs to know that his Chief Whip will take a bullet for him if necessary and as I'd led David Davis's campaign to stop David Cameron becoming leader of the Conservative Party, this was definitely a compliment.

As David outlined his plans for me, my face fell and I slumped back into the chair. 'I really don't think I'm the right person,' I told him. 'I'm delivering for you at DfID and international development brings out the sunny, optimistic side of my nature. I'm not sure I can return to the serpentine world of whipping, which brings out the darker side of my character. Besides, I don't know half the new intake. I've been offshore for the last two and a half years doing my job in development.'

But David was clear. 'They'll all want to get to know you as chief.' And then, rather slyly, he said, 'Besides, if you do it, William Hague won't want to stay in the Foreign Office for ever. Please think about it and let me know as soon as possible. If you agree, I'll cook you dinner tonight in the flat and we can talk about the forthcoming reshuffle.'

Over the next hour I received calls from William Hague, George Osborne, and Ed Llewellyn, all urging me to put aside any doubts and accept. I decided I'd go back to Nottinghamshire and talk to my wife and try to work out how to get out of this. As Steven, my DfID government driver, powered north up the M1, I called two of my closest friends, Jeremy Sillem and Mark Malloch-Brown, whose judgement I particularly respected. Both urged me to accept. As I mulled it over in the car, I remembered I'd already declined to move to Defence when a vacancy had occurred in 2011 on the grounds that I was only halfway through the reforms of DfID, which we'd spent five long years crafting in opposition. It goes without saying that ministers should try to do what the Prime Minister wants. I realised he'd be perfectly within his rights to say, 'I'm fed up with Mitchell not doing as I ask; I think I'll get rid of him at the next reshuffle.'

As we got to Junction 15, I told Steven to turn round and go back to London. I then called David Cameron and said I was on my way back. 'OK, I'll do it; what time is supper?' We agreed that I'd do my last planned visit as DfID Secretary to Ghana and leave the department for the Chief Whip's office, all to be announced before the reshuffle began. He made clear that while I would have no say in who he would then sack (I was distressed that he had decided to fire my junior minister at DfID, Stephen O'Brien), I would be involved with him and George in deciding who should be promoted.

No Whips' Office can operate effectively if the parliamentary party know they can always go around it and talk directly to the Prime Minister's personal staff in Downing Street – worse still if those staff make a habit of ringing backbenchers directly from No. 10. Both David and George understood this and agreed that the role of the Chief Whip and his office now needed to revert to what it had been in the past. I described this somewhat unwisely as turning the office back into an officers' mess rather than the sergeants' mess it had recently become. We agreed that whipping would no longer be interfered with from Downing Street but would be left to me and the office. It would be the Whips' Office under my leadership that would handle the parliamentary party and would have a key role during reshuffles determining who would be promoted, particularly at junior level. This traditional role, very much the case under Mrs Thatcher and John Major, had been eroded over recent years as power had seeped away from the office. This was partly because we had been in opposition for so long. I had made clear that if they wanted me, this reversion was non-negotiable, and the Prime Minister had agreed.

But as I was to discover to my personal cost and pain, while he and George understood and agreed this, the Downing Street political officials did not really accept this change and deliberately undermined me from the start, for example telling the Prime Minister almost as soon as I was appointed that I was 'throwing my weight around'.

There is a tendency for senior Downing Street officials appointed by the Prime Minister to regard MPs as legal necessities and with a degree of contempt, while trying to keep power and decision-making tightly drawn to themselves. This is set out beautifully, if inadvertently, in Sasha Swire's recently published diaries, where you could be forgiven for thinking that she and the deputy chief of staff were running the country. Indeed, in these circumstances it is important that the Prime Minister is utterly clear that the Chief Whip is joined at the hip with him. I am sure that David Cameron understood and agreed with this in theory. But not least because he inevitably was so close to his politically appointed officials, whom he saw all the time, it did not work out as I hoped in practice. It has to be said that under Boris's leadership, very strong defence has been given from the centre to wounded colleagues, who he ensures are surrounded by a military square.

Following our agreement, I went off to meet the most important person in any Chief Whip's life, the Chief Whip's principal private secretary, Roy Stone, and to see the new accommodation, now at 9 Downing Street following the forced eviction from our traditional home at No. 12 back in 1997.

When my appointment was announced, on its own, ahead of the

reshuffle, there was a generally supportive reaction from the press, with some amusing references to my alleged nickname, 'Thrasher'. Only one journalist, the shrewdest observer of the Tory tribe, not least because he was once of it, Matthew Parris, doubted that it was a good idea to make me Chief Whip.

The Prime Minister and I had agreed that a fresh start within the Whips' Office was required. This was not because there was anything wrong with the old office and its members but because most of the talent there would benefit in career terms from being repotted. This was to rebound on me personally later because many of the whips let go did not become departmental ministers but returned – at least temporarily – to the back benches. From such decisions grudges are born.

We decided to keep the old deputy, John Randall, to act as 'the institutional memory', but I had persuaded Greg Knight to return as the No. 3 on the assumption that he would resume his old role as deputy as soon as possible.

Over the next week or so, we put together a formidable team of mainly new whips and allocated departments and duties. We went off together to dine as a team at Gran Paradiso (now closed) in Wilton Street, and I made arrangements for the entire Whips' Office to have a weekend away team-building at the home of Gilbert Greenall, who had so generously hosted my DfID team in opposition at his spacious country house.

With hindsight, the most important discussion I took part in as Chief Whip in No. 10 centred on the European referendum. David's instincts were clearly to go for it, while George Osborne was against ('You might lose'). I remember saying I did not think the referendum could possibly be lost but it was wrong to use a national vote in this way to resolve what was essentially an internal Tory Party issue.

On Wednesday 19 September, I had agreed to spend most of the day seeing those who had lost out in David Cameron's reshuffle. It was effectively his first shake-up after a period of two years and had inevitably been extensive. I found the task difficult, as some of those whose services had been dispensed with were close personal friends and all were obviously upset. The reshuffle had been effectively executed (execution being the word) and included one drive-by shooting of someone who had to be sacked just to ensure the numbers were right, as a result of our discovery that we had one more minister than we were allowed (it was put right at the next reshuffle).

I remember going in to see David Cameron, who was lying horizontal on his sofa, looking completely knackered. He opened his eyes and said, 'If you've come to tell me I've got to sack anyone else, I simply can't do it.'

It was my task to tell those who'd lost out why they'd been removed and advise them what to do next in the hope they'd not go off and cause trouble from the back benches. But it was also important to be straight with people and tell them the truth. Two of those I saw that afternoon had been in tears and there was little I could say for their comfort.

Late for a dinner where I'd agreed to speak to an audience about international development, I raced out of No. 9, grabbed my bike and rushed down towards the gates of Downing Street as fast as I could. I had no inkling of the havoc the next forty-five seconds would unleash.

CHAPTER 11

FORTY-FIVE SECONDS TO DISASTER

In the scheme of things, it was a minor incident. But it was a spark that lit a huge bonfire of consequences.

This is not an easy chapter to write. I shall not talk about what happened at the gates of Downing Street or the libel trial. The one thing I am not doing here is adducing evidence, sifting through material and refighting old battles. I cannot do so anyway for legal reasons; nor do I wish to do so. But I will try to describe what it was like for me and for my family to be in the eye of a media storm. I have long since buried the sheer awfulness of these events, and reflecting on them is like a dog returning to its vomit. Nor was this episode unhappy – ghastly – just for me but for all the others involved, including the police and all our families. I have tried where possible not to name police officers individually. None of it should ever have taken place. It was my weakness – arrogance, indeed – that started it all off.

My brief altercation with a police officer on duty at the entrance to Downing Street lasted less than a minute. Although words were exchanged over the matter of how I could get my bicycle out of Downing Street and what I perceived to be an unhelpful attitude by the officers, the problem was resolved and I left Downing Street with my bicycle through the pedestrian gate. This led to my resignation from the government and to two libel actions costing me over £2 million. The whole affair ended in a mess, with four police officers being sacked for gross misconduct, one going to prison and several others disciplined, while I lost my libel battle. The judge preferred the evidence of the officer, with the consequence that I lost my action against *The Sun* and he was awarded £80,000 damages. He was vindicated by the judge's decision, and it is not the purpose of this chapter to do other than to accept that vindication. I have no intention or desire to refight old battles or reopen old wounds for anyone else involved.

It was the following afternoon that Ed Llewellyn, the Prime Minister's chief of staff, telephoned me. 'Houston, we have a problem' was his succinct analysis. *The Sun* had got hold of the previous night's altercation. I displayed considerable naivety: 'Is it a big story?'

'Yes, massive.'

Downing Street officials had known about this since late the night before but had not thought to alert me until then.

The general view in Downing Street was that the public would not believe the word of a Tory minister over an extract from a police logbook and I immediately issued a statement, acknowledging that I had not treated the police with the respect they deserve, and apologising. We decided that I would lie low and wait for any storm to blow through – which was another massive miscalculation. But I thought it would be, as so often in these cases, a two-day wonder.

I returned to our home in Nottinghamshire, where Sharon and our two daughters were preparing for Rosie's 21st birthday party on Saturday evening. None of us had the faintest idea of what was about to take place.

The balloon went up at midnight as *The Sun*'s front page emerged. A banner headline: 'Cabinet minister: Police are plebs' covered the whole front page with a paragraph saying, 'A million-aire cabinet minister was threatened with arrest after an astonish-ing foul-mouthed rant at armed cops in Downing Street. Chief Whip Andrew Mitchell, recently promoted by PM David Camer-on, raged "You're f***ing plebs."' It was the start of thirty-three days of continuous media assault. A tsunami of vitriol assailed me and my family from all directions as my reputation and character were assassinated. As Conor Cruise O'Brien once said, being the subject of the attention of Britain's tabloid press is like being picked up and minutely examined by a giant skinhead. The hideous caricature that emerged at their hands prompted almost 1,000 hostile emails including death threats over the weekend. I clung to the hope that my family, friends, constituents and the many I had got to know in my seven and half years immersed in international development would simply not recognise the awful picture the tabloid press were painting of me.

That Thursday night, I tried to get hold of David Davis, whose razor-sharp intellect, toughness and clarity in adversity and ency-clopaedic knowledge of the police from his time as shadow Home Secretary I badly needed to engage. However, he was incommuni-cado in the United States, honing his flying skills on an intensive refresher course. It took me six days to get hold of him. He then stayed up all night wading through the blizzard of media coverage.

Throughout this time the media mob was in full cry. I soon stopped reading any of it and could not bear to turn on the TV. Murdoch's Sky News was camped on Whitehall and had my name running incessantly along the bottom of the screen.

Ken Clarke, who was wonderfully supportive throughout, rang to say that although he had been regularly whacked on the front pages of *The Sun* and the *Daily Mail*, he had never achieved the double whammy of being attacked simultaneously on both. The situation was made yet worse by the awful news that two brave policewomen had lost their lives in a dreadful attack in Manchester two days earlier. And if that wasn't enough, there were very few other news stories around.

That Friday, photographers and journalists started camping outside our home in Islington. They were always polite but intimidating. At the peak there were eighteen outside. They stayed on and off for a month. At first we sought sanctuary with friends nearby in Kentish Town and stayed for a week. But for the subsequent three weeks we returned home and tried to get used to the presence of the press. They would start arriving at 5 a.m. and still be there at midnight. We would peer out of an upper window and most mornings a sinister black Audi would be there with photographers and a TV crew. On occasion they would follow our daughters or my wife in cars or on foot. They interviewed the neighbours, begging for any adverse comment. My neighbours were generally wonderful, though one was persuaded to say something disparaging which was then blown up out of all proportion. A TV film crew visiting a shopping centre in Sutton Coldfield found virtually no one who would speak out against their MP. The experienced and respected editor of the *Royal Sutton Coldfield Observer*, Gary Phelps, handled the issue professionally and decently, while the Labour parliamentary candidate declined to use it for personal or political advantage.

Meanwhile, other journalists headed off to Swansea, where they visited my in-laws and begged for unfavourable comments. My 92-year-old mother-in-law was forced to hide in the back of her house while being shouted at through the letter box for something – anything – hostile that she might say. They pursued my 84-year-old dad, suffering from dementia, but who came from a generation who believed it was part of their civic duty to talk to the press.

I had been planning to return to work in Downing Street a week after the incident on the assumption that by then everything would have died down. With no sign of this, the Downing Street head of communications wanted me to do a doorstep interview outside Whitehall at 8 a.m. I foolishly agreed. My elder daughter Hannah offered to drive her dad down to London and we left Nottinghamshire at 3 a.m. so as not to be late. En route George Osborne called to say the proposed doorstep interview was a mistake, but by then it was too late. As we arrived in London, I learned to my horror that I was not only top of the news – above the Liberal Democrat party conference, which started that day – but being carried live on countless channels. I had been advised to apologise – to grovel – as hard and as far as I could. I tried. I apologised again for what I had said and tried to be dignified. I am not good at grovelling, and it showed. The interview was a disaster. As I reached the safety of the Cabinet Office, my phone rang and the broadcaster Iain Dale asked, 'Who the fuck told you to do that?' Far from bringing down the curtain on the story, I had given it yet more legs. Sky TV spent hours broadcasting on and off, live outside my office in Whitehall.

The cumulative effect of all this quickly asserted itself. By Day

4, driven out of our home, I could not sleep. I stopped eating and started smoking again. The weight dropped off me and I lost more than a stone in three weeks. Sharon lost about as much. On several days I simply could not get out of bed. I would sit for hours with my BlackBerry in one hand and my ancient mobile in the other. Virtually all press calls went through Henry McCrory, a senior party official trusted by the press and loved by the party, with vast experience of dealing with difficult problems. Henry called regularly. 'Ah, Andrew, another one I'm afraid – the *Mirror* has dug up someone who says that in 1987...' and so it went on as day after day new and yet more ingenious ways were found to keep alive a relatively minor story which served other agendas and blackened my name.

Night-time was the worst: we would sleep for a couple of hours then lie awake tossing and turning, chewing over the sheer horror of it all – worried about the effect on our family and contemplating the destruction of my ministerial career. As I faced the wall at 3 a.m. after another day of yet more creative and wild attacks and aware of even more lurid stories pending in the morning, I wondered if I could take much more of this.

During the early days I received a call from the Midlands Police Federation. After solicitously commiserating with me over the obvious unhappiness caused to me and my family, he asked for a meeting to 'clear the air and look to the future'. I agreed but took the precaution of putting it off until the Friday after the Conservative Party conference in Birmingham. Also, as a constituency MP I offered to make a constructive contribution by taking their reservations about our police reforms directly to Theresa May, the Home Secretary. The Federation's regional chairman agreed that the meeting would be private and the location not disclosed to the press. It was with dismay but not surprise that I discovered a few days before the meeting that the Federation had not only revealed the time and place but lined up as much press as they could muster. I considered postponing or cancelling the meeting because of the Fed's bad faith but concluded that it might look like cowardice.

Worse ensued. On Friday 12 October, Fleet Street's finest made their way from London to Sutton Coldfield. The royal town had not seen such media attention since the Queen visited for Scouting's 50th jubilee in Sutton Park in the 1950s. There were no fewer than nine TV camera crews outside my office for this 'private meeting'. At several points in the day we were above the Jimmy Savile scandal in the news bulletins. The Federation did not disappoint. Throughout the party conference and outside my constituency office they had paraded wearing 'I'm a pleb' T-shirts. Arriving more than half an hour before the appointed time for the meeting, the three Federation representatives gave the camera crews and journalists their pre-briefing: that they would demand to know what I said at the gates; if I failed to tell them then I must go. Once I had completed my constituency surgery, the meeting with the Federation started at 5 p.m. – after a suitable expression of amazement from the three of them about how the press had discovered the location.

During the next forty-five minutes I gave them my account of what had happened. When I asked if they would like to talk about the root cause of their disagreement with the government, they expressed no interest whatsoever. Bringing the meeting to a close at 5.45 p.m. sharp in order to give the nation the benefit of their views at the top of 6 p.m. news bulletins, they told the journalists that

I had refused to tell them what I had said at the gates and that I should resign or be sacked.

As it happens, a Conservative Party press officer had attended the meeting, sitting quietly in the background, and had taped the whole encounter – something Sharon had insisted I should arrange. Once the tape came out, a very different story emerged which led to the three officers being summoned to appear before the Home Affairs Select Committee in the House of Commons. Subsequently, two of the officers were recalled to Parliament to correct misleading statements and inaccuracies in their committee evidence. In a statement, the chairman of the select committee said:

> We were appalled by the evidence given ... It is now clear that [two of the officers] misled the committee, possibly deliberately. We have recalled them to correct the record [about the meeting in Sutton Coldfield] and if they do not, they will be in prima facie contempt of Parliament ... We have referred the police officers to the IPCC.

Before then, however, it was with a mild sense of relief that I went back to Parliament on Monday 15 October for the new term. I had realised that the conference season would be a very difficult time as the other political parties took advantage of my predicament. Not attending my own party conference in Birmingham was thought wise, as the Chief Whip is the one member of the Cabinet who doesn't have to speak, but it was another mistake. While clearly my presence would have been a distraction, hiding away drained away any remaining authority, and a Chief Whip without authority is of little use.

Back in Parliament, the scale of my problems became clear. While most of those who knew me well were supportive, the new intake from 2010, who were more than half our backbench strength, hardly knew me at all. As one journalist put it, 'The newspapers had been saturated by anecdotes of arrogance and meanness. It seemed that nobody had anything nice to say about Andrew Mitchell.' And for a certain type of parliamentary colleague, nothing so lifts the spirits as the prospect of a public hanging for those in ministerial office.

On Wednesday, the 1922 Committee convened – the regular weekly meeting of all Conservative backbench MPs. Twelve colleagues spoke about the position of the Chief Whip. While most were supportive, four were not. At the Chief Whip's usual private meeting afterwards with the officers of the 1922 Committee, I asked for a supportive statement, which the chairman and his colleagues, while personally sympathetic, felt they could not give. During the course of that day, I decided I needed their clear backing to remain in post. Had I stayed on, I believe the parliamentary party would strongly have approved of the changed nature of the Whips' Office which I had agreed with David Cameron. But these were early days and few had yet appreciated the benefits of what we planned to do.

Meanwhile, my team in the Whips' Office had been put in an impossible position. All except two were personally loyal (I had appointed most of them), but they were clearly torn as their flocks returned mixed views.

One colleague, of a churchy disposition, grabbed my arm as I walked through the Cloisters and, looking me in the eye, urged me to stay in post; after ascending the stairs to the Members' Lobby and spying his own whip there, he urged him to convey his view, anonymously, that the Chief Whip must go. By now Labour were threatening an Opposition Day debate the following week with a motion under an arcane procedure to cut the Chief Whip's salary. I was faced with the unattractive prospect of whipping a reluctant party to support my pay packet. It was clear my position had become untenable.

The next morning, I consulted four trusted colleagues. I made arrangements to see the Prime Minister on his return from an all-night negotiating session in Europe. I left town to go to Chequers, pursued as ever by an attendant photographer, and arrived at around 4.30 p.m. On arrival, I gave my resignation letter to be typed by the secretary on duty. 'Have you done many of these before?' I asked. 'Oh yes, quite a few actually!' We released it together with the Prime Minister's generous response just after 6.15 p.m. The letter made clear that I could no longer continue to put my family and colleagues through the upsetting and damaging publicity.

I considered making a resignation statement in the House of Commons. Indeed, I drafted one. But in the end I concluded there was little point. My parliamentary colleagues would have sat there wishing I would let the matter drop and the inhabitants of the Press Gallery would not have been kind.

Once I had resigned, I thought that the sheer relief of not being at the centre of the storm would lift my spirits, but it was not to be. I considered throwing in the towel and resigning from Parliament, but my constituents and, in particular, my local Conservative association had been extremely supportive and made clear that they wanted me to continue to represent them.

I began to find each day difficult and while I put on a brave face in the House of Commons, my friends there knew it was an act. Throughout the storm of vitriol, nine journalists had defended me or were sceptical about what they were hearing. But they had been drowned out by the tabloids. Chris Mullin, the respected former Labour minister and veteran exposer of police misconduct, wrote in *The Times*: 'No sensible Prime Minister should surrender to the mob, and the mob in this case is being orchestrated by the Police Federation, as big a bunch of headbangers as one is ever likely to come across.' I was fiercely defended by Dotun Adebayo, the journalist and broadcaster who together with his lovely family have become our good friends. I am lucky to be blessed with a large number of wonderful friends, most of whom are not involved in politics. Many were indignant and horrified at what had gone on. Most felt that, at the least, the scale of press assault (let alone my resignation) far exceeded any fitting punishment for the exchange at the gates of Downing Street. It cannot have been easy for my friends in the House of Commons to defend me publicly, but several of the braver ones did, including Henry Bellingham, Crispin Blunt, Ken Clarke, David Davis, Alan Duncan, Nigel Evans, Rob Halfon, Michael Howard, Jeremy Hunt, Bernard Jenkin, Sir Richard Ottaway, Mark Pritchard, Dominic Raab, Jacob Rees-Mogg, David Ruffley, Sir Nicholas Soames, Jack Straw and Charles Walker.

Privately, support came from other unusual sources: friends in the Labour Party, including members of New Labour who had worked in Downing Street, Shami Chakrabarti, members of minority communities and the chair of the English Collective of Prostitutes (the first time I had had the pleasure of meeting her), who expressed her support as we sat in the green room waiting to appear on the *Today* programme (separately) on unrelated matters.

On a particularly low evening, Sharon and I set out for what we thought was a quiet dinner at the home of a friend. On arrival, we were greeted by nearly eighty close friends: people I knew from international development, friends from Parliament, people who supported our family, my old dad. They had gathered in secret and burst out of rooms as we arrived. Our friends were such an important source of support for us.

For much of the period between the incident and my resignation, I had ceased to function properly. Within hours of the media storm erupting and my going to ground, I lost my sense of judgement and determination. For the first time in my life, I was widely recognised on the street, shouted at and on one occasion spat at outside the Angel Tube Station. I felt like a hunted animal.

Several times, however, I was stopped by black people in the street, who were universally supportive. As I walked behind Sadler's Wells Theatre, one came up to me: 'Now you know what it is like for us.' But overall there was scant sympathy for the well-heeled, arrogant Tory toff portrayed in the press.

During this time, I continued to try to look after my constituents – I was conscious that many of them had worse problems than me – and to maintain my dignity in public and in the House of Commons.

Shortly afterwards, I went with six friends for a weekend break in the wine-growing areas of France. During the car journey from Dijon to Beaune I sat next to Fiona Stourton, an old friend and distinguished film-maker in the independent sector. Her company made films for the Channel 4 *Dispatches* programme. She later told Sharon that she thought I was completely traumatised as I agonised incoherently about it all.

It was when I started talking about 'an email from the Downing

Street onlooker' that her ears pricked up. I explained how this
email had arrived at the outset of all of this in Downing Street and
how it had fundamentally undermined my relationship with the
Prime Minister and gravely damaged my position with the No. 10
staff. Once this email had arrived, it had all the appearance of the
last nail in my coffin. As I railed on and on about how on earth
the email of a passing tourist could stand up the police account,
Fiona started to listen more attentively and asked to see a copy of
it. Amidst my ramblings there was little evidential material, but
an email was different. It was this email that gave the claims such
credibility; an eyewitness account before the matter became public.
I could not work it out. And the receipt by Downing Street of such
apparently incendiary evidence completely cut the ground from
under my feet.

Not long before the deadline for the publication of *The Sun* on
that dreadful Friday morning, this email from a resident of Ruislip,
one of his constituents, had arrived in Deputy Chief Whip John
Randall's inbox. It purported to be a detailed account of my altercation the day before, which the sender and his nephew claimed they
had witnessed outside the gates of Downing Street. Larded with
detail, it vividly stood up the police log and *The Sun*'s front page.

The email was very precise: it explained that the author had been
accompanied by his nephew, who was visiting from Hong Kong,
while outside the gates of Downing Street. His nephew had mistaken me for Boris Johnson, but the author, claiming a keen interest in politics, had correctly identified me. The obscenities attrib-
uted to me matched the police log. He had been disgusted by my
behaviour, he said, as had other tourists at the gate, one of whom
may have 'inadvertently' filmed me ranting away.

After first telling the Downing Street team, John Randall rang me to relay the content of this email. I was absolutely horrified by what he told me and remember shouting that I was being stitched up by the writer of the email. An attempt was made by my deputy to question the author. He declined to cooperate but sent a second email to say that he stood by the first. Following this exchange of emails, my deputy told Downing Street that the email was 'credible'.

I was brushing my teeth early on the following Tuesday morning, in the bathroom of the house where I had gone into hiding from the press, when David Cameron called. He had been shown the Ruislip email. He, not surprisingly, found it compelling and decisive. He phoned me to say that I would have to go. After a tense six-minute conversation in which I categorically refuted the email – 'David [I normally called him 'Prime Minister'], how will you feel in six weeks' time if this email is exposed as bogus?' – he agreed to put my sacking on hold and institute enquiries through the Cabinet Secretary.

At the end of our weekend in France, Fiona Stourton took away a copy of the email. The following week she discussed this at a Channel 4 planning conference. She pointed out that I was a friend, so she would have to recuse herself from any investigation, but she made clear that there were aspects of the email that she thought did not stack up. I later learned that at that meeting most people thought that a Tory toff would behave precisely in this way, but that Dorothy Byrne, the commissioning editor, read it several times and, turning it over in her hands, said that there was something about it that did not ring true. Shortly afterwards, I received a call from Channel 4, who said that they were interested in the email but could not do anything without the CCTV footage, which had been viewed by Downing Street but no one else. Could I secure a copy of it? In addition, they made clear that Fiona would no longer be involved because of our personal connection and that another experienced producer, Karen Edwards, would lead any team investigating it – if indeed they decided to do so. They also underlined the need for confidentiality if their investigation was to be able to uncover anything.

I set about trying to see the CCTV footage. Jeremy Heywood, the Cabinet Secretary, agreed that I could see it but would not allow me to have a copy, 'for national security reasons'. It seemed to me that a Chief Whip alleging that he had been stitched up was something of a national security matter itself. When finally I saw the CCTV together with Sharon, David Davis and a lawyer, we were astonished. There seemed to be serious discrepancies between the email and the situation recorded by the CCTV: in particular, there were not 'several members of the public'; nor were there 'members of the public looking visibly shocked'.

I went to see David Cameron at his flat, together with Sharon, late one Sunday night to ask them to release the CCTV footage of the incident involving me. I told him I intended to give the CCTV footage to independent and experienced journalists who I hoped would investigate all of this without fear or favour. David agreed to my request.

Once *Dispatches* had viewed the tape, they decided to launch a full investigation. They approached Michael Crick, one of Britain's longest-standing investigative journalists, to ask him to front the programme. With his long experience of Westminster and politicians, Crick was cautious, believing that the story needed careful testing and that scepticism is the first tool of journalism. He said later that his experiences had left him no more sceptical of politicians than he was of policemen. Over the years, we had met professionally but did not know each other well. I was informed by *Dispatches* of his involvement and told that there would be no further contact with me until they had got to the bottom of the story.

They did tell me, however, that they were putting serious resources into their investigation and asked that I give them a free hand and not contact other media outlets in my pursuit of justice. *Dispatches* researchers took the email and started investigating its author and its content. Ed Howker was put on the case and started to search official records. He subsequently discovered that the author of the email was a serving police officer in the same unit as those guarding Downing Street. Crick tried to interview him and failed. Together with Phil Braund, the television and print journalist, they went to his home and tried to doorstep him. Finally, they managed to get him on the phone, having secured permission from Channel 4 to tape the conversation and film Crick on the phone in view of the clear public interest.

During this call and Crick's cross-examination, the author admitted that he had not in fact been anywhere near Downing Street, as set out in his email. The email was therefore a total fabrication. Although not broadcast, the film of Crick turning to the camera in astonishment at what he had learned was widely viewed by the production team.

Crick also arranged to meet and interview one of the three Police Federation representatives who had attended the meeting in Sutton Coldfield, who enthusiastically agreed to take part. After letting the police officer state his case on film, Crick quoted from the taped conversation and the police officer was reduced to stuttering incoherence.

Meanwhile, Downing Street was pouring cold water on the whole thing. The head of the Downing Street press operation, Craig Oliver, called Channel 4 to warn them off pursuing the matter on the grounds that 'there is no story here, nothing in the CCTV, and Mitchell is fucking obsessed'. Channel 4 quietly declined to be bullied by the Downing Street machine. As Crick said later on his programme after making these astounding revelations, 'Some "no story".'

No incident could more clearly indicate the importance of an independent and free press able to stand up to government power. In many parts of the world a call from the government press team is sufficient to stop further enquiries.

The following Monday night, the bombshell story about the email broke on *Channel 4 News* – for which they later won a prestigious award. Apparently, David Cameron watched open-mouthed in the Downing Street flat as the story blazed across the television. What the Channel 4 programme showed was that the corroboration provided by the email was a fabricated account of the event. But the Channel 4 programme could not reach a conclusion on the words used in the incident itself.

Even I had only become aware of the full story during the course of the day; Channel 4 and Crick had held it very tight. But the story very nearly didn't make it. It had to be broadcast that night before the matter could become *sub judice* and kicked into touch. Channel 4 spent the day completing the film and dealing with lawyers. While the full film was to go out later, the principal part had to fit into twenty minutes to form the second half of their news that evening. The production was beset with huge technical problems, which meant that when the news began at 7 p.m., the physical discs had not reached Channel 4's studio on Gray's Inn Road. Crick and Jon Snow had to ad-lib at the top of the programme for eight minutes as the disc negotiated the London Christmas traffic on a motorbike. It reached the Channel 4 studios and was uploaded with less than a minute to go before the deadline. Glued to our television at home, Sharon and I had no idea of the drama behind the scenes.

The police watchdog, the Independent Police Complaints Commission, were supportive too, even if they did not have the resources needed for a thorough investigation of their own. The IPCC commissioner, Deborah Glass, noted that although the investigation did not find evidence of an organised conspiracy to bring down a Cabinet minister, 'there was clearly collusion between certain officers', adding that 'a largely inaudible altercation, lasting less than a minute' had been turned 'into a national scandal which has not only caused injustice to Mr Mitchell. They have brought shame upon the police service.' (I stress that whatever mischief other officers got up to, there is no suggestion that Toby Rowland was involved in misconduct or that his account of what I said was influenced by others' wrongdoing. As I say at the start of this chapter, PC Rowland was vindicated in the High Court, and I bring no challenge to that outcome.)

Had I decided to walk away at this point, my reputation would have been largely restored.

Suing *The Sun* for libel turned out to be a fatal mistake. I should have left matters as they were following the Channel 4 exposé. It was one person's account against another's and after assessing the evidence, including weighing up the contradictions in the police evidence, the trial judge, Mr Justice Mitting, was to conclude that the police version was to be preferred to mine. But my feeling gave way to abject terror as I discovered the extraordinary costs to which I suddenly found myself exposed. We had only ever been willing to enter the legal arena on the express understanding that we would face no financial liability. But one bill arrived for £20,000 on a Tuesday, followed by another for a further £20,000 two days later. We had been assured by our lawyer that in the event that we lost we would be covered by insurance. Much later the insurer tried to avoid paying up. Another set of lawyers helped us to oblige them to do so.

Everything now seemed to go wrong: it felt like we were on a conveyor belt to hell. We faced daily horror at intergalactic fee levels as we realised we were betting much of our life savings on a judge's assessment of our evidence. I became terrified of the arrival of letters. We received some generous help with these fees from wonderful friends who felt that an important principle was at stake and who believed in me. But as costs mounted, we realised that we badly needed to settle. In addition, there was evidence against me. The police, with extraordinary diligence, had dug up reports of a small number of incidents going back over the previous decade when I had been high-handed when driving or cycling into the House of Commons. Many such incidents take place when harassed MPs are late and rush in. Sometimes officials would cover themselves, in case MPs complained, by getting their retaliation in first. Nevertheless, one of these incidents was broadly accurate.

We got very close to settling, thanks to the good offices of George Osborne, but in the end agreement eluded us.

Sir Hugh Orde, the highly respected former president of ACPO, negotiated a form of words which both I and the police officer agreed to accept, but to my disappointment we were not able to reach final agreement. In addition, the Police Federation was now under new management and had been cleaned up by Steve White, its new chief. But he had narrowly won the leadership and his influence did not extend over the London branch of the Fed. He came to see me and Sharon privately, intent on doing a deal and putting it all to bed. But it was not to be.

In his judgment, Justice Mitting considered that the police officer was 'not the sort of man who would have had the wit, imagination or inclination to invent on the spur of the moment an account of what a senior politician had said to him in a temper'. He ended by saying he was 'satisfied at least on balance of probabilities that Mr Mitchell did speak the words alleged or something so close to them as to amount to the same, including the politically toxic word "pleb"'.

I was at the back of the court surrounded by my family and friends, who had turned up in support. When I left the Courts of Justice to meet a phalanx of cameras and photographers outside, I thanked my legal team, made clear I was bitterly disappointed by the judgment and said it was 'time to bring the matter to a close and get on with our lives'. I was subsequently obliged to pay £80,000 to the police officer and faced legal bills of around £2 million. We took out a hefty mortgage.

Nearly two years later, on the evening of 7 September 2016, I was astonished to be hailed across the drawing room of a London club by the same Justice Mitting with the words 'I hope we are not on bad terms.'

Here we were in the most establishment of settings and the judge behaves as if we were at prep school together and all is forgiven in a 'good chaps' sort of way. His decision was all in a day's work for him, never mind the huge emotional and career cost to me – not to mention the financial one.

In the months that followed, my health collapsed and I started to suffer from serious depression. To begin with I thought there was nothing to be done about it except to just crack on. After all, there was a clear reason for my depression: I had lost my ministerial job, and the savings that Sharon and I had worked so hard to make throughout our careers had been wasted on extraordinary legal fees. It all felt like an updated version of Charles Dickens's Jarndyce v. Jarndyce and it drove us to the brink. I was also extremely worried about the effect on both Hannah and Rosie, let alone Sharon, of what my career and actions had done to them. But eventually, at Sharon's insistence, I sought medical help. Looked after by a brilliant psychiatric consultant, the late Jeremy Pfeffer, I began to recover.

Our next discovery was that the legal profession had a whole extra wheeze for making money that we had never heard of. Once legal issues were completed, lawyers would then make money arguing over the levels of their invoices. There appeared to be a ready assumption that legal fees are over-inflated. Special barristers deal with 'costs', so the legal profession could now make even more money by wrangling over them – at length. Expensive letters went back and forth between both sides as we tried to settle with the Police Federation and News International's lawyers. In the business world you meet around a table, have a negotiation and settle. I had done such arbitrations at Lazard. But that would be far too simple and besides would deprive lawyers of the eye-watering earnings involved. In the end we went round the back of the lawyers in dealing with News International and once the intervention of Rebekah Brooks was brought to bear a reasonable compromise was reached.

I had lost my job; there were huge financial consequences, and I felt my reputation was in tatters, but there was nothing for it but to get on with life. I auctioned my rickety old bicycle for £20,000 to raise funds for Nyumbani, a charity in Kenya founded by a Jesuit priest and strongly supported and guided by Jeremy Hunt to provide a home and education for AIDS orphans there. On occasions when my morale slipped, Sharon was there to tell me to man up and get a grip. My flamboyant friend Greg Barker advised, 'Just think of it as a divorce, Andrew, but luckily you get to keep the good doctor.' David Blunkett told me that it takes three years to recover from a searing political resignation, and I thought at the time how long that seemed. But I remember waking up one morning after exactly three years and realising I was over it.

And in the process, I found I'd resigned from the British Establishment.

CHAPTER 12

DIRTY MONEY AND
DIRTY WARS

O nce the dust from Plebgate had subsided, I picked myself up
and focused on those issues I thought most important, while
looking after my constituents, who had generously stood by me
during my troubles.

Since March 2011, I had been heavily involved with the emerging disaster in Syria. I had watched the crisis develop from the
Department for International Development, surrounded by senior
officials who repeatedly warned that a humanitarian catastrophe
was looming.

Like many, I had watched Obama's brilliant Cairo speech in
2009 with rapt attention and optimism. The President had held out
the hand of peace and friendship to the Arab world after the errors
of Iraq, seeking a new beginning in relations between the US and
the Muslim world. Then the touch paper of the Arab Spring had
been lit in Tunisia, with all the promise of change in governance
throughout the region. With hindsight, I wonder how we could
have been so naive.

As the wind fanned the flames of dissent in Syria, President Bashar al-Assad's regime clamped down. Horrific stories of human rights abuse and state-sanctioned murder started to surface from across the country. Citizens brutally and violently driven from their homes began pouring across the border. One of the key points of exit was into Jordan, near a place called Zaatari, and it was here that the Jordanian authorities agreed that refugees could be helped and accommodated.

I had set off, as Development Secretary, in August 2012 to visit Jordan and see what Britain could do to help. Before heading to Zaatari, I met the Jordanian Foreign Minister, who was grateful for our assistance. He reminded me that in terms of water resources Jordan was one of the poorest countries in the world and that the looming refugee crisis could well overwhelm the state; could the EU help? I arrived at Zaatari and saw the terrain which today houses the largest camp for Syrian refugees and one of the biggest in the world. Touring the area with the young impressive Australian charged by the UN to set up the camp, I met Syrian families who had come across the border in the past few days, shot at by the Syrian Army as they fled. The stories were uniformly shocking and all too credible. These were not poor African camp dwellers like the ones I had seen so often in parts of the Democratic Republic of the Congo or Somalia; they were people from a relatively wealthy society – the children wearing designer clothes and almost all clutching mobile phones.

During the day the temperatures soared and dust got everywhere. At night-time in winter it fell below freezing. It was clear that tents would not suffice; portable buildings would be needed by the thousands in the coming months, as traumatised Syrians poured in. I agreed to double the amount of British money we had initially allocated to help. The UN team urgently needed to secure accommodation, food, medical help and a structure to build and equip a small city. To this day it remains the case that the UK has contributed more support and help to Syrian refugees than the whole of the rest of Europe added together.

At the National Security Council meeting in London in summer 2012, when Syria was the principal item on the agenda, a sympathetic David Cameron let me have my say. I argued that there were three actions the UK should take. First, we needed to increase, massively, the amount of humanitarian support we were providing. In particular we needed to make the case for other wealthy countries to open their wallets. The need was not just in Jordan, Lebanon and Turkey – the countries into which civilians were fleeing – but within Syria itself, where the internally displaced were frequently stranded in the open. Also, the host countries would need intelligent support. The one thing life in a camp easily allows is the education of children; they are literally a captive audience. But at the start of this crisis teachers who had fled Syria and found themselves in the camps were not allowed by the local rules to teach – such work had to be done by the nationals of the host country. No plans were made to allow refugees to work or receive training – particularly young men. Efforts to help Jordan to export to the EU or set up EU-sponsored employment zones took ages to advance. It was not only the camps but the host countries that needed sympathetic attention.

Second, I said, we must make an early attempt to disrupt the culture of impunity. Technology, and in particular mobile phone photography, meant we could hold to account human rights abusers for their actions – no matter how long it took. Whether it be electronic intercepts of instructions to bomb, or pictures of soldiers brutalising civilians, the evidence must be kept and compiled for use in a courtroom on a future occasion. Who had believed in the Bosnian crisis that we would ever be able to bring the war criminals to justice? Yet many had ended up in The Hague. It was agreed that the Foreign Office would handle this – probably from Beirut. Both these two propositions carried the support of the Prime Minister and the NSC.

Third, I suggested, we should make clear that together with our allies we reserved the right to move naval and air assets to the eastern end of the Mediterranean and to RAF Akrotiri and use Cruise missiles to take out concentrations of weaponry, military and command structures if we had evidence that they were being used to attack innocent civilians.

This final proposition did not receive much support. Nick Clegg thought it particularly inadvisable. But as we left the Cabinet Room, the Chief of the Defence Staff, General David Richards, with whom I had established a considerable rapport during the Libyan campaign, whispered in my ear, 'I don't think we'll be hearing any more suggestions from the military that you are a pacifist tree hugger!'

Of course, just weeks later I moved from DfID to become Chief Whip, and stood down shortly afterwards, but I continued my interest in the Syrian refugee crisis from the back benches. The situation went from bad to worse as the catastrophe unfolded. It was not long before nearly half the Syrian population was on the move. Eventually 5 million people would be internally displaced, with around 5 million more in surrounding countries. More than

1 million others (including much of the cohort of Syrian graduates) would make the perilous journey across the Mediterranean in leaky boats, placing themselves in the hands of the modern-day equivalent of the slave trader in the hope of pitching up on a safer and more prosperous European shore. Almost every mistake that could be made now followed.

The UN tried to mediate through the much-respected Kofi Annan. He came close: Assad agreed to go, but only once negotiations on a new settlement had been secured. This was vetoed by the Americans, with the support of Britain, on the grounds that Assad would still be there for the negotiations. It was a dreadful error of judgement by the two governments, as subsequent events have demonstrated. Next, Obama made clear that if the Syrian Army used chemical weapons, a 'red line' would be crossed. A year later, Assad's forces did just that, killing almost 1,500 people, including 400 children, in a sarin gas attack outside Damascus. The use of these appalling weapons was against all international agreement, but the world did nothing, thereby sending a clear signal to the Assad regime that they could do whatever they liked.

A coalition of the US, the UK and France planned to launch air strikes against Syrian forces, but an embarrassing defeat for the UK government in the House of Commons put paid to British involvement, and with little appetite in Congress for further action in the Middle East, the Americans backed down as well. I strongly supported David Cameron's instincts on military intervention, but the long shadow of Iraq and a certain lack of definition (coupled with borderline duplicity by the opposition) persuaded the Commons to deny the government its wish.

To complete the tale of international dysfunctionality, the

European Union totally failed to measure up to its responsibilities. Boatloads of immigrants washed up on the Continent. They came to rest mainly in Italy, on the island of Lampedusa, or in Greece. Both countries were largely left to cope on their own. There was little sense of European solidarity, and the appalling result of European governments' failure to act meant displaced people making their way up through middle Europe towards Germany, Scandinavia or Calais in the hope of a better life.

Together with Clare Short, who set up DfID after Labour's 1997 election win and was a considerable and respected figure in the international development community, I made a joint visit to Gaziantep in Turkey and the Syrian border in early 2016 to see the logistical difficulties and to visit refugee camps in Turkey. We met some of the brave humanitarians who were delivering tents, food and medicines into embattled areas throughout Syria. We saw for ourselves the immense generosity of the Turkish people taking in millions of Syrians both in overwhelmed border towns and in some of the best-run and most humane refugee camps either of us had ever seen. Clare Short and I come from very different backgrounds and do not have many political views in common, but we were entirely united in our outrage at the failure of the international community. Without much difficulty we managed to produce a joint op-ed for *The Times*, agreed and crafted between us during the night flight back from Turkey to London.

Back in Syria, the fighting had zeroed in on Aleppo – one of the great cities of the world – where fierce resistance had erupted. It became clear that the Syrian regime, aided by Russian air power, was deliberately targeting hospitals. With red crosses emblazoned across their roofs, hospitals could not possibly be mistaken for military targets. There could be no doubt that war crimes were being committed, and committed with impunity. The low level of international support for the internally displaced was compounded by British anti-terrorism legislation making it difficult to send money and supplies to areas of deepest need within Syria.

As Aleppo was pounded back to the Stone Age, a British doctor, David Nott, was operating in one of the hospitals targeted by the regime. As the sirens sounded the alarm for yet another attack, David was urged to take cover. But he was operating on a small child who would die if he left in mid-operation. Exhausted and fatalistic, David refused and, with the anaesthetist, continued with the operation. The hospital was hit, but they – and the baby – survived.

When David returned from Aleppo, he was invited to lunch with the Queen. He told the story on *Desert Island Discs*, in one of that programme's most memorable episodes in more than seventy years. David Nott has acted ever since to prick the international conscience of the world over Syria. He certainly pricked mine. His evidence enabled me to persuade the Speaker of the House of Commons to grant, most unusually, an emergency debate on what was happening in Syria, which then took precedence over all government business.

After the 2015 election, Jo Cox, who had just been elected to the House of Commons, came to see me to ask whether we could team up to run a new all-party group, Friends of Syria, and I readily agreed. We worked closely together until Jo was murdered in 2016. She was a bundle of energy and determination and I adored her. On one occasion we went together to take tea with the Russian Ambassador and to remonstrate about the appalling war crimes committed in Aleppo. He had previously complained that I had described Russia's actions in the House of Commons as no different in principle from the bombing of Guernica by the Nazis in the Spanish Civil War. We agreed that Jo would do most of the talking, while I conversed with the fourth person in the meeting, who was probably from Russian intelligence. We left an hour later, Jo with her head held high and a seasoned Russian diplomat reduced to incoherence as he tried to defend the indefensible.

After she died, there were tributes to her in the House of Commons. Once the front benches had spoken, I did the main contribution on behalf of the Tories. It was all I could do to get through it without breaking down.

*   *   *

Syria was not my only preoccupation internationally; the other major crisis, in which Britain was rather more directly involved, was that of Yemen. I knew little about the country when the war started in late 2014. It had provided a low drum beat of concern while I was at DfID, but because the President, Ali Abdullah Saleh, was a personal friend of Alan Duncan, my Minister of State at the department, I had left him in charge of our day-to-day involvement. I carefully watched over our humanitarian aid spending there, which was significant, and over safety issues, which became increasingly serious until I decided the last DfID representative had to leave. The final straw came when an RPG round went through the back window of a DfID Land Rover.

Under Ali Abdullah Saleh, the country had remained reasonably unified, but the Saudis took a strongly proprietorial approach to Yemen – basically because they bankrolled the entire country. As Yemen started to fall apart, the Houthis – a Yemeni resistance movement who oppose Saudi influence in the country – took over the capital and increasingly part of the north. The Saudis went to war. But being unwilling to put large numbers of troops on the ground, and preferring to conduct warfare from 30,000ft, the Saudis were always going to be fighting a losing battle.

The US and Britain are responsible for supplying much of Saudi Arabia's armament, in the process underwriting thousands of high-quality jobs in the British defence industry. Throughout this struggle I have never called for an arms embargo on Yemen. But the status quo has become increasingly difficult to defend.

Saudi Arabia has every right to protect itself. It is a rich country surrounded by enemies and is well able to buy the arms that it needs. If Britain supplies weapons, we can at least influence their use in accordance with the rules of war and our arms export licences are the toughest to secure in the world. That at least was my theory. In practice, the Saudi coalition was bombing this poor country and destroying whatever infrastructure they had. As the war gathered pace, night after night the Saudi Air Force pounded away, killing civilians and destroying the basic essentials for life and disease control. I became increasingly concerned that the war was unwinnable by the Saudis, who were being outmanoeuvred politically, militarily and in the court of public opinion. The dangerous Shia/Sunni divide loomed large too, with the Saudis driving the Houthis into the arms of the Iranians. The Houthis are Zaidis, but in these circumstances they and the Iranians have become natural allies.

The international community gave official support to President Hadi, the elected leader of Yemen. But Hadi's was the only name on the ballot paper at the election and most other states have continued to recognise him long after his mandate expired. In theory he has a toehold of rule in Aden but actually he spends most of his time in Riyadh or on an Emirati warship. He is the only President I know of who has to make a state visit to his own country.

To me, the issue was made worse because Britain held the pen on Yemen at the United Nations. The world looked to us for leadership on this and yet we gave all the appearance of being owned for commercial reasons by the Saudis. Indeed, on one occasion at the UN a British statement on Yemen had to be rewritten by the Russians before it could proceed because it was hopelessly one-sided. Meanwhile, Yemen was being blockaded by land, sea and air. The Saudis accused the Iranians of arming the Houthis, but it was not clear how significant arms could be delivered in the face of the blockade. Some small fast boats were getting through, but nothing of size.

Meanwhile, hideous evidence of a mounting famine was becoming clear. The port of Hodeida, through which the bulk of Yemen's food arrived from overseas, was similarly blockaded. We reached the ludicrous position where one arm of the British government was supporting the destruction of this port while another, DfID, was using British money to pay to re-equip and reopen it. I started asking questions in the Commons about whether this was really the sort of cause we should be supporting.

In December 2016, I was asked by Jamie McGoldrick, the head of the UN in Yemen, whether I would make a visit to see for myself what was happening on the ground. No European politician had been able to visit the capital, Sana'a, and the northern areas. McGoldrick had apparently shown the Houthis the reports of what I had said in Parliament and they agreed that I could pay them a visit in the New Year. Meanwhile, I had always regarded myself (and still do) as a friend of the Saudis and was on good terms with the Saudi Ambassador in London in spite of obvious disagreement. The Saudis who controlled Yemen's air space agreed that I could go, and Oxfam, which has a significant presence there, helped organise the non-UN aspects of my visit.

The night before I left, a Foreign Office junior minister called, ostensibly to offer a briefing but in reality to suggest that I would be on my own and that the British government would do nothing if I got into trouble. The only way to get to Sana'a at the time was via Djibouti, a former French colony on the Horn of Africa. No Brits tend to visit and I was well entertained by the honorary British Consul – a Frenchman with outstanding connections whose services the Foreign Office had managed to secure at virtually no cost. I flew into Sana'a on a plane chartered by the World Food Programme. The other passengers were at the grittier end of the humanitarian system. We travelled across the sea to Yemen with two Saudi war planes passing alongside.

As we landed, I saw the airport littered with burned-out hulks on the side of the runway. I was whisked into the city to the UN headquarters, where the different arms of the UN explained their deployment. This was followed by a briefing with Oxfam and the other NGOs working on the ground there. As we drove through Sana'a, I saw the devastation caused by nightly bombing raids. I called at the meeting house where a funeral gathering had recently been attacked by Saudi jets, killing 180 mourners. On that occasion the aircraft went round again for a second bombing run just to make sure.

This and other alleged war crimes have been investigated – not by an independent international team but, at British insistence, by the Saudis, a process akin to a student marking their own homework and entirely lacking any credibility. That night I stayed in UN accommodation hearing from the experts in the field. They told me there was clear evidence of famine and cholera on the ground; the humanitarian services were being gradually overwhelmed. Travelling through Sana'a that afternoon I had noticed emaciated children leaning listlessly against doorways, the older ones chewing khat, a low-octane stimulant drug much loved in that part of the world.

During the night I was awoken by three separate bombing attacks. I knew I was safe sleeping in UN accommodation, but it must have been terrifying for the families in Sana'a who faced the ever-present danger of becoming collateral damage.

The next day I made the journey to Sa'dah, the northern city and Houthi stronghold, travelling in a UN convoy with a heavily armed Houthi escort at both ends. The Saudis had agreed to deconflict the convoy on its way there and back. Driving through beautiful countryside, I saw the exceptional Yemeni architecture. Every few miles we passed through roadblocks manned by khat-chewing armed soldiers. We stopped at a camp organised and run by Oxfam, who had cleverly agreed to restore water to a large nearby town in return for local agreement that around 2,000 displaced people could be accommodated on this arid plain, supplied and assisted by Oxfam and British philanthropy.

We arrived in Sa'dah in the late afternoon. The city had posters up, some in English (perhaps for my benefit), saying 'the British and Americans are killing our children'.

That evening I met representatives from welfare groups working in Sa'dah. With the aid of an interpreter, I learned the terrible humanitarian cost the city had paid. One of those who came to talk to me was a woman dressed from head to toe in black. With eyes blazing she pulled out from the folds of her robe two pieces of shrapnel. 'These are your country's gifts to my people,' she said. That night I slept in the basement of the UN compound – a fortified encampment against whose walls petrol tankers would cluster each night, in the hope that the Saudi Air Force would not bomb the succulent target positioned there.

The next day I met the Governor and we went together to meet the group responsible for demining and defusing ammunition in the area. This initiative had been led by a former British Army major and funded in part by the British. As I was told in detail about their work, the bizarre absurdity of the situation was reinforced. The Governor and I made our way through the rubble to a school he said had been destroyed by British munitions – the markings on which they had carefully preserved as evidence. I was taken into a large tent where forty eleven-year-olds were being taught, their textbooks – indeed, their tent – paid for by Britain. As I came in, they stood up and started chanting in much the same way as younger children might stand and recite a nursery rhyme. 'What are they saying?' I asked.

The interpreter explained, 'They are chanting "Death to the Saudis and death to America" – but out of respect for your visit they have been told to cut out the third stanza.'

Passing along the devastated city streets (reminiscent by now of my visit to Mogadishu), we arrived at a hospital teeming with staff and patients. The medical charity Médecins Sans Frontières had withdrawn a short while before because it was too dangerous for their staff to remain. I climbed the steps to the top floor of the building to visit what is the most upsetting place in a developing world hospital: the ward dealing with malnutrition. As I saw these suffering children, mostly accompanied by their mothers, with pain and misery in their eyes, I was told how proud I should be that the ward was partly funded by the British.

At the end of the visit, the Governor took me up onto the ancient walls of the city for a final view of the devastation and served from an ornate pot the best cup of coffee I have ever tasted; before the war, coffee was one of Yemen's leading exports.

As we left for the long journey back to Sana'a, my interpreter asked if I remembered the woman who the night before had shown me the shrapnel fragments. I said I did indeed. 'Well,' he said, 'I did not accurately translate what she said.' What she had actually said was: 'These are your gifts and tomorrow we will get you.' I told him it was just as well he hadn't told me, as the city tour would have had to be cancelled – too many people could have been put in harm's way.

Once back in Sana'a, I went to meet the Houthi Foreign Minister, Hisham Sharaf Abdullah, with whom I got on well. He was American-educated, smart, cynical and persuasive. We went together to see Saleh Ali al-Sammad, the Houthi leader, who told me that in spite of Britain's 'appalling' conduct, he wanted the UK (and the Russians) to mediate with the Saudis. He said that as a token of goodwill he would agree to withdraw all Houthi assets 20 kilometres from the Saudi border and cease sporadic missile attacks on Saudi territory. In return he expected an end to indiscriminate Saudi bombing. The night before, a bus with school children had been hit while returning to Sana'a, killing twenty-eight, their bodies laid out at the side of the road, together with their satchels and school smocks. Apparently, the target had been a petrol station.

I promised to brief the Foreign Office and thanked him for letting me come. He was generous about my visit and gave me a magnificent Houthi knife, which the UN managed to get back to the UK. From our conversation it was clear that he was a dove when it came to the peace talks. Alas, he would be killed by the Saudis in an air strike in April 2018. My final visit was to see the former President, Ali Abdullah Saleh, at a secret location. He owned numerous fine houses across Sana'a which the Saudis were busy identifying and destroying. Hisham Sharaf Abdullah and I were obliged to change cars a couple of times en route, hidden from Saudi eyes in the sky, under a bridge.

Ali Abdullah Saleh had largely recovered from the attempt on his life and his experience in Saudi Arabia, where he had effectively been incarcerated by the Saudis. But he was not well. His party, the GPC, was allied with the Houthis – much to the fury of the Saudi leadership, who had bankrolled him for years. We talked about ways of de-escalating the conflict and about how a new constitution could be developed. It was not an encouraging conversation. The former President subsequently fell out with the Houthis and was murdered in December 2017.

Once back in the UK, I briefed the Permanent Secretary at the Foreign Office and at their invitation visited the Saudi government in Riyadh. I saw the Saudi Ambassador to Yemen, who was effectively in charge of the politics of the war under the Crown Prince MBS, as well as the head of the Saudi central intelligence agency. The British Ambassador to Saudi as well as his counterpart to

Yemen, who was living in Riyadh, came with me. At the meeting I respectfully tried to suggest that the Saudis would lose this war, were guilty of perpetrating a famine, radicalising Yemeni youth and losing badly to the Iranians, who for precious little effort were humiliating them. This message was heard in mainly silent distaste and irritation, though the head of the intelligence service did give me his magnificent worry beads as a present when I left.

While Britain can be proud that around the world its values are respected, our recent involvement in Yemen has been both confusing and disreputable. Elsewhere, our country has done much good by helping desperate people in some very dark circumstances. Let us hope that our profoundly unwise involvement in and support for the Saudi coalition in Yemen may be redeemed by the part we play in securing peace and prosperity there in the future.

* * *

If Britain's involvement in Yemen supporting the Saudi coalition is a badge of shame, America's engagement in Guantánamo Bay is probably one of its greatest errors.

By 2015, more than 100 of the original 780 captives remained in the notorious military detention camp – including the last British prisoner, Shaker Aamer, who had been seized by bounty hunters in Afghanistan and held by US forces without trial or charge for more than thirteen years, during which time he was allegedly tortured. David Cameron had asked President Obama – twice – to release him back to the UK, and though the President had agreed, nothing had happened.

After the 2015 election, I had hoped to return to the government and David had generously indicated that was shortly his intention. Wondering what I might do in the interim to help, and mobilised by my newfound antipathy to state abuse, I joined Shaker's cause. David Davis and I found ourselves as the two Tory officers for the All-Party Group to Free Shaker Aamer under chairman John Mc-Donnell and secretary Jeremy Corbyn. David and I would turn up to meetings of the group on the fifth floor of 1 Parliament Street, populated largely by left-wing activists who viewed David and me, at least at the outset, with considerable suspicion. They were little comforted by John's assurances that 'despite being Tories, these two are OK'. I learned from these meetings that John McDonnell was an effective organiser.

It was agreed that a parliamentary delegation should go to the US to see if we could secure Shaker's release. John McDonnell was not well enough to come, so David Davis and I were despatched as the Conservative team, along with Jeremy Corbyn and Andy Slaughter for Labour.

I had known Jeremy Corbyn since 1983 when he was first the Labour candidate for Islington North and I was chairman of the local Conservative association. I have always liked him and, although I agree with few of his views, respected his political consistency. My wife has been a GP working on his patch and they both spoke extremely well of each other. Andy Slaughter has a reputation as a forensic lawyer who has skilfully interrogated government ministers and is respected on our side of the House. When we four rugged backbenchers set off, I was the only former Cabinet minister in the group, but not long after, two of our number became respectively Leader of Her Majesty's Opposition and the Cabinet minister responsible for the Brexit negotiations.

There was clearly a pecking order of seniority on this visit as far as the organisers, the international legal action charity Reprieve, were concerned: on the flight out to Washington, David and I sat perfectly happily at the back of the aircraft, noting that Andy Slaughter was placed in business class. There was no sign of Jeremy. On arrival, David and I were given adjacent rooms in the hotel while Andy was placed in a luxury suite and Jeremy allocated the presidential suite on the top floor. David and I concluded that perhaps he had been transported across the Atlantic in a private jet.

In Washington, we visited the Hill and had meetings with Senator John McCain, who was particularly interesting also for his insight into the misbehaviour of the British intelligence service in Libya in the rendering of Abdel Hakim Belhaj back to Tripoli – evidence I subsequently passed on to the British police. Much later Belhaj's wife received compensation from Britain and an apology from the Prime Minister.

John McCain strongly supported our position on Shaker and urged us to make our case to the administration with vigour. There were other equally important meetings with Congress. One senator said he wanted Guantánamo closed because it was not fair on the US guards having to work there. Over lunch for the four of us in the garden of the beautiful British residence in Washington, the not surprisingly wary and nervous British Ambassador, Sir Peter Westmacott, was helpful. It must have been one of his more unusual delegations of MPs. We particularly wanted to meet the US Guantánamo envoy, and the Ambassador arranged for this to take place. Twenty minutes before the meeting, the envoy indicated he was not minded to attend, but the Ambassador sprang into action and persuaded him to do so.

We met at the State Department. The Guantánamo envoy arrived, stretched out his arms and yawned. Five officials from the State Department sat on his right and three from the Department of Defense on his left. 'Gentlemen, what can I do for you?' the envoy languidly opened the proceedings. Over the course of the next hour, the four of us in our different ways expressed outrage at the way the US were treating their oldest allies. If he is guilty of something, charge him, we said; he has been locked up for thirteen years without due process; he has never seen his son; the British Prime Minister has asked for his release; our country has stood shoulder to shoulder with you in Afghanistan, shedding blood and spending treasure. Other prisoners were being released to third countries, including in Latin America, where the US were paying the host country to take them. How could the US treat the UK in this way?

The US response was deeply suboptimal. They alleged that Shaker had been a note-taker for Osama bin Laden. It was far more likely that he had been in the wrong place at the wrong time – when the Afghans were handing over any foreigner to the US for a financial bounty. There was some suggestion that the Brits would not constrain him (to which we replied that we operate under the rule of law) and that he would disappear back into the terrorist underworld (at which we pointed out that we have intelligence services too).

As we were wheeled out of the meeting, the senior State Department official ran after us and said, 'Thank goodness you guys said what you did – it is the Department of Defense that is the problem.' We reiterated the point that our visit should not have been necessary and that they should release him at once.

In a wash-up afterwards, we concluded that we would probably fail in our attempt to get him out but at least a note had been taken by the American system and an argument made. The envoy had looked particularly irritated at being berated in front of his colleagues, but he had no answer to the legitimate questions put to him save for the inertia of the US legal system and American might.

That night, Reprieve took the four of us out to dinner. During the course of the meal, David and I asked Jeremy whether he intended to stand for the leadership of the Labour Party. A vacancy had opened up following the general election and Ed Miliband's resignation. Jeremy replied, 'No! It's John McDonnell's turn.' Such decisions were made by the left of the Labour Party when they decided who should carry the torch in any leadership election. When the meeting took place, John McDonnell was not well and nobody else wanted to do it, so Jeremy stepped up. The rest, as they say, is history.

A couple of months later and to our considerable surprise we learned that Shaker was to be released and a plane sent to collect him. A few days after he returned, he came into the House of Commons to thank his supporters for their help. The meeting was held in the shadow Cabinet Room and hosted by John McDonnell. Dominic Grieve, David Davis and I attended briefly along with many of the committee of largely Labour activists who had campaigned for so long for his release.

Since his return, Shaker Aamer has said little. He has chosen to focus on his family and children after more than thirteen years of captivity in the camp which has arguably done more than anything else to undermine the moral leadership and reputation of the

United States of America. Shaker's only public statement of note has been to say that anyone who wishes to harm the UK and its citizens 'should get the hell out'.

*　　*　　*

It is usually difficult to secure change to government legislation from the back benches, but in a hung parliament with good cross-party cooperation there are unusual opportunities. I learned early from my involvement in international development that huge sums of money were being stolen from poor countries by corrupt politicians, dishonest businessmen and greedy warlords. Lack of governance enabled businesses, particularly in the extractive industries, to pay 'commissions' to smooth their way.

Anti-bribery legislation in America and Britain (introduced in the latter by the Cameron government) has had some effect. The Extractive Industries Transparency Initiative has done much to help by introducing greater openness: asymmetric knowledge has been tackled, so that both sides, not just sophisticated business, know the value of the assets to be extracted. This should lead to a fair distribution of profit between the extractor and the host country and thereafter a proper use of revenue for public services and goods to the advantage of their citizens; that at least is the theory.

During my time at DfID, we gave strong support to police involved in tracking down stolen funds. One of the most prominent cases was that of James Ibori, the Governor of the Delta State in Nigeria, who had used his wife, his lawyer and his mistress to launder his ill-gotten gains. We worked hard to identify and recover stolen funds and to see that they were returned to the Nigerian government. Such work is extremely painstaking and drawn-out, with the criminals all too often one step ahead of the law enforcement agencies.

During the 2013 G8 summit, held in Northern Ireland, David Cameron and George Osborne had tried to secure a significant boost for transparency in the international effort to identify and track down illicit funds – both to tackle tax evasion and to intercept money stolen from Africa and Africans. The United Kingdom showed the way by introducing open registers of beneficial ownership, meaning that significant company holdings and property in Britain could not shelter anonymously behind a wall of secrecy. It was a landmark moment for transparency. But we could only do this for our own UK-based interests. A company registered in the British Virgin Islands could still get away with anonymity even though it owned British assets. The National Crime Agency in Britain believed that between 2 and 5 per cent of global GDP is the subject of money laundering. Of course, no one knows, but even if they are half right, the figure is colossal.

Across the House of Commons on the Labour benches, Dame Margaret Hodge MP was pursuing a similar agenda to mine. Margaret had been a minister in the Blair government and a highly effective chair of the Public Accounts Committee. She had a formidable reputation for skewering those who came before her committee either ill-prepared or intent on obfuscation. She was concerned both by the non-payment of tax by wealthy tax evaders and by international companies who shielded their profits to deny the payment of tax where such profits were earned. From our different perspectives we arrived at a unity of purpose.

Over a cup of tea in Margaret's palatial office in Portcullis

House, surrounded by photographs of her children and numerous grandchildren as well as her late husband – a man venerated in Islington as a public-spirited lawyer – Margaret suggested we should team up. Theresa May's government was backtracking on the Cameron–Osborne agenda for openness, and the publication of the Panama and Paradise Papers had helped to uncover the extraordinary levels of theft and malfeasance perpetrated by the rich, powerful and corrupt.

In particular, the British Overseas Territories (mainly in the Caribbean) were unwilling to implement open registers on the grounds that the closed registers they had already set up were quite sufficient. They pointed out that their registers of ownership were available to answer any questions from law and order and revenue authorities within twenty-four hours, and on a matter to do with terrorism within an hour. But the problem with this argument had been vividly exposed: closed registers certainly enabled the legal authorities to secure answers to specific questions, but the Panama and Paradise Papers showed clearly that closed registers would not expose enough of the criminal landscape to enable anyone to join the dots and uncover the ever more expert and cunning devices of money launderers.

The EU responded well to these arguments and published Economic Directive No. 5 to usher in open registers across Europe by 2022. On behalf of the Overseas Territories, the Foreign Office refused to help and the government decided to resist any question of imposing these registers on them.

Margaret and I carefully prepared an amendment drafted with the support of experts which said that if the Overseas Territories did not themselves set up open registers by the end of 2021, then they would be imposed on them by an Order in Council – an arcane device using the royal prerogative by which Westminster could, if necessary, assert its will.

In discussion with Boris Johnson, then Foreign Secretary, we agreed to extend these provisions to the end of 2022 to take account of the recent hurricanes which had done such terrible damage to the Caribbean islands and their economies. We then lay in wait for a suitable Bill to amend. Sure enough, one appeared and I went off to see Julian Smith, the government Chief Whip, to explain why I thought the government should accept our amendment but also to make clear that if the government refused to do so, I was pretty sure we had the numbers to force this through. As a former Chief Whip, I apologised for the gamekeeper turned poacher approach, but as he had previously been a PPS in my team at DfID I hoped he had some personal sympathy on the issue and would not see it as a gratuitous attack on the government.

I quickly gathered enough like-minded senior Conservatives (also allowing in my calculation for 10 per cent of them to be burned off in a government fightback). Margaret thought her relationship with her own Whips' Office was somewhat strained and sent me in to negotiate with the Labour Chief Whip. I knew and liked Nick Brown from our time on the Finance Bill back in 1988, when late at night he would entertain the committee in the evening session after dinner with a witty and incisive cross-examination of complex government financial manoeuvres. He promptly agreed to support our amendment, saying that he would regard it as a badge of shame if the Conservative government were to win as a result of all Labour Members not being there.

My next port of call was Vince Cable and the Liberals, who

were completely on side, followed by Ian Blackford for the SNP. 'Yes, Andrew, we are definitely on side, but I will have to go now as I am on Skye dipping my sheep.' Subsequently, the Foreign Office tried to persuade the SNP that supporting our amendment would somehow undermine Scotland's relationship with Westminster, but the Nationalists were not dissuaded.

The weekend before the debate and vote were due to take place, government ministers and whips rang up the Tory signatories to the amendment and tried to persuade them to withhold their support. A few recanted but not enough. On the Sunday I was taking my elder daughter, Hannah, to see the double Harry Potter show at Cambridge Circus. As we came out at half-time, I saw that David Gauke, the Lord Chancellor, had phoned several times. He had rung to say that we were causing him serious trouble over open registers, and the Crown Dependencies were complaining to the palace. Would we consider excluding them? I told him we were not planning to include the Crown Dependencies in this amendment. 'Ah that's fine,' he said and rang off.

On the night before the debate, Theresa May had another go at dissuading the SNP in a meeting with Ian Blackford at No. 10. This was also unsuccessful. The Chief Whip rang me to ask if I was definitely going to proceed; I confirmed that we were and believed we had the numbers.

The next day, the debate started at 4 p.m. after Question Time in the House of Commons. About five minutes before kick-off, the Chief Whip came into the Chamber and up the gangway and sat beside me. 'OK,' he said, 'we surrender – but don't rub our noses in it.' I quickly texted Margaret across the Chamber, who looked up in delight and surprise, just as the Speaker called her to set out our case. The government graciously accepted and the measure went through. According to my calculations, we would have won by seventeen votes.

After our modest victory, Margaret and I then set out to persuade the Crown Dependencies (Guernsey, Jersey and the Isle of Man) that they too should embrace these measures. Their governments were affronted by the suggestion that we should seek to make them do this, and their Chief Ministers came to London to see both Margaret and me to voice their opposition. We suggested to them that their well-governed territories were open to abuse by money launderers and villains looking to warehouse dirty money. As part of the British family of nations they ought to embrace the same laws of transparency as the UK.

Margaret and I flew to the Isle of Man for a visit followed by day trips to Guernsey and Jersey. On each occasion we would meet the politicians first for what was invariably a constructive chat as they worried about the effects on their local economies. We tried to persuade them that they had much to gain from embracing this transparency. We also pointed out that as the footprint of secrecy narrowed, and the Cameron–Osborne agenda advanced towards becoming an international standard, they would inevitably face greater exposure, while deposits in their jurisdictions would come from ever more dubious sources, including drugs, people trafficking and the sex trade. We had a rather tougher time in meetings with the professionals and practitioners, who clearly thought we were out to steal their lunch. The lawyers were the worst.

Not long after we completed these visits, Margaret spotted a Bill which the government required as part of the Brexit legislation and which we could amend to impose open registers on the

Crown Dependencies if they did not voluntarily introduce them. The government spotted this as well. Unusually, the business for the following week was not informally available on the Wednesday afternoon and only came to light on Thursday morning at the start of Business Questions in the House. I had smelt a rat and had already had some discussions with Conservative colleagues whom I thought likely to support even when faced with a much tougher counterblast from government ministers than on the earlier occasion. We quietly set about assembling a team of colleagues who we knew would withstand the pressure. I asked my Tory colleagues to sign up to the amendment only if they were adamant they would not allow themselves to be burned off. By 4 p.m. we had assembled nineteen Tories, eighteen Labour, seven Lib Dems and enough SNP support to demonstrate the seriousness of our purpose.

The government went into over-drive (Crown Dependency Lieutenant Governors had complained to the Queen's private secretary), but by Sunday night not one Conservative MP had recanted. Over the weekend Ken Clarke had been phoned by no fewer than three Cabinet ministers.

And so it was that on Monday, faced with imminent defeat, the government pulled the business and the House rose early after Questions and Statements. I cannot remember any other occasion when this has happened in the past thirty years.

Meanwhile, Margaret and I had also been trying to press our case by other means. Thanks to Ken Macdonald, the distinguished former Director of Public Prosecutions and Warden of Wadham College, Oxford, we secured a compelling legal opinion that suggested that Westminster had the absolute right to legislate for the Crown Dependencies by Order in Council when it affected

UK security or good domestic order. What with our efforts, the EU directive and some strong and influential front-page support in the *Financial Times*, sentiment amongst the Crown Dependency ministers had been changing. The Deputy Chief Minister of Guernsey, Gavin St Pier, invited me to the Trafalgar Day dinner at the East India Public Schools Club. This was a first for me. Union Jack waistcoats predominated and we sang 'Jerusalem' at least twice. Over the port, Gavin indicated that the Crown Dependencies would introduce open registers but wanted until 2023 to do so. They hoped this would end any question of precedent-setting legislation from Westminster. I took this back to Margaret and we agreed that this would do.

There was one final shot required. The Foreign Office had played dirty over the Overseas Territories. Our amendment, agreed by the House of Commons, and now law, said that if the Overseas Territories did not set up these registers by the end of 2022, then an Order in Council would oblige them to do so. The Foreign Office, however, had sneakily interpreted this as meaning that by the end of 2022, if these registers had not been introduced, an Order in Council would then be issued stating that implementation would be one year later. This was clearly not what Parliament had intended.

Accordingly, it was arranged with the Speaker that points of order about this would be raised in the House. One Labour and one Conservative former Development Secretary (Hilary Benn and myself) and one Labour and one Conservative former chair of the Public Accounts Committee (Margaret Hodge and David Davis) in turn got up to complain to the Speaker that this sleight of hand by the Foreign Office was an abuse of Parliament which should not be tolerated. Speaker Bercow – at some length – made clear that the Foreign Office interpretation was clearly not the will of Parliament. However, in the end we concluded that we should not let the best be the enemy of the good and the Overseas Territories got a further year. As it happened, once Dominic Raab became Foreign Secretary the Foreign Office changed tack and have now become supporters of this measure.

In the fight against dirty money and money laundering – theft by any other name – we must gradually focus on eradicating these tax havens. As we do so, money laundering will be driven to more dubious and less well-governed locations. Villains will sleep less easy worrying about the safety of their ill-gotten gains. That is why it is so important that respectable locations under the British flag bear down on it. Credible research suggests that London, the Overseas Territories and the Crown Dependencies may inadvertently be conduits for up to 40 per cent of worldwide money laundering.

The Americans are also taking an interest in what the UK has now done, as I discovered when I was recently invited (courtesy of the Foreign Office, to my surprise) to meet and discuss this agenda with senators, representatives and members of the powerful Banking Committee in the US. America is not yet at the stage of introducing open registers, but there is now sufficient concern about these practices in several states, and anxiety about dirty money, to ensure that the wheels are turning there too in the fight against secrecy and the money laundering of profits from often horrendous crimes.

CHAPTER 13

WHAT I HAVE LEARNED

I hope I am following the precedent set by Norman Fowler, my predecessor as the Member of Parliament for Royal Sutton Coldfield, who wrote a book in what was very much his mid-career. I do not regard this as 'thank you and goodnight'. There are many causes for which I wish to continue campaigning – the issues that most affect my constituents in the royal town as well as more general matters which I believe greatly affect my children's generation and where we who are currently 'at the crease' need to do better – not least around human rights and civil liberties.

I have been part of most of Britain's Establishment – prep school, public school, the University of Cambridge, the City of London, the Privy Council and the Cabinet. But I have somehow become more internationalist, less Anglocentric, less trustful and less respectful of the organs of state, and generally less certain. But overall I am definitely an optimist.

I think the 2020s could be the most exciting decade in which to be alive. But in terms of the ferocious twin challenges of pandemics and climate change, as well as inequality and the dangers stemming from populism, nationalism and the emasculation of the international rules-based system, it is also, paradoxically, a world fraught with new dangers.

I was born in 1956, in the midst of the baby boom, four years before Harold Macmillan's 'Winds of Change' speech which ushered in the dismantling of empire, though the winds of change were already very much in evidence. It was the year Britain's questionable moral authority and military might were laid bare by the fiasco of the Suez Canal, while in Hungary the Soviets were brutally suppressing a popular uprising. In the same year, rock and roll took off, and the social and cultural hierarchies of post-war Britain began to fracture. 1956 has since been voted the best year in which to be born, with the children of the 1950s the most content of any subsequent generation.

Life for the vast majority on our planet has improved. Before Covid stalled progress we had never been better off. This is mainly because India and China are powering out of poverty and the extremes of misery across the poor world are at an all-time low. Since 2000, more than 1 billion people have gained access to energy, more than 90 per cent of girls are now in primary school, deaths from malaria – a huge killer of children – are falling and, thanks to Bill Gates, polio is heading for eradication. Deaths from HIV/AIDS have reduced by 50 per cent. Ninety per cent of people now have access to clean water, and greenhouse gas emissions decreased by 13 per cent in the developed world between 1990 and 2018. Since 2014, deaths from terrorism have fallen by 20 per cent. If education, health, cleanliness and security are the keys to liberty – especially for women – then we are at an all-time high. In 1815, one person in 100 lived in a democracy. Now half the world has that privilege and more women ran for office in 2018 than in any previous year in human history.

Between 1988 and 2008, the world signed 650 peace agreements. Negotiations during those twenty years brought more conflicts to a close than in the previous 200. But over the past decade, any illusions that the peace dividend from the end of the Cold War could be realised and a new era of tranquillity ushered in have been blown away. Syrian warfare, Yemeni misery, Libyan turmoil, the Iraq and Afghanistan conflicts, the expansionist rise of China and Russia and the use of chemical weapons have all destabilised our world. Recently, non-state actors kidnapped 276 female Nigerian students aged sixteen to eighteen, underlining the nature of terrorism and undermining our hopes for progress. A two-state solution to the Israel–Palestine issue in the Middle East continues to elude us.

At a time when all these problems for the next generations call for greater cooperation between nations and highlight the benefits of an international rules-based system, narrow nationalism and populism have been on the rise. From President Putin to President Trump to President Xi Jinping, this is the era of the strongman. And for those of us who bemoan this set of circumstances we have to accept that President Trump, although failing to secure re-election in 2020, received the second highest vote ever from his fellow Americans in a free and open election.

As Covid has attacked the hopes and aspirations above all of younger people, it is perhaps little surprise that they are the first generation since the end of the First World War that does not expect to be better off than their parents.

It is particularly dispiriting, therefore, to see my own country at this point deliberately relinquishing its leadership in international development and in tackling the discrepancies in wealth and opportunity which continue to blight our world. Indeed, globalisation and new technology have meant that knowledge is effectively universal, and so is the understanding of the scale of deprivation throughout parts of the world.

While America is the military superpower, Britain had increasingly been seen since 2000 as a development superpower, casting a light in some very dark and conflict-ridden places, respected around the world for its soft power knowledge, leadership and effectiveness. As President Trump's Defense Secretary Jim Mattis memorably noted, whenever development aid was reduced, he had to order more ammunition. Soft power transforms and saves lives; its exercise is very much cheaper than hard power. Sending troops to combat terrorism in Mali while cutting back on aid and development in the same location is a failure of strategic understanding. Helping to build safer and more secure societies and more prosperous and better-governed countries also makes us safer and potentially more prosperous here in the United Kingdom. And while it is not a straightforward equation, helping to build peace and prosperity in the longer term cuts immigration to the richer parts of the world.

Against this background it is astonishing that a British Prime Minister would deliberately dismantle UK leadership in this area. The decision to abolish the Department for International Development, taken secretly and with no consultation, is in my view a quite extraordinary mistake which has been greeted by our friends all around the world with dismay and incomprehension – a view echoed by the hundreds of thousands of British people who strongly support our great international charities, church and faith movements, and for whom this remains a priority. They are proud of Britain's superpower development status and the amazing impact Britain has had on tackling the twin scourges of inequality and poverty which disfigure our world – much of which will now sadly be lost.

Not even to have, as Mrs Thatcher did as Prime Minister, a department for development within the Foreign Office with its own ministerial lead – the Overseas Development Administration – deprives Britain of a centre of expertise and knowledge which has been respected around the world for its international leadership. This was not just because it was a highly regarded government ministry but because it drew together the expertise of Britain's great universities, with their wealth of vital research and knowledge, the capacity for effective intervention on the ground by British international charities, and the unrivalled ability to fashion policy of British think tanks and institutions. It is no surprise that those leaving university who wished to join the British governmental service gravitated overwhelmingly towards the Treasury and DfID. Nor was it just the best of the civil servants that DfID attracted. Because of its strong international reputation, the most experienced civil servants from around the world served in the department, often returning to the UK and giving the British government huge influence in key international organisations like the IMF, the World Bank, and the United Nations. In my first days as DfID Secretary of State, I rather resented when senior civil servants came to tell me that they were leaving for a prestigious international posting. But I soon realised that the flow of people in and out of the department enhanced British influence and spread understanding and the values we supported into the most important and influential international bodies. With DfID destroyed (let no one think that adding a silent 'D' to the FCDO changes anything), there has been an exodus of expertise and knowledge that will not be easy for a future British government to reassemble – destroying at a stroke a key aspect of Global Britain. It is hard to think of any coherent reason to justify such an act of vandalism.

It is also true that while British diplomats are amongst the most effective in the world, serving our country with great dedication, they are not particularly renowned for managing money well. It was generally accepted around Whitehall that 'while the Foreign Office does prose, DfID does money'. Already hard-pressed Ambassadors and High Commissioners taking on the responsibility for multi-million-pound programmes should not fill taxpayers with the confidence that the money will always be well spent. Indeed, the aid and development expenditure that attracts negative attention from the British media has almost always been money spent by departments other than the Department for International Development who lack the knowledge and financial acumen of those who worked in ODA and subsequently DfID. Expenditure in China – largely wasted and unnecessary in development terms – has for the past ten years mostly been a decision of the Foreign Office.

Not content with the destruction of DfID, which the Prime Minister described from the Despatch Box in the House of Commons as a 'cash machine in the sky' spraying around taxpayers' money, Boris Johnson then proceeded to break a promise made by Britain at the UN and a clear manifesto commitment made at the general election just over a year previously – one also enshrined in law – to provide 0.7 per cent of our gross national income for international development. It was suggested that the Covid crisis necessitated this cut. But it was the only expenditure reduction to be announced in the late 2020 comprehensive spending review. And it saves just 1 per cent of the £400 billion borrowed to combat

Covid. The decision also ignored the fact that the 0.7 per cent had been reduced anyway as a result of the British economy contracting steeply during the pandemic. So this was in my view clearly a political and not an economic decision, designed apparently to please those in the so-called Red Wall seats. While it is true that many do not relish taxpayers' money being spent overseas, polling shows that in about the same numbers our fellow citizens do not believe humanitarian aid should be cut. And anyway, as Members of Parliament, we owe our constituents our judgement and should stand by the promises we make.

Because of the way the development budget is configured, with long-term agreements with major international agencies being unaffected, most of these cuts fall on British humanitarian support and so we have seen the unconscionable decision of British ministers announcing cuts of more than 50 per cent in our humanitarian aid to Yemen – a country in the throes of a famine – in the certain knowledge that this will lead to children dying of starvation and in agony as a result. This is surely not the message we aspire to send the world about our values as a nation.

While I did not vote to leave the European Union, this was not out of any affection for the institution itself. As a minister I had seen the sclerotic nature of the Brussels administration and the airs and graces unelected officials bestowed upon themselves. I did think it would have been better for Britain to have exercised more effort in extending its influence within the EU rather than spending our time bitching about it, but I never doubted for a moment that following Brexit we would be able to make our way economically and politically in the world. We can punch above our weight through the influence we secure from our role as one of the five permanent members of the UN Security Council, our position as the second most influential member of the NATO alliance and our pivotal role in the Commonwealth, which as a significant north/south representative organisation punches well below its weight. We also gain immensely from the prominence of the English language, London's pre-eminence as an international financial centre and its legal reputation for settling commercial disputes. In or out of the European Union, Britain remains a major European power.

So it seems all the more extraordinary to me that a British government would destroy its own reputation as a successful international development superpower just as it set out to show the world what 'Global Britain' means.

As our country took the chair of the G7 group of nations in 2021 and hosted the occasion in Cornwall, Britain decided, alone of the G7 countries and in the heart of a worldwide pandemic, to cut its support to the poorest countries. Rather than a confident, assertive act of post-Brexit leadership and British vision, we gave all the appearance of shooting ourselves in the foot and retreating from one of the few areas where our country was internationally lauded and respected. It is little surprise that every living British Prime Minister condemned the decision without qualification.

The final step in this tragedy of errors – dismantling the rules governing development spending – is likely to be taken shortly. The OECD Development Assistance Committee (DAC), set up by the Americans after the war and composed of thirty countries, determines what does and does not qualify as aid and therefore as part of the 0.7 per cent spending. In many ways the rules are more important than the money, since once the rules are dismantled, the stronger voices in Whitehall will plunder the budget – which will then be spent on battleships and bullets and not on international development. If Britain leaves the OCED DAC, a key thread will then have been removed from the international system and from international development. It is true that charity begins at home. But it does not end there. And Britain's huge knowledge and effectiveness in this vital area, which have chimed so well with our influence and national feelings of concern and pride, will have been comprehensively demolished.

One of the key opportunities stemming from Brexit is to put more power into Parliament: that is to say, into the legislature rather than into the executive as decision-making reverts to Westminster. The House of Commons has changed in recent years, much of it for the better. In 1987, I joined a House of Commons that was broadly male and pale. Nowadays, a TV picture of the packed Chamber shows that we look more like the country that elected us, although we have further to go to achieve genuine diversity and gender equality.

Over the years, I have learned that there are three potential stages to a career in the House of Commons. Not everyone is able or wants to pass through all three. The first part encompasses the early years before high office may beckon. The second is your time on the front bench – in government if you are lucky. The third comes after office. Sometimes you may move from the third phase back to the second; often from the second to the third before you wish to do so.

In Stage 1, if you are wise, you will get to know your constituency well and dig in against future political adversity. There is no such thing as a safe seat any more. Tribal political allegiance is at an all-time low. Gone too are the days when you can neglect your constituents. Jo Grimond, the former leader of the Liberal Party, once described meeting a young Conservative MP at King's Cross station who was looking particularly down in the dumps.

'Hello,' he said. 'You're not looking very happy. What's the matter?'

'I've got to go to my constituency,' the young Tory said. 'And I know perfectly well I am going to have to go there again in three months' time too.'

These days any MP – regardless of party – knows that they neglect their constituency at their peril. Whatever else we may do in politics and on the national stage, our constituents and the work we do for them are the baseload of our role and come first. I have learned that much of the job satisfaction from being an MP comes from going the extra mile to help a constituent and through preserving and improving something that matters to those you represent. Members of Parliament are often approached by people who say, 'I have come to see you as my last resort'; people who have fallen through the safety net of state protection or have fallen foul of the system. This is the essence of an MP's constituency work. While the slings and arrows of fortune will affect your progress at Westminster – for good or ill – your reputation in your own constituency is entirely down to you. In many a pub the cry has gone up: 'MPs are all a shower, useless – though ours here is not so bad; she sorted out my aunt's pension problem, helped my daughter find a nursery place. But most of them are a waste of space.' Research still suggests people have a higher regard for their own MP than for the rest. It must be said that many of my colleagues are kinder and more decent than the public image allows. I once entered Sir David Amess's office to hear David dictating a letter to a constituent: 'Dear Mrs Allan, I am writing to say how sorry I have been to learn of the death of Percy. (New paragraph.) Percy, your much-loved budgerigar...'

At Westminster during the first phase, you will learn to tread the tricky pathway between standing up for your own beliefs and sucking up to your party hierarchy. A quote supplied to the media supporting your own party will generally be of little interest, but if you speak out against the government and off the record, you will be surprised and delighted to note that the press describe you as a 'senior and respected member of the House of Commons'. You may even be referred to as a grandee. The sight of a younger member enthusiastically declaiming an unspeakably loyal and partisan question to a grateful minister causes the bile to rise in the throats of the more long-serving but will win an adoring glance from the whip on duty. Not quite cashable promises of preferment will waft your way and encourage you.

You may soon become the parliamentary private secretary to a junior minister. Always hope to serve in the Whips' Office if possible before moving to a ministry. You will learn so much about procedure and about human foibles. The threat to vote against your party will lead to serious and early efforts to dissuade you, since the Whips' Office, like the Jesuits, believe that if you catch 'em early, you keep them for life. When the Chief Whip solemnly informs you that your budding career is over, remember that, like the Mafia, 'it is not personal, only business'. And never forget, if the whips know you have voted against your beliefs in the hope of sucking up to the system and securing promotion, they will smile warmly at you but lose any respect for you.

If you are wise, in your early months and years you will spend time in the Chamber listening and watching. Knowledge of parliamentary tactics and procedure will always serve you well. If you make a point of order, the Speaker will always be more tolerant if you hold up a copy of Erskine May, the parliamentary bible, to support your argument. Using an older edition with different page numbers will get you further tolerance as the clerks struggle with the pagination. Above all, contribute on the issues about which you know and to which you bring experience from outside. The Commons is not meant to be a college of further education. Such issues will hopefully include those of most interest and concern to your constituents. Do not get carried away by the House of Commons. Ensure you remain rooted in your constituency and your friends and family. In the first half of any parliamentary term the Tearoom divides between the ambitious and those whose talents have yet to be recognised or who have been passed over. But in the second half it is between those nervous of losing their seats and those with reason to be more confident.

The September sitting of Parliament – introduced by the New Labour government after 1997 – was driven by complaints in the *Daily Mail* that MPs were off on a three-month holiday. It is an entirely unnecessary parliamentary session and has led to a deterioration of the fabric of the Palace of Westminster because the summer recess no longer affords due time for restorative building work. It also means that select committees and Members of the House of Commons cannot use September to travel and probe while comparing our policies with those in other countries wrestling with the same problems.

During one recess, Tony Banks, a larger than life and extremely amusing Labour MP, went with my father on an all-party mission to the Argentine Parliament in the hope of improving our post-Falklands War relations there. Meeting Tony in the Tearoom queue, I said I hoped he would look after my old dad on their mission. Alarmingly, he replied, 'Ah, yes. Don't you worry about that! We've done a deal. He's going to teach me about wine and I'm going to teach him about sex.'

If you reach Stage 2 and become a minister, appearing at the Despatch Box and being held to account by your colleagues should ensure that you don't get too big for your boots and suffer from 'ministerialitis' – a disease which causes you to think, like the Pharisee, that you are a cut above your fellow Members of the House of Commons. Answering questions is easier than it looks – you can always be reasonable. But you will rightly be extremely wary of misleading the House. If you do, you must immediately return to the Despatch Box, correct the record and apologise. By now the House of Commons will have made up its mind about you and have a view about you both in general and as a minister. It is decent and fair on such occasions.

As a junior minister, try to secure responsibility for an area which is either too complex for your Secretary of State to follow on a daily basis or one in which they are not particularly interested. That way you will get more chance to drive policy and display individual initiative. Above all, look after your private office and they will look after you. One minister so antagonised and mistreated his officials that when the moment came to deliver an important speech in the House of Commons, he turned over page 7 to see the words 'You're on your own, Minister.'

When the question of your promotion arises, remember that views will be gathered about your performance from the Chief Whip and the Permanent Secretary of your department as well as in No. 10. As always in politics, merit and ability are only part of the equation and sometimes don't feature at all. Your face needs to fit and you need to be in the right place at the right time. Such matters are overwhelmingly an issue of good fortune.

As a member of the Cabinet, always remember what it was like to be a junior minister and try to keep them busy. Most junior ministers believe they would do a far better job than their Cabinet boss if only their talents were properly recognised. Some of them will actively plot against you. I was fortunate in having Alan Duncan, a highly capable junior minister, who was not really interested in my job because he believed he would be more suited to being Prime Minister. Nevertheless, I kept him occupied.

When the time comes to return to the back benches – almost always, alas, not in the way or at the time you had hoped – nurse your wounds in private and resist the urge to become bitter. It will corrode your soul and you will be in danger of becoming bad company. Besides, this third stage could be amongst your most enjoyable times in Parliament.

If at this point you can resist the temptation to chuck it all in and depart for pastures new, you now have the chance to make a real contribution to the parliamentary process. You might seek to chair a select committee, which is now almost a separate parliamentary career in its own right. But above all you may acquire an authority born of your independence of thought. Influential backbenchers like David Davis and Margaret Hodge are able to make the political weather. It is hard but possible. You can stand up on the issues you come to believe are important – in my case, international development, human rights and civil liberties. As co-chair of the Friends of Syria and the All-Party Groups on Rwanda and Dignity in Dying – a cause whose time I believe is now overdue – I have the opportunity to make common cause with people from other parties and from the House of Lords. A degree of detachment and independence from slavishly following the party line will make your views generally more interesting – including to the media. But of course you will not forget that you are in the House of Commons because you serve your constituents as a member of your political party rather than because of the brilliance of your views.

And while you are enjoying Stage 3 of your parliamentary life, you can engage too with younger, newer members whose interests and views you hold in common – encouraging and helping those who are making their way up the greasy pole and dispensing useful advice when you have served your time. Shortly after I was elected to the House of Commons, a journalist wrote something unfriend-ly about me in their paper. I bumped into Ken Baker, a senior col-league, who asked me why I looked down in the mouth. I showed him the piece and said I was going to send them a biting riposte. 'Oh, I wouldn't do that,' said Ken. 'Take him out to lunch. That's a much better investment.'

I have made many friends across the House of Commons amongst members of other parties. I won't embarrass them by naming them, but working together across Parliament can be re-warding on many different levels.

Not long ago I visited Twycross Zoo, which is much loved in Sutton Coldfield for the educational input it provides for children as well as its strong involvement in conservation. My old friend

Geoff Hoon, a former Labour Chief Whip, is the chairman of Twycross. As we toured the zoo, we two former Chief Whips from our respective parties lugubriously watched a tiger enthusiastically gnawing its way through the leg of what looked as if it had once been a cow. As whips do, I asked him: if he was able to nominate five former colleagues from the House of Commons to be fed to the tiger, whom might they be? After a moment of reflection, he assured me that they would all be from his own party, and I took little time to admit that my five would all be wearing a blue rosette.

Being a whip gives you an understanding – not always welcome – of human nature. I was brought up to believe in the Christian view that people are essentially good. But over time I have learned that it is better to expect the worst of my fellow human beings so that one can delight in being proved wrong when that turns out not to be the case. In general, whipping experience suggests that men seldom tell the truth about sex or money. This view of human nature has probably also coloured my view of the state. We are led to believe that the state is essentially a force for good and that it will make the right decisions in our interest. But the state is made up of human beings like us, with their own views and prejudices. The state gets things wrong.

During the Covid crisis, Parliament, with considerable misgivings, gave ministers extraordinary powers over our liberties: to say we could not travel, could not hold those we loved, could not be with our partners even when dying, could not see our children. Throughout that time, Parliament could not discharge its duties to scrutinise the executive properly and help them to get it right. Ministers learned that absolute power, as ever, is absolutely divine.

I first understood just how dangerous it is to hold this rose-tinted view of the state when in 2005 Parliament was seriously asked to give the executive the power to hold someone in custody for up to ninety days without any charge being laid against them. As the scales fell from my eyes, the next proposition was that all of us should carry identity cards – by law – with sanctions against us if we failed to do so. This would have been a preposterous extension of state power at the expense of an individual's liberty which would not have made us safer, and in due course I was similarly wary about Covid passports.

I have learned that individual liberties – acquired and in some cases fought for over the centuries – should not lightly be discarded. I have also learned from my interest and involvement in international development the critical importance of a free press as the single most important guarantor of our freedoms. All around the world where a free press exists and journalists are able to go about their investigations unfettered and unthreatened, basic freedoms are safer.

My colleagues complain regularly about the BBC being biased – usually against the governing party. I have never really believed this to be true and like many am continually impressed by the rigour and accuracy of BBC journalism, but the BBC is very much a part of the Establishment and, because of its relationship with the government over funding, wary of offending. When I had my difficulties with the police, it was *Channel 4 News* – fiercely independent of everyone – which took up my case and, importantly, investigated it. The BBC was not remotely interested.

It is fair to say that I have had my ups and downs with the British press, not only on the receiving end of major storms but also enabling me to have my say when I have been at odds with my own party and government. But I have learned that an unruly, disrespectful, cynical and cacophonous press corps is the price we pay for our freedoms and is essential for exposing bad behaviour and even wickedness and corruption amongst the wealthy and powerful.

Of course, this can be uncomfortable. When I was a whip in the 1990s, one of my flock told me the press were certain he was having an affair and were pursuing the matter. I sympathised and lazily assumed it was probably true. He told me his life was being made a complete misery. His wife didn't believe him, his children were upset; indeed, he nearly had a nervous breakdown. In the end, it emerged that the press had simply muddled up two MPs with similar-sounding names.

Nevertheless, in discussions at the most senior levels in Downing Street, fear of how an issue could be portrayed on the front page of a British newspaper acted as an important restraint in the best interests of us all. The free press is in my view more important in sustaining our individual liberties than judges, the police or politicians. While I bridled at Freedom of Information as a government minister, I have learned its importance as a member of the legislature.

So, finally, I have learned what we all know to be true in theory and which I have tested in the fires of experience and sometimes adversity: that the love and friendship, support and advice of friends and those we respect and adore is the very essence of life. Be cynical about everything except love, and while we rely on it for many aspects of our well-being, never forget that the state is not a divine all-knowing entity. It is our servant not our master and should be given powers over us only when absolutely necessary.

ACKNOWLEDGEMENTS

I would never have written this book without the encouragement of Michael Crick. Michael told me that if I did not write down some of the stories I had told him over the years from Westminster politics, he'd be inclined to do it himself. Once I'd produced the chapters on whipping and on Boris Johnson, he and his – now my – brilliant agent Bill Hamilton suggested I write more. I am grateful to Michael and Bill for introducing me to a world I knew little about and for their encouragement.

I am indebted to Olivia Beattie, my editor at publisher Biteback, and Suzanne Sangster and Vicky Jessop, who so ably guided me through the process.

Duncan Budge, Anne Chant, Charlie Falconer, my parliamentary colleague Sir Greg Knight, John McLaren and Jeremy Sillem all generously read the text and made invaluable suggestions, as did Alan Field – one of the first generation of the 'Mad Men' of Madison Avenue. I am so grateful to them, as I am to Karen Grieve and Janet Walker, who laboriously typed up the manuscripts – in part via WhatsApp in Australia. Any errors or omissions are of course my own.

I am also indebted to three of England's leading libel lawyers, John Stables, David Hooper and John Campbell, for their wisdom, experience and general advice.

Above all to Sharon, working in the NHS alone in London for three months of lockdown, who returned to her family to find my handwritten manuscript awaiting her wary attention!

Andrew Mitchell
October 2021

INDEX